"Thank you for sharing your experiences with the world and giving us a safe place to laugh at the teenage years of parenthood!" Cat Smith, KSVY Sonoma, California

"Such a funny book, hilarious from start to finish. Recommended." Wendy M. Rhodes, author of Dr. Pritchard, The Poisoning Adulterer (UK)

"Great book, and I can definitely relate as a parent! Plenty of laughs, and relatable points. It's one I'd recommend." Gemma Johns, author of The Marriage Sabbatical (Australia)

"A hilarious account of being a parent as well as a roadmap for want-to-be parents. This book is a guidebook for everyone: those who are parents, those who wish to be parents, as well as those who wonder what being parents would be like. Whether you've raised teenagers or only been one so far, you'll find something to laugh about. And if your parenting style is to be their friend, aren't you in for a surprise." Ashima Jain, short story writer in India

"I love how open, honest and just downright relatable this book was." Rebekah Fisher, Book Reviewer, Australia

"Having a teenage daughter myself, I was interested in seeing the experience of someone who had gone through it and come out the other side — hairless or otherwise. I recommend this book for anyone with a teenage daughter. It makes you feel less alone." Sam Hurrell, UK Book Reviewer

"I loved the title of this book and couldn't wait to read it. I highly recommend this book even if you don't have children. It is very funny and well written." Sylvia Garai, NetGalley Book Reviewer, Romania

HOW
I LOST
MY HAIR
RAISING
TEENAGE GIRLS

AND THE LESSONS I LEARNED

ANDREW McKINNEY

For more information contact andrewmckinney2019@gmail.com or through the website www.howilostmyhairraisingteenagegirls.com

Published by AM Press Ltd., Brampton, ON, Canada

Cover by ANA CHABRAND DESIGN HOUSE

Library and Archives Canada Cataloguing in Publication
Title: How I lost my hair raising teenage girls / by Andrew McKinney.
Names: McKinney, Andrew (Author of How I lost my hair raising teenage girls), author.
Identifiers: Canadiana (print) 20210397888 | Canadiana (ebook) 0210398000 | ISBN 9781777996406 (softcover) | ISBN 9781777996413 (ebook)
Subjects: LCSH: McKinney, Andrew (Author of How I lost my hair raising teenage girls)—Family. |
LCSH: Parenting—Anecdotes. | LCSH: Fathers and daughters—Anecdotes. | LCSH: Teenage girls— Anecdotes.
Classification: LCC HQ798 .M345 2022 | DDC 646.700835/2—dc23

This is for my lovely wife, Karen, beautiful children Eric, Meaghan and Jacquelyn, and best friend, Steven, whose unwavering faith in my ability to do something that I had never done before convinced me I could as well.

INTRODUCTION

MY WIFE, KAREN, and I have raised three children: one boy and two girls. Although I've threatened my daughters with writing a book for years, particularly during the teenage ones, I made the decision to do so only recently. Blessed with a life full of funny anecdotes, and a family that has a good sense of humour, I wanted to capture these stories for us and others to read and laugh about. Believe me, I do not think my family is any more special than anyone else's, but perhaps some of these stories will remind readers of similar incidents in their own lives.

It hasn't been all laughs, though. There was a lot of worry and stress too, and I've tried to capture these moments honestly. Life moves too quickly, and sometimes it feels like an accelerating treadmill, as you struggle with the demands of work, children and aging parents. Each new stage appears suddenly. Just when you're comfortable with one, they move to another with new issues. We were the first generation of parents to deal with cell phones, and that added new challenges in parenting.

We made mistakes, we know that, but we've learned some life lessons along the way. Readers still dealing with raising children can hopefully benefit from these. Others may recall their own bittersweet memories of similar trials and tribulations. Oh, yes, I should add that all these stories are absolutely true. There was no need to fabricate anecdotes for this book. As they say, truth is often stranger than fiction.

The names and places were changed, however, in order to protect the innocent and the not-so-innocent. For me, it's similar to being in a witness protection program and hoping my daughters don't find me.

Andrew McKinney

THE DAY YOUR KIDS LIE

"Don't lie to your mom, and if you ever do, don't assume you got away with it." - designpress.com

MY EYES GREW misty as Tia, the rebellious teenager, and her mother embraced in a bear hug of love, apology and forgiveness in the movie *Uncle Buck*. Then Tia shared a loving goodbye with her uncle, emerging from a battle of wills to a more mature, respectful relationship. She had left her bratty nature behind as well, all within a week.

I shook my head. Hollywood lies; no question about it. All conflicts get resolved and wrapped up in neat little bows by the end of every film. Unfortunately, real life isn't that easy.

As the credits rolled, I shut off the in-flight entertainment system, closed my eyes and leaned back in my seat.

The movie made me consider how my family would greet me when I arrived. Karen and the girls might be out, depending on their activities. Eric, our oldest, was attending McMaster University in Hamilton and was not expected home this weekend. Raising the kids was challenging, but at least none of them had behaved like the brat in this movie.

The biggest issues with Meaghan were getting her to school and to do homework. A grade ten student, her marks weren't bad, and she was popular enough, but for some reason she struggled. Jacquelyn, our youngest, was the fastest learner of the three but had become lazy. At thirteen, she valued social activities more than grades, and she was the most sociable in the house.

"More port, Mr. McKinney?"

I opened my eyes to see a smiling flight attendant standing by her drink cart. "Sure, thank you," I said, holding up my glass.

Business class has its perks, I thought as I pushed a button to recline the chair and raise my feet. Sadly, I never slept in these metal pods but contented myself with movies or reading instead. The seating was more like metal coffins than pods, particularly when you lie down surrounded by padded walls. Airlines claim the pods provide more privacy, but I suspect they prefer them because they can squeeze more people into business class.

An announcement cut my rumination short. "Ladies and gentlemen, we have begun our descent into Toronto, and we'll be landing in about fifteen minutes. Local time is 11:36 a.m., the weather is sunny, and the temperature is plus twenty degrees Celsius."

I adjusted my watch from Zurich time. Thanks to the time difference, I'd be home early for a change.

*

The taxi rolled west along Highway 401, and I looked out the window at the sun dancing on the grass and trees. The thrill of arriving on a warm Friday afternoon lightened my heart. And what a pleasant change to relax and let someone else do the driving. The driver turned off the highway and began his way through the small town of Streetsville. With quaint shops on both sides of the main street, it's quite picturesque. There's the historic, red-bricked Robinson-Bray house, where they serve high tea with sandwiches and scones accompanied by Devonshire cream. We've had a number of enjoyable visits there.

I leaned forward. "Turn left at the lights and then right at Maple Street."

A man of few words, he simply glanced in the mirror and nodded. Seconds later, when I pointed out the house, there was even less response. It was easy to spot; the mighty blue spruce stood out from the numerous maple trees on the other lawns. I paid the fare, and a barking frenzy erupted as the driver lifted my bag out of the trunk. Milo had sensed I was home, and I caught sight of his head in the bay window.

When I opened the door, Karen was standing in the entrance. "Hello, dear," she said and pointed to the dog. "Oh my, someone's happy to see you."

"Yes, I can see that."

We hugged as I pulled my suitcase in behind me. Then her smile quickly turned to a frown. "Shut up, Milo!"

The racket abruptly halted, and our beagle nosed around my legs with his tail wagging.

I leaned over to pet him. "There, there, Milo," I said and smiled at Karen. "He's telling me off for leaving him, that's all."

She laughed sarcastically. "Oh yeah, that's just what I was thinking."

I knew what she meant. With the stress of work and three kids, I often lost my patience too when he barked, which was every time the doorbell rang. I sat on the bottom step of the stairs, cupped his head in my hands, and gazed into his soulful eyes. "See, Milo, I'm the only good one. Remember me when dogs take over the world."

He studied me briefly before dropping his head to sniff my shoes, trying to determine where I'd been and if I'd played with other dogs.

To one side of this commotion, Moochie sat on her haunches,

eyeing us while her black tail swept the floor. Cats are funny; they always appear to be judging us and finding we don't quite measure up. But dogs just love us and eagerly show it.

Karen shut the door and yelled upstairs, "Girls ... Dad's home!"

Tall with delicate features and attractive blue eyes, even dressed in a T-shirt and jeans without makeup, Karen was beautiful. When I married her, my friends told me I lucked out, which may be the greatest compliment one man can give another. Much to my annoyance, some even said it to her face, which led to no end of teasing from her.

"Did you have a good trip, Andrew?" she asked, brushing back her light brown hair.

I had attended a weeklong meeting for quality heads at the Swiss site of our multinational pharmaceutical company.

"Yes, it went well but was tiring. Let's just say I'm glad to be—"

A commotion reminiscent of stampeding horses interrupted me as my daughters came running downstairs. Meaghan first; blue-eyed with raven black hair, she would turn fifteen next week. Jacquelyn, blonde and blue-eyed, was right behind. Although nineteen months younger, Jacquelyn was three inches taller, which grieved Meggy to no end. Both were gorgeous, yet with that curse of teenage insecurity, the youngest fretted she was too tall and the oldest that she was too short. I'd tell them not to worry. They'd be fine, but it didn't seem to help. My arms were pinched as they grabbed me in quick hugs, joyful smiles and greetings. Then as fast as they arrived, they were gone.

"Take your father's bag with you!" Karen shouted at the departing legs, shooting me a look of exasperation.

Meggy reappeared and snatched the bag with a grin before racing off again.

"Well, that was fast!" Karen said, laughing.

"That's doesn't bother me. I'll see them at dinner, and we'll have the whole weekend together." I touched her arm. "Listen, it's beautiful outside. Let's take Milo for a walk."

Karen hesitated. "You go. I'm going to start dinner."

"But I'd like to walk with you. Tell you what, let's make it a short one."

"Alright," she said, grabbing the leash from its hook in the closet.

As we strolled along the sidewalk, the leaves were putting on a display—shades of yellow, brown, orange and brilliant red hung on the branches and drifted downward to form a multicoloured carpet on the lawns and road. The sight made me smile. Autumn is one of my favourite times of the year.

"Funny, the leaves weren't falling when I left, and I've only been gone a week."

"Oh, you were probably too busy to notice," Karen mused and stopped to let Milo sniff on a lawn. "I swear that dog sniffs more than he walks." She smiled at me. "After sitting so long on the plane, you must have craved a walk."

"Yeah, that's about it," I said and inhaled deeply. "You know nothing evokes my childhood memories of Halloween better than the musky-sweet aroma of decaying leaves."

"Yes, or when the wind sends piles of leaves spiralling upwards like mini tornados."

We walked Milo a few more blocks and then headed back.

*

When we returned to the house, the TV was playing in the family room. Karen walked to the kitchen, and I popped my head into the room to say a quick hello before going upstairs. Jackie's blonde hair bounced as she glanced over from the computer station. Laptops were expensive in those days, so we all shared a desktop unless I brought my work one home. Both girls were proficient with MSN messenger, but Jackie was amazing. She'd look at you and talk while typing a hundred words a minute; it left me speechless. Our IT department still used the two-fingered hunt and peck method, and I chuckled every time I saw them.

I strolled over to observe her accuracy.

"What's DITR?"

"Nothing." She shrugged and kept typing.

Meaghan smirked from the couch. "It means Dad's in the Room."

I peered closer. Well, I'll be damned. The back-and-forth correspondence had halted; she was just typing random words for camouflage.

"Shut up, Meggy!" Jackie barked over her shoulder. Then throwing me an annoyed glance, she mumbled, "Now I have to change it."

I walked away snickering; DITR—I had no idea they used codes.

*

The next morning, I lay staring at the clock. Five a.m. illuminated in bright, red numbers. I calculated this to be eleven in the morning Swiss time and climbed quietly out of bed. No point struggling to sleep any longer; my internal clock needed to recalibrate. An early riser, anyway, I find Monday mornings easier if I don't oversleep on the weekends. So, I crept downstairs, made a cup of tea and lay on the couch with the radio turned down low. The quiet was enjoyable. In a few hours, the world would come back to life, and my newspaper would arrive, but until then, it was pleasant to relax in the dark and watch the neighbourhood awaken.

A cry erupted from the basement—*Mrrrrrrawr.*

Damn cat. She must have heard me and wanted to be fed. I ignored her, but the sounds grew louder and angrier—***Mrrrrrrrrrrawr!***

Either she was learning a new tune or becoming impatient. A few more minutes of caterwauling, and I couldn't stand it anymore. I hurried downstairs before she woke up the entire house.

I stood behind the laundry room door, slowly cracking it open a bit to see where Moochie was when it banged me in the head. Glimpsing freedom, she had burst out. Cursing, I watched the black fur ball disappear upstairs. That cat could move fast when she wanted to. The sound of a tail banging against the side of a cage made me turn around again. Milo sat watching me expectantly.

"Okay, I'll let you out, boy," I said and bent down to open the latch. He wiggled joyfully around me for a few seconds before bouncing upstairs. I started after him and heard a racket above; he must have bowled the cat over in his mad dash to the door. I let him out into the darkness and almost fell over as I turned around. Stupid cat. She'd been weaving between my legs, purring for breakfast. Usually ignored by her, I was now her new best friend.

Before I could prepare their meals, the sound of howling startled me. In a panic, I yanked the patio door open again. "Quiet, Milo. Get in here! You'll wake the neighbours."

He marched in indignantly and waited at his eating spot while I fixed their bowls. It always amazes me how impatient animals get at feeding time. Moochie gets fed first at the opposite end of the kitchen. If I didn't separate them, she'd try to swallow the dog's food before her own. Even then, as I lowered the dish, she pushed at it with her nose, almost knocking it out of my hand.

"You little pig!" I muttered as she greedily devoured the meal.

Milo was better behaved but didn't finish his kibbles, so I scooped up the bowl before Moochie could get them. She could strike like lightning when there were leftovers, but today, I hummed a merry tune, for I had beaten her. Now that their demands were met, they lay down in their beds, and I resumed my spot on the sofa.

Karen got up a few hours later, and we enjoyed a lazy day with the girls.

*

By Monday, I had recovered from my trip. I whistled in the elevator on the way up to my office; I was looking forward to getting back to my desk and catching up. I surprised my staff with a box of chocolates, and we sat together in the small kitchen area to sample them and chat about issues that arose during the past week. Meanwhile, Karen ran the girls to their respective schools. When I called her in the afternoon to touch base, she told me that they had settled into their new school routines. The day flashed by as I struggled to catch up on tasks and projects, and my energy began to wane. By five o'clock, I was drained. No point in overdoing it, I decided, so I called it quits and headed out.

When I got home, Jackie was at her usual station at the computer with a map on the screen in front of her.

"Are you doing a project?" I asked.

She smiled as she studied the screen. "Yes, it's on Poland."

"Oh, that's interesting."

Her brow furrowed, and she appeared to be concentrating, so I left her alone. Karen would enjoy this project because her father was born there. The wonderful aroma of fried chicken drew me into the kitchen.

Karen smiled when I told her, "Oh good, I want to read it when she's done."

We relayed this to our daughter during supper, and she seemed pleased that we had shown an interest in the assignment.

*

We tried to limit the kids' computer hours, but it remained a challenge. While our parents' generation fought with kids over the amount of TV they watched, today it's computers. Jackie spent a lot of time on our desktop, but we didn't mind if it was for school. For the next few weeks, whenever I came home, there was Jackie—hard at work with the map of Poland on the screen. Funny though, the picture never changed, and I grew increasingly suspicious.

Finally, I confronted her. "That's a map you pull up to trick me, isn't it? You're not even working on a project, are you?"

She threw back her blonde head and cackled. "You just figured that out now? Ha-ha-ha, that's funny!" Her eyes danced with a mixture of merriment and deviousness.

Her expression was so comical that, at first, I couldn't help chuckling myself. Then I made her shut it down.

I tipped Karen off too, so she wouldn't fall for it. "That kid's so fast, she can switch the screen before you even notice."

She giggled, unconcerned, but I was stunned. When the kids were small, Jackie never lied. If I wanted to know who broke the lamp, I only had to wait a moment before she'd tell me the entire story, with elaborate details, much to the dismay of her disgruntled siblings. Today marked a pivotal change in behaviour. She was no longer 'honest to a fault', and I would need time to adapt.

*

I soon experienced this craftiness again, only this time it was both of them. We discovered the girls were using their phones at night, so I insisted they leave them on the kitchen counter until morning. There was much protesting.

"Sometimes, when I can't sleep, I like to use it," Jackie insisted.

I scoffed. "You're thirteen. Who will you text? Your friends will be asleep."

"Actually, all my friends are on it. I often get texts from Katie."

"Yeah, mine too." Meggy agreed, fixing her eyes on me from under the dark hair she meticulously straightened every morning.

"Really?"

This shocked me, but I recovered swiftly. "All the more reason to turn it off, so you have a good night's sleep. I shut mine off so work won't bother me."

After more discussion, they acquiesced, and I tried to keep the triumphant look off my face as they placed their cell phones on the counter.

"It goes to show you," I said to Karen as we got ready for bed, "persistence and a solid rationale always win the day." She gave no response.

It didn't take more than a few days to discover the girls were sneaking downstairs to retrieve their phones.

Now I was irritated, but I stifled my annoyance and calmly reprimanded them, dripping as much disappointment into my voice as I could muster.

With their eyes downcast, I concluded, "From now on, I'll collect the cells at bedtime."

I believed they got the message, and I wasn't angry. It was our own fault. We should have created rules for the phones at the beginning. Set the limits early, and there's less resistance later on. I'd try to remember that in the future.

*

That night I went to bed secure in the knowledge that the phones had been removed from temptation. We turned the lights off to go to sleep, which can take me a while. Karen, on the other hand, drifts off in minutes. As I slipped into that place halfway between drowsiness and sleep, a feeling of apprehension came over me, and my body tensed up. Something wasn't right—was there a noise downstairs? Did someone break in?

I sat up and listened but didn't hear a sound. I relaxed and settled down again. Still, the uneasy sensation persisted. Finally, and I don't know why, I propped myself up on one elbow and blurted out, "Jackie, get out of here!"

Stunned, I watched my blonde daughter jump up from the foot of our bed and march out of the room without a word. I glanced at Karen, but she was fast asleep. Shaking my head in disbelief, I lay down again. Then I wondered—had that really happened, or was it my imagination? A moment later, I dozed off.

*

When the alarm buzzed in the morning, I shuffled around the bed toward the bathroom and tripped over something on the floor. The culprit was Jackie's fluffy pink bunny, lying helplessly, arms stretched out and a scared expression on its face. I picked it up and placed it on the pine chest by the wall. As I shaved and dressed, I laughed out loud whenever I pictured my blonde commando crawling across the floor with the bunny tucked under her arm. Oh, she'd make quite the Ninja, that one. And once discovered, how swiftly she abandoned her beloved rabbit.

At dinner, I couldn't resist teasing her about the nighttime raid. "Why were you trying to steal the phone back? You realize if you succeed, you'll just lose it longer."

Jackie paused eating.

"How did you know I was there?" she asked with a sly smile.

"Fathers always know. We have a special 'Spidey-sense,' and mine was tingling, so I figured something was up."

She rolled her eyes. When they were young, I used to say I could tell if they were lying by looking into their eyes. They believed me for a few years until they proved otherwise.

I spooned more vegetables onto my plate. "Imagine my surprise to find Dreamers when I woke up."

"Yes, I love my bunny."

"And yet ...you left bunny behind to take the fall."

"Yeah, ha-ha, that's right. She had to get the blame."

*

I dropped the matter and didn't add any punishment since the attempt had been foiled.

When I popped in to say goodnight, Jackie was in bed with the stuffed rabbit.

I sat down on the edge of the mattress. "Has Dreamers recovered from the trauma of being deserted?"

She nodded, a quiet smile on her lips.

"Do you still sleep with her?"

"Oh yeah," she said and sighed. "She's the best to cuddle with. We cuddle like this..." Turning on her side, she pressed her face against the bunny's head and pulled her knees up until they touched Dreamers.

My eyes crinkled in a smile. "That does look comfortable. Well, nighty-night, honey."

"Good night, Daddy."

When they act like little children, it's hard to be angry. Thank goodness for that. It helps us remember how much we love them and that they're just kids, after all.

As I walked down the hall to my bedroom, I thought—*okay, she's broken the virtue of honesty, which, although surprising, is hardly the biggest worry for a parent.* Still, a little voice inside my head seemed to whisper, *"Better buckle up. It's going to be a bumpy ride."*

DON'T BITE THE HAND THAT FEEDS YOU

"Women and cats will do as they please, and men and dogs should relax and get used to the idea." - Robert A. Heinlein

O N THE TUESDAY before Christmas, I looked out the bedroom window. A heavy layer of snow engulfed the lawns and road as if a white blanket had dropped on the neighbourhood overnight. Draped over roofs and cars, glistening in the morning sunlight, it brought a smile to my face. Everything looks cleaner, more pristine, covered in white. I cranked open the window and took a deep breath of frosty air. There was a trace of wood smoke; someone had a fire last night. How wonderful to be alive on such a glorious day. Glancing at the clock, I realized it was getting late, so I hustled downstairs, grabbed my coat and hollered goodbye to Karen.

"Be careful driving!" she shouted as I bolted out the door.

While backing out of the driveway, a neighbour walked to his truck and started brushing it off. He returned my wave with a friendly smile. I pulled the steering wheel to the right and heard the soft crunching sound of the snow before my tires found the ruts carved out by previous vehicles. My breath came out in steamy white puffs, and I shivered. The van was as cold as a tomb, even though the heater blasted away on the highest setting. It would take a few more blocks before hot air gushed out. Once I reached the office, I knew everyone would commiserate over coffee. Canadians love to complain about the weather. But it looked like a wonderful winter's day to me; perfect for skiing if I didn't have to work.

*

During the week, I chatted with people at the office and easily plowed through my tasks and meetings. Eric was coming home from university this weekend, and the news raised my spirits. The harmony in our house was better when he was around. His easygoing and joyful nature had a way of dissipating the tension between us and the girls. However, he was no angel. Like most older brothers, he took pleasure in teasing his younger siblings.

On Friday, Eric walked through the front door, and Milo began a barking spree as if embarrassed at being caught off guard by his sudden entrance. Eric put his bags on the stairway landing and eyed the dog with amusement.

"Milo, it's me. Calm down!"

"I guess he misses you," I said.

We all gathered at the entrance to greet him.

"It's okay, Wonder Snout," he said in a soothing tone. "I miss you, too." The use of his pet name for Milo made me grin.

"Oh, my, you've got a beard!" Karen announced with surprise when they embraced. She stood back and appraised the stubble. "You know, it looks good on you."

He beamed, and I felt a surge of pride. "I agree. It gives you a more mature appearance. I must say, you are a handsome devil."

And attractive he was. Six-foot-two, with a slim muscular build, short black hair and hazel eyes; the close-trimmed beard outlined and complemented Eric's features perfectly.

"How are you, Poppo?" he asked, wrapping an arm around me. "My, my, you are a little man, aren't you?"

His eyes twinkled mischievously, and I had to laugh. At five foot-ten, I felt like a dwarf when I stood beside him. "I'd look bigger with more hair," I argued. "Besides, your generation's taller because you eat better. That's why dinosaurs grew so big, you know. It was the food. Soon young people will all be twenty feet tall."

"Oh, is that so?" he said, chuckling as the girls hugged him.

"Your dad was the runt of the litter!" Karen piped in with a smirk.

"Yes, and you were the grunt of the litter!" I quipped right back. Karen giggled, and it pleased me to have tickled her funny bone.

*

The next day when Eric came downstairs, Jackie was standing in the living room talking animatedly to me about a friend. While I listened, Eric crept up behind her, grabbed her shoulders and pretended to gnaw on one like a dog with a bone. I broke out laughing at the sight of him chewing away, one eye closed in a maniacal expression.

"Get away from me," she wailed, pushing him off. "You think Eric's perfect, Dad, but see what he does!"

I waved my hand. "That's just how brothers express affection, honey. Maybe it's a guy thing, but my brother used to punch me on the arm to show he liked me."

My mind flashed back to the time that Peter taught me how to use the lawn mower when I was eight years old. In those days, mowers didn't have an ignition shut off.

"Okay, that's pretty good," Peter said as he surveyed my handiwork on our front lawn. "Now you have to shut it off."

"How do I do that?" I looked up at his tall frame.

He pointed at a black wire on one side. "Just reach down and pull the distributor cap off the spark plug with your hand."

I obeyed and immediately leaped into the air from an electric shock.

Peter guffawed and added with a big smile, "See, now you'll always remember not to touch it. Next time, use a stick or something else to knock it off instead."

I stared at him, not accepting the implication that he had done this for my own good. Although we had a lot of fun together, and I knew he loved me, it seemed that older brothers couldn't resist the temptation to play a trick on their younger siblings now and then.

*

We went into the kitchen, where Meaghan was sitting with her hair up in a bun.

He weaved towards her, muttering, "Ooh, a bun... I've got to... bite the bun."

Within seconds, he had clamped his teeth on it and emitted a menacing moan.

"You weirdo. Let go of my bun!" Meggy yelled and lifted her arms to fight him off. "Stop! You'll mess it up."

Eric released it with a snicker, and I couldn't help smiling at his playfulness.

"Why do you let him do that?" she said to me accusingly.

"Hey, I had nothing to do with it," I protested, adopting a hurt expression. Then, in a serious tone, although I confess not with much enthusiasm, I added, "Eric, leave their hair alone."

"Chill out, girls. It's no big deal," Karen snapped as she brushed past us on her way to the sink. "It's just your hair bun. Get over it."

"Oh yeah, 'cause Eric's your favourite," Meggy whined.

I thought I should add something, but he'd already moved on to the refrigerator.

"I'm hungry... what's there to eat?" he asked, his lanky frame bent over and his head in the fridge.

"It's only an hour till dinner," I said, glancing at the clock while he foraged around. "There's some soup I made."

Jackie was also observing him. "Keep your hands off my sub."

"Too late," he said, not even bothering to turn around. "I had that for lunch."

"Dad! He's always eating my stuff!" Jackie squealed, and her face got red.

I nodded solemnly. "Eric, you should leave their food alone."

"It's not my fault," he replied briskly. "They don't put their names on it. So, how do I know whose it is?"

"You know it's not yours! " Jackie snapped, but her protest was in vain. Having found cheese and crackers, Eric was in the process of carrying the food to the table, mindless of her complaints.

Karen laughed, and she sat down beside him. "I once saw a cartoon about a teenage boy. The father stepped on his foot, the boy's mouth opened like a garbage can lid, and he dumped an enormous plate of food into it. That's the best description of a teenage boy's appetite I've ever read."

*

Eric cringed, but the anecdote stirred up memories for me. When I was seventeen, my brother and I got summer jobs at the steel plant where my father worked. Hired as a Fitter's Helper, I fetched and held things for the Fitter, who built components of buildings and bridges. Two years older and tall for his age, Peter had the plum job of operating a forklift. Fortified by a scant ten-minute training, he zipped across the shop floor with his mind set on the task of transporting angles, plates and beams.

In the beginning, my mother prepared us five sandwiches each for lunch and the usual two for Dad. After a week, we asked for more. Beautiful, with a gentle manner, at five foot-five, Mother won the title for the shortest member of the family, and she bore it with good humour. She made the lunches faithfully but must have struggled with the idea that her skinny sons could eat seven sandwiches apiece.

She brought up the subject over tea on Sunday in the living room. Mom and Dad sat on the sofa, I in an adjacent chair, and Peter slouched in another armchair with his long legs stretched out in front.

Mother's eyes focused on us. "Boys, I don't mind making the sandwiches, but if you're not eating them all, please tell me," she pleaded and then, with a touch of alarm in her voice, added, "because I'm using a *whole* loaf of bread every day just for you two. I'm not complaining, but I don't want any thrown out."

"Oh, we're eating them, Mom," Peter replied, nodding vigorously. "You can keep making them."

I agreed and went on to explain. "I have two for breakfast at about nine o'clock. Then we meet in the car at noon and eat the rest."

Her eyes widened, and she stared for a moment in disbelief. "Alright," she said, and her features softened. "I just wanted to make sure they weren't being wasted."

Mom doted on us but was often in awe of our voracious appetites, whereas Dad was proud of them. One day, I passed the cafeteria and heard his voice, so I stopped to listen.

With a lightheartedness in the Irish lilt, I heard him say, "I know what you mean, Bill. Listen, if I find a bit of cake or a cookie in my lunch box, I figure either it's going stale, or the boys didn't like it!"

The ensuing roar of laughter made me feel sheepish, and I hoped he had enjoyed the odd fresh treat now and then, even if it was one we liked.

*

By the time I finished the story, Eric had completed his snack. Karen slumped in the chair and gazed up at him, enjoying his company.

I pointed to Milo, who nosed around under the table. "Want to join me walking him, Sonny?"

"Sure, I'll come, Poppo," he said, pushing his chair back.

Our beagle isn't the easiest to walk. Either he constantly stops to sniff or gets excited and pulls hard on the leash. As we made our way through the neighbourhood, he seemed to pick up a scent, which intrigued me. After all, skunks, rabbits, foxes and coyotes live in the nearby ravine—perhaps he was tracking one of these.

I motioned towards him. "Look, Eric."

"The Hound of the Baskervilles has found something!" he teased.

Eric's eyes lit up with amusement as he observed the beagle. Fur raised on the back of his neck, nose to the ground, he weaved in and out of the snow-covered lawns and sidewalk, following the trail. His intensity increased, and he whimpered before stopping to scrutinize the smell of a particular spot. I peered down the sidewalk while he did this. About a hundred feet ahead marched an immense black dog alongside its owner. Given the thick, coarse coat, I judged it to be the Newfoundland dog that lived in the area. Then it dawned on me — this was who Wonder Snout was pursuing!

"Milo, you idiot. Look up." I gestured with one arm. "Your prey is right in front of you."

But our hound would not be deterred. He was on the hunt and continued with full concentration, oblivious to the obvious. Meanwhile, the big dog turned a corner and disappeared.

"See, Milo, this is the reason dogs will never take over the world — you're imbeciles," I said scornfully.

*

As we neared the house, our canine slowed down, I suspected, to take a crap.

I held the leash out. "Hold this, Sonny, while I get the poop bag ready."

While I pulled a plastic bag out of the holder, I heard Eric ask, "What's he doing?"

I looked up to find Milo lumbering across the yard in a crouched position. He was pooping alright but continuing to move forward as he did.

"He's stealth pooping," I cried. "If he could talk, he'd say — *Pay no attention to me. I'm not crapping. I'm just shuffling along. Nothing to see here!*"

Eric chuckled and muttered, "Stealth crapper." Then, he threw his head back and roared with laughter, and I joined him.

I did feel a twinge of guilt, though; it might have been my fault. Whenever Milo tried to crap near the house, I'd tell him off for not waiting for our back yard. Oh well, at least Eric had a funny story now and a new nickname to take home to McMaster on Sunday.

As we walked to his car to see him off, he put his hand on my shoulder. "Remember, Dad, I'm the only good one," he said, then laughed heartily.

*

But even though I'm Milo's favourite, I like to think Moochie loves me, too. Having grown up with cats and dogs, I feel an affinity with both animals. Besides, I'm the one that feeds her. She often lies on my belly if I'm on the couch or sits in my lap when I'm in the armchair, which was just what we were doing on Friday afternoon. While stroking her, I noticed some of the fur on her face had turned grey, giving her a more grizzled appearance. Her eyes were closed, and her mouth formed into a smile; she lay still and purred blissfully. Her expression of complete ecstasy filled me with pleasure as well, and I let out a sigh of contentment. Almost sixteen, Moochie never left the house, except that one time we forgot she'd been on the patio with us. Meggy spied her through the window at dusk, pacing back and forth and glancing in desperation at the house. She raced out and saved the abandoned kitty from neighbouring raccoons. A little plump,

Moochie would have made a tasty meal indeed, a thought that likely crossed her mind, too.

I relaxed, alone in my thoughts with the warmth of her body on my lap. Then, suddenly, Moochie's head whirled to the side, and a piercing pain shot into my wrist. She'd had enough petting, and unlike any cat I'd ever known, she never gave a warning nip. No, not Moochie. She would go straight for the kill, especially with me. I pulled my arm away and jumped up, flinging her off my lap, and ran to the bathroom to run cold water over the bleeding wound. My eyes were drawn to a particularly deep hole caused by one of her fangs. Blood continued to seep out despite the icy current flowing against it. *Not much hope of getting antibiotic cream in there* — I thought. *The blood would only push it out.* Nonetheless, I patted the area dry with a towel, put cream on and bandaged it.

"Better see Dr. MacEwan," Karen cautioned on her way by with a laundry hamper, "or you'll get an infection like last time."

I glanced at the clock and hurried to the phone in a panic. It was going to be close. The doctor quit early on Fridays, and his office remained closed all weekend. Thankfully, his receptionist, Chelsea, answered and listened patiently as I explained the situation. She put me on hold but returned after a few minutes.

"Can you come in right away?" Chelsea asked in a voice that rose musically at the end.

"I'll be there in ten minutes," I gasped.

Grabbing my keys, I hollered upstairs, "Karen, I'm going now."

"Go ahead. He must be waiting for you," she called back. "I'll shut the door."

*

As I waited in the examination room, I considered my situation. Stupid cat. Didn't she realize I was the one that fed her? There had to be something wrong with her. The door burst open and startled me as Dr. MacEwan rushed in with a white lab coat draped over his slim five-eight frame. He dropped into the chair, swivelled around, and fixed his gaze on me. There was a twinkle in his eye.

"I heard you got bitten. What was it — a lion? A tiger?" he asked in his Glasgow accent.

"No," I sputtered in surprise. "It was Moochie, our cat."

I pulled up my sleeve and held out the injury. Two years younger than me, Dr. MacEwan was the best doctor I'd ever had, and his sense of humour was a bonus. He delivered all three of our children, which is a rare feat these days.

A mop of black hair hung down his forehead when he bent over to examine the wound. "It's fairly deep, so I'm giving you some antibiotics. Cats have a lot of bacteria in their mouth." He wrote out a prescription, tore it off the pad and handed it to me. "I hate cats," he said with a disagreeable expression. "I don't understand why anyone has one."

I pulled my sleeve down and sighed. "I can't say I disagree with you."

Still sitting, hands on his knees, he seemed in a jovial mood. He shook his head and smiled. "With all the stress from three kids, a goldfish might have been a better choice. But if you ever get another cat, choose an older one, preferably one with no teeth!"

*

Fortunately, Moochie had never bitten anyone else, not even Milo. They got along pretty well, but there was always underlying competitiveness for food and affection. This point was brought home on Monday while I was preparing to leave for work and noticed the dog on the floor beside the stairs leading to the basement.

"Milo, get out of there!" I cried in alarm. "Someone will trip over you."

He gave me a disgruntled look but didn't move. So, I nudged him with my foot. Karen happened along, headed for the linen closet.

"Watch out. Milo has a nasty habit of lying by the stairs. It's dangerous."

"Oh, he's just bullying the cat. He does that," she replied carelessly as she searched inside the closet. Confused, I surveyed the hallway. "What do you mean? The cat's not here."

She sighed and turned to face me, speaking slowly and deliberately, as if addressing a person of limited intelligence. "When Moochie goes downstairs ... to the kitty box ... he sits there and won't let her back up. He growls whenever she comes near the steps."

"Honestly?" I glanced down the stairs in surprise and then at the dog. "Oh, Milo, why do you bully the cat?"

He rolled those sad beagle eyes at me, then straightened up and sauntered off. Sure enough, a minute later, Moochie came creeping nervously up the stairs. I pondered this for a minute. I really should stop Milo from bullying her, but then again... maybe it was her just deserts for being such a demon cat.

THE DAY IT ALL STARTED

"Once they start to get boobs, the bullshit begins." - Karen McKinney

IN FEBRUARY, KAREN started taking Jackie to the Scarborough Hospital for scoliosis treatments. A keen-eyed dance instructor spotted this condition, where the spine curves sideways, in her case to the left. The doctors x-rayed her back, measured the curve and made a cast for her to wear at night. Intervention during the growth stage would straighten her spine but required multiple visits, checks and adjustments over six months. This was the only treatment available to prevent the condition from getting worse and becoming painful in later life.

After the initial visit, I came home to find Karen sitting on the chesterfield, arms crossed and fuming.

"That Jackie is a little brat!" she cried.

My brow furrowed as I hung up my coat. "Why? What happened?"

"I drove her to Scarborough. They checked her spine, then directed us to another room for measurements. But she refused to go."

"She didn't get measured?"

"Oh, she went. I wasn't going to run there again just for a fitting, but I had to fight with her. And then she walked along the corridor twenty-five feet ahead, as if she didn't recognize me. I guess she's reached the age where she's too cool to be seen with her mom."

The exasperation showed visibly on her face, and I felt sorry for her.

"Why didn't she want to get measured?"

"Well, I found out when we got home that she was in a hurry to go to a party. Can you believe it?"

I shook my head. "I'm sorry, but you were right to insist. It sounds as if she might have IAS."

"IAS — what's that?"

"A condition teenagers get. That spoiled attitude I call Irritable Ass Syndrome."

"Oh, she has that in spades," Karen said, cackling.

Yes, that was the day it all started. The day our happy and loving daughters turned into possessed demons. I remember it well.

*

A month later, my cousin Eileen was hosting a family gathering at her home in Richmond Hill. Everyone was excited. Besides being an opportunity to connect with relatives we don't see often, her dinners are a feast like no other. True to form, she laid out the table with copious salads, mains and desserts, each bearing its own hand-printed nametag. After saying grace, the guests converged on the buffet. Children always make the fastest start, and our brood was no exception. In fact, they led the charge. We stood back with the other parents, watching and admiring their zest for food. Then the next generation followed, and I slipped in behind Karen as she eased into the line. While loading my plate, I overheard her tell my cousin Debra about the hospital incident. A short, brown-eyed brunette of Irish descent, Debra had three daughters, and the youngest two were Meggy and Jackie's ages.

"I know what you mean," Debra commiserated as they made their way through the abundant dishes. "They walk ahead of me in the mall, too. And last month, I took Kristal shopping. After the saleslady helped us find a nice blouse, I said, 'What about a training bra for your boobettes, dear?' Well... after the woman left to get one, she turned on me like an animal, her face full of anger and hissed, 'Don't you *ever* talk to me that way in the store again!'" Debra's voice shook as she told the tale, but she giggled at the end.

Ah, mothers and daughters — that special bond. Afterwards, Karen surprised me by saying that she found the conversation comforting. Just hearing our girls behaved no worse than others relieved some of her stress. It seemed a bit odd to me, but I was happy it helped her.

*

The days rolled into April. Eric finished his exams, and we prepared to move him to an off-campus house to share with three other boys. All first-year students stay in residence but then vacate to make space for the next crop of freshmen. I must admit I wasn't enthusiastic about spending my Saturday doing this; it seemed as if we'd just settled him into the residence. But it ended up being more fun than expected.

After loading the van with boxes of linen, kitchen items, clothes, a desk and chair, I motored out of the residence parking lot. We were experiencing one of those warm weeks of early spring, and all traces of snow had vanished, leaving green grass behind. It was a glorious day for a move. Students lounged on the lawn and basked in the sunshine or milled about, revelling in the thrill of not wearing a coat for the first time in months. It brought flashbacks of my own university days, and I felt myself smiling.

Approaching Eric's street, I noticed many small, older buildings similar to how Karen had described his new place. Constructed after the war for a different generation, they had fallen into various stages of disrepair and were rented now to undiscerning youths.

"It's nice it's so close to campus, Eric," I said as we pulled into the driveway.

"Yeah, it's only a fifteen-minute walk." His brown eyes smiled at me, and he fumbled for his keys. Then he jumped out to unlock the door and hurried back to unload. I carried a large plastic bin into the kitchen, and Karen followed with another container full of kitchen utensils. This was my initial visit, so she excitedly pointed out the new drapes and two refrigerators in the extra-large kitchen. Two roommates had already moved in, and Eric introduced us. I marvelled at their height, which I estimated at six-two and six-four. No doubt, we were rapidly approaching the next dinosaur era.

"It's a nice place. You guys were lucky to find it," Karen said and broke into a warm smile, "and those girls left it spotless."

Tall, good-looking young men with curly brown hair, they responded with shy grins. Karen drew them into conversation, and it soon became apparent that they were serious students, not party boys like so many others.

Karen was right about the cleanliness. Four girls had rented previously and washed and vacuumed thoroughly before departing. The floors practically shone. I returned to the van to get the bed linen. When I opened Eric's bedroom door, I was struck by how small, bare and lonely a room appears when emptied of humans, furniture and accessories, as if it were waiting for another occupant to bring fun, life and personality into it. An object to the right caught my eye. Lying across the windowsill with its long tassels hanging down to the floor was a black whip. My jaw dropped, and I stared for a moment before picking it up.

I hurried into the hall and waved it at Karen with a grin, "Look at this ... isn't it a hoot? Those girls knew four guys were moving in, so they left this in the bedroom for a joke."

Eric came into the hallway at that moment, lugging a large cardboard box. He stopped in his tracks and gawked. "Whaaat?"

Karen laughed, and her blue eyes darted from him to me. "Oh my, I wonder what they were thinking!"

*

Monday, I sped faster than usual on the drive to work. I couldn't wait to tell my staff about the move. And I didn't have to wait long. Two of my Quality Specialists were in the small kitchen area when I arrived. It contained a sink, microwave and coffee maker on the counter and a wooden dining table with six chairs. Set in the corner of the office floor, large windows on two sides provided ample lighting, making it very pleasant for lunch, coffee or a quick breakfast. I inhaled the rich smell of a mocha java blend as I entered.

Suzanne, an attractive brunette who had a son Eric's age, stepped away from the machine to let Sarah take a turn. We exchanged greetings and enquired about each other's weekends, and I told them about Saturday's move. Their eyes opened in surprise when I described the 'present' the girls had left in the window. Sara smiled, brushed her long blonde hair away from her eyes and took a sip from her mug. "A whip. Now that's interesting."

Suzanne gave a throaty laugh. "You're lucky they left it so clean." She leaned against the counter. "We moved Zackary last weekend, and when we got to his new place, the previous tenants were still in bed. We had to wake them up!"

"That's terrible. Didn't they have somewhere they had to move to as well?" I asked, horrified.

"I guess they'd graduated and weren't in a rush to leave," she said with a shrug. "Oh, eventually, they packed up their things and got out, but it was a real pain. We had to go for breakfast and wait until they dressed."

"I've never heard of such a thing. Poor you!" I imagined myself in that situation; I wouldn't have taken it so well.

Sara had two daughters in high school and had been listening to us quietly.

Suzanne turned to her with a big grin. "See what you have to look forward to?"

"Yeah, that's just what I'm thinking," she giggled.

I left them joking good-naturedly and hurried to my office for a conference call.

*

The move turned out to be a pleasant change from the antics of our daughters. Emotions in the house had been going up and down in peaks and valleys, which made the weeks fly by faster than usual. Too soon, the hot days of June descended, and Jackie graduated middle school. This was a proud moment and marked the last days of her early youth before the high school years would begin. Karen and I attended the ceremony, which was held in the gymnasium. With much scraping of chairs and bantering in hushed voices, the audience prepared themselves for the customary speeches. Afterwards, the lights dimmed for a slide presentation representing the past year. During a series of fall pictures, a close-up of Jackie's beautiful face filled the screen; fall leaves in the background, blonde hair poking out from under her toque and a big angelic smile on her face. A collective gush of admiration erupted from the crowd, and we glowed with pride.

Afterwards, when we were in the van preparing to leave, I said, "Well done, Jackie. You looked gorgeous in that picture — did you hear the crowd?"

"Thank you, Daddy," she said and smiled. I started the engine.

"We're very proud of you, daughter," Karen said and reached back to hold her hand.

I nodded, "Yes, and just think, in September, you begin high school. Where has the time gone?"

"Oh, that reminds me," Jackie said while she gazed out the window. "I don't want Hillside anymore. I want to go to Streetsville."

"What are you talking about?" Karen said, whirling about in her seat. "Hillside is a great school, and you passed the audition!"

"Oh well, I don't want to go there anymore," she responded sullenly.

Karen and I exchanged glances, and I gripped the wheel and stared at the road ahead.

*

Hillside Regional Arts School was the best around, and if you lived outside the boundary, you needed to audition. Eric had gotten in with his trumpet, and they accepted Jackie into the dance program months ago. When the girls were younger, they took dance lessons passionately for years. But last year, they both became bored with them and stopped. However, dance remained Jackie's ticket into a better school. But now, despite our efforts and her success, she dug her heels in and insisted on the local school, which was quite dangerous. Police were on-site every day. Karen and I were dumbfounded.

There were bullies in my day but nothing like today's gangs. Now when kids reach high school, drugs and safety become the chief concerns of parents.

Although vague about the reason, we suspected this boy, who Jackie claimed was not her boyfriend, would be going there. We met Aaron Dobransky a few years ago when he rang our doorbell trick-or-treating. Shorter than Jackie but good-looking with fair hair and quiet confidence, he was taking her to their prom. So, he sure seemed like a boyfriend.

"Is it because of Dropsky? Is that why you said no to Hillside?" Karen quizzed her on the weekend, her voice grating with annoyance.

"His name isn't Dropsky; it's Dobransky!" Jackie hollered back with her features twisted into a scowl.

Karen never could get his name right, which astounded me, given her Polish and Russian heritage. And because of her, I confused the name, too. Later, she admitted to me that it was her way of getting even with Jackie for all the aggravation she received.

Karen brushed aside the outburst and kept her eyes on our daughter. "Whatever — is that why you won't go there anymore?"

"That's not it at all. I have friends going to Streetsville."

"Yes, but your best friends are registered for Hillside — Katie, Vicky and Natalie..."

"That's not all my best friends. You don't know everything. Sue and Haley will be at Streetsville." Jackie put her head down and brooded. She had become moodier this year, and the fact that Karen felt she knew the details of her life obviously irked her.

Whatever the cause, this was the first time one of the kids refused to listen to us, and we found it upsetting. At her age, I certainly never disagreed with my parents. And not just because they were authority figures; I also respected their opinion. For the time being, we let the matter drop but remained determined to change her mind.

*

The next weekend, as we sat with both girls in the living room, Karen looked innocently at our blonde daughter. "Remember my friend Alice?" The girls had been playmates with Alice's youngest child, Scott, when they were young.

"Yes," Jackie said lifelessly while playing with her hair and staring at the carpet. Karen had more patience for her indifference than I did; it always made my blood boil.

"Okay ..." Karen carried on undaunted, "she sent Mathew, her oldest, to Streetsville. He told Alice that he knew every pair of shoes in the school. When she asked him to explain, he said, 'Because I have to look at the floor when I walk down the hall. If you glance up and someone thinks you looked at them the wrong way, you'll get the shit beaten out of you. So, I know every shoe in the school.'"

"Yes, Mother," Jackie sighed and looked away. But the story must have struck a chord because she soon blurted out, "Okay, okay, I won't go there. But then I want to go to Rick Hansen."

I looked at Karen; she was the expert on schools. "Okay ..." she said thoughtfully, "that one seems to be alright."

And so, we reached a compromise, and the crisis abated.

*

On Thursday, I arrived home early and couldn't find Karen in the usual places. I paused in the hallway to consider where she might be. Her car was in the driveway, so she should have been home; *perhaps she's gone for a walk.*

"Hi, Poppa," Jackie chirped brightly as she zipped past.

"Where's your mother?" I shouted after the blonde comet, but she didn't hear me with her earbuds in.

A soft voice answered from another room. "She's in the back yard, Dad."

"Thanks, Meggy. How are you?" I asked, poking my head into the room.

"I'm good," she said, shooting me a smile before turning back to her program.

I walked into the kitchen and peered out the window. Our beautiful gardens were in bloom. Yellow, orange and red marigolds provided splashes of colour along the rear fence, intermixed with purple chrysanthemums. On the right side, trumpet vines climbed up the wooden fence beside hanging baskets of mixed begonias, while pansies and hydrangea blossomed below. I stood there captivated. Karen entered the view from the side. Her tall, slender frame moved across the yard, bending down every few minutes with a little shovel to pick up dog poop and put it in a plastic bag. Milo lingered nearby, watching her labour with great interest. I smiled appreciatively. Although I tried to avoid this chore, she gathered up these landmines daily.

When she saw me, she motioned to the patio door, walked over and poked her head in. "I swear Milo must invite all the other dogs in the neighbourhood over for pooping parties because that's way too much crap for one little beagle to make!"

"Perhaps we're feeding him too much," I said with a laugh.

"You're right. Maybe we should cut him down, ha-ha. Oh, and there's something else," her eyes searched my face. "Don't get mad, but Jackie says she doesn't want to come with us out west." Then she pulled herself up straight. "Don't worry. I'll talk to her."

"Okay," I nodded, letting the news sink in.

She closed the door and resumed her work in the yard. The news caught me off guard and left me baffled. I wandered into the family room, where dozens of our vacation pictures graced the walls. The best was B.C. and Alberta; the scenery had been spectacular, and fifteen large photos from that trip alone graced the walls. I studied one of Jackie and me canoeing an emerald-blue lake with mountains in the background, and the memories came flooding back, creating a lump in my throat. They'd been great bonding experiences for all of us. We'd talked about another trip for a long time, finally making reservations this year for the last three weeks of August. But this turn of events presented a problem. I felt a pang of regret. I had taken it for granted when the kids were small that we could bundle them up and take them wherever we wanted. Once they were older with jobs or boyfriends, we knew it would be harder. But Eric was on board. In fact, he'd already gotten the time off from his summer job. Now, out of the blue, Jackie dropped this bombshell, and I realized I didn't want it to end, not yet anyway. She was only fourteen. Surely, we had more years of holidaying together ahead.

*

There was a noise in the other room. Karen had come inside, and although the girls were out of earshot, she came up close and whispered, "Jackie's coming with us. Staying behind is *not* an option." Her blue eyes blazed and locked onto mine.

We'd seen what happened when you left a teen home alone. When the kids were little, we took them for a stroll through the neighbourhood. As we reached the part of the street where it curves towards the park, a burned-out building stood ominously on one side. The garage and half of the top floor were black, and charred timber stared out from open walls.

"Looks like they had a bad fire," I said.

"Oh, that's awful," Karen moaned and studied the damage. "Those poor people. I don't know what happened, but they won't be living there for a while!"

We got the story from the owner a few months later when we passed by again. An older lady was gardening outside. Karen struck up a conversation with her about flowers and then asked about the restoration that was underway. The poor woman poured out her heart. She and her husband had travelled to Florida, leaving their sixteen-year-old son behind. And he had a party. Somehow a fire started in the garage and proceeded to burn down half the house before the fire trucks arrived. They ended up grounding him for a month.

"That's it," Karen said as we resumed our walk. "There's no way we're ever leaving our kids alone at that age."

So far, we never had. But now we had to convince Jackie the trip would be a lot of fun. We discussed the situation over the weekend. Jackie insisted she was old enough to stay home and didn't want to leave her friends. We suspected 'friends' meant the 'boy,' who apparently was not her 'boyfriend.' In response to further queries, her answers were nebulous, so it remained a mystery. But as the French say — *Cherchez l'homme!*

*

I thought about how my parents would have handled the situation and decided to talk it over with Karen. She looked at me from the couch where she sat in cream-coloured slacks and a blue shirt, legs crossed and hands clasped around one knee.

"I'm not sure we should force her to come if she doesn't want to," I said and noticed her eyes narrow. "Jackie might learn a lesson if we leave her home. After all, it'll be pretty boring here."

"I'm not having my house destroyed!" she said with a sarcastic laugh. Evidently, the memory of the neighbour's fire still burned strongly.

I rolled my eyes. "That won't happen. Your mother can stay here and chaperone."

Karen straightened up and crossed her arms. "Don't you remember what happened to Iris' daughter?"

Iris and Rod were neighbours who often attended the theatre with us. Of German descent, Iris was attractive: tall and thin, with long black hair and a daughter just as beautiful. A vague recollection of the event surfaced as Karen talked. "They went away for the weekend, and Mikala invited some friends over. We were at the cottage, but the other neighbours told us about it. The noise kept them awake until three in the morning. There was loud music and drunken kids yelling outside and peeing in the bushes."

"Someone called the cops," I admitted.

"Yes," Karen's eyes lit up, "Mikala texted some classmates, who texted others, and it got out of control. The police told them it happens constantly with social media. News spreads like wildfire, and before you know it, you have an army of uninvited, obnoxious teenagers crashing the party."

I threw my hands up. "Okay, okay, you win. We'll tell her she has to come."

But we deferred that discussion until the next week to let the dust settle with Jackie.

*

Surprisingly, when we brought it up, Jackie agreed without protest. Karen suspected it resulted more from peer influence rather than our efforts.

"I overheard her on the phone with her friend Vicky — that family never travels," Karen snorted. "I'll bet she said, 'What are you, nuts? Who wouldn't want a holiday?'"

I slumped in my chair and put my head back. "Well, whoever did it, I'm grateful."

And so, we had surmounted another hurdle, and we could now start getting excited about our upcoming vacation. In my heart, I was hoping this trip would be a tonic for us, a panacea for the early signs of teenage angst, but it didn't quite work out that way.

GO WEST, YOUNG GIRL

4

"You know it's time for a vacation when you start looking like the person on your driving license…" - *26 funny travel quotes*

I STOOD BEHIND THE huge SUV with the trunk open and assessed the situation. Although we had specifically reserved an extended minivan, when we arrived at the rental desk in Vancouver, they didn't have one. They upgraded me to a large SUV instead.

Although an 'upgrade' sounded good, it became immediately apparent when I lifted the tailgate that there wasn't sufficient trunk space. I scanned the interior, and my heart sank — *how will I fit all the suitcases in?* With no alternative, I squared my shoulders and loaded the largest first. The muscles in my back strained as I heaved the behemoths up. "Ugh!"

Once I got each up, I pivoted and arranged them in such a manner to take up minimal space. But out of the corner of my eye, I spied more carts bursting with bags and suitcases, rolling ominously towards me. After ten minutes, I dropped a bag on the ground and waved my arms. "There are too many bags! There's no way I can fit them all in. Can't you people pack lighter?" Karen stared at me in bewilderment while I ranted. "Maybe we should leave some in an airport locker?" I wondered out loud.

A look of annoyance came over her face, and she brushed her light brown hair back. "We'll manage somehow. We always do. So, don't get uptight. I'll hold a bag on my lap."

She's the eternal optimist, and frankly, at times like this, it really pissed me off. "Great! That takes care of *one* bag. What about these other *three*?" I scowled at the sinister luggage waiting at the side. My outburst met icy silence.

Having vented my frustration, I re-entered the fray, pulling some cases out and rearranging them angrily in a struggle to create more space. I repeated this operation again, squishing soft pieces into narrow cracks. I may have said a few nasty words under my breath; I'm not sure. This was the same nightmare I went through whenever we packed for a holiday.

"You say 'don't worry,' but *I'm* the one who has to fit them all in," I blustered between gasps. This horror continued while a gnawing fear mounted inside me that I wouldn't succeed. Then, a few minutes later when I frantically grasped for another bag, there were none. I stared in disbelief, but the ground was bare. I looked around and under the vehicle, just to be sure, while the family waited inside. Eric and the girls had satchels on their laps and under their feet; Karen held a backpack in her lap and two bags by her legs. My heart was racing as I climbed in the driver's seat and surveyed the pile behind me. I could only hope they wouldn't come flying at me if I hit the brakes.

"See? I told you we'd fit them all in." Karen's mouth tightened; her blue eyes blazed. She showed me the tiny spot for her feet. "Look, I'm not complaining."

I pulled out of the parking area and sighed heavily. "It's ridiculous, that's all. We bring too much luggage, and we do this *every bloody time*. In the immortal words of Dr. Evil, *it's frickin nuts!*"

She put her hand up. "Alright, stop! I have to read the map." Then she glanced up and pointed. "Here, turn left."

I wrenched the steering wheel around. We always made a good team, with her navigating and me driving. I peered out over the hood, which seemed to go on forever. "You know what's funny? This SUV is huge — an El Grande version — and yet there's not enough luggage capacity." As we motored onto the main road, I felt like I was driving a tank, and it seemed too big to fit safely in our lane.

"Is there any room on your side?" I said, glancing at her. "I'm afraid we'll get hit head-on."

She looked down at the pavement by her side. "Okay, you can come over a few inches but no farther."

It was an ordeal, but fortunately, the ferry dock wasn't far, and I began to relax. Once onboard, I could sit and enjoy the crossing to Victoria. The first day's always the worst. I was bound to grow accustomed to this vehicle during the next few days.

*

After squeezing the humongous vehicle into the bottom of the ferryboat, we climbed the iron stairs leading to the upper decks.

"Wow, look at this!" Meggy shouted as I stepped out of the stairwell. Her black hair swung about as she danced across the deck snapping pictures.

I was speechless, and felt my jaw drop as I beheld the panoramic view of the Pacific Ocean. Faced with its sheer size and scope, we seemed tiny and insignificant. It's a wonder of nature, and cameras cannot capture the enormity of its size.

Karen leaned over the railing and squealed, "Keep your eyes peeled. You might spot dolphins. They jumped in front of our boat when I went to Florida with my parents, and they were *bee-u-tee-ful*," she cried, singing the last word.

We strolled the deck and inhaled the warm, salty air. When I held the railings, I could feel the vibration from the engines, and their continuous hum resonated in our ears as the boat cut a path through the placid blue water.

I gestured towards the horizon. "The sun's starting to set, Meggy. I'll bet you'll get some great shots in a few minutes."

And indeed, we did. An incredible scene unfolded on the horizon before us; an undulating array of colours spread across the clouds and sky. Cell phone cameras were in their infancy, so I had brought my digital SLR camera along, and we fought for turns in our attempts to capture the spectacle from different angles.

"Let go, Dad. You're obsessed!" Meggy shrieked and giggled as I wrestled with her.

In short order, the Gulf islands emerged, silhouetted in evening mist with streaks of red and yellow from the sunset. I attempted to count them, but they continued far out of sight. We remained on the deck, trying to imprint the haunting images in our memories before they disappeared. Not a shabby start to Vancouver Island; the vistas from the ferry alone were worth the fare.

*

Victoria was charming. We walked along the harbour and passed the grand Empress Hotel. The next day, we visited the home of Emily Carr, the famous post-impressionist Canadian painter, who was heavily inspired by the indigenous peoples of the Pacific Northwest Coast. Karen and I always found her paintings of totem poles, like Blunden Harbour and Totem Walk at Sitka, to be dark and haunting. Although the kids simply tolerated this excursion, Karen and I really enjoyed it. We walked slowly through the various English-styled small rooms, with high ceilings, ornate mouldings and a parlour and sensed her early family life in the late 1800s.

The next morning, as we cleared our dishes off the breakfast table in our rented condo, Karen outlined a plan for the day. "Let's go to Butchart Gardens. I've heard great things about it."

Eric nodded. "Sure, I'm up for that."

But I wasn't as enthusiastic. I tilted my head to one side. "To be honest, I don't want to. It's hot, and flowers aren't really my thing."

Karen stuck her chin out. "Fine, then we'll go without you. But you'll be sorry. It's over a hundred years old and a National Historic Site," she read from a brochure. "Originally a limestone quarry, the owner's wife turned it into a garden after they exhausted the stone and beautified what had been an eyesore."

I mulled my options over; being left behind was not appealing. "Okay, if you really want to see Butchart that badly, then I'll go," I said.

She beamed. "Good, I think it will be fun."

My mind began to warm to the idea. "You know, come to think of it, my mother raved about it on a trip years ago."

And I'm glad I gave in; the floral gardens were gorgeous. When we walked down the entrance ramp to the sunken gardens, Karen stopped to gesture at the colourful grounds. "Look, dear, it takes a woman to create something beautiful like this out of something ugly."

I smirked, trying to think of a clever comeback, but none came. Even the kids were drawn to the pictorial display before us and hurried eagerly ahead to explore. The gardens were divided into different sections and were more varied and interesting than I expected. After a few hours, we stumbled upon a quaint tea house, and Meggy suggested we have lunch. Sitting down at a large table in a room, the kids' faces beamed with delight as sunshine poured in through wide windows. After placing our orders, we chatted about our favourite parts; mine had been the Japanese garden. Our server reappeared shortly bearing two heavy pots of tea and platters of sandwiches and set them down beside the fine china. We ate, talked and sipped our tea in this wonderfully relaxed setting. It wound up being a pleasant respite after all the walking we had done and helped prepare us for the long drive ahead the next day.

*

In the morning, we headed across the island to spend time on the West Coast but not before stopping at a few sites along the way. At the first one, we stood and stared at the rooftop of a country market and counted goats as cars zipped by on the roadway behind us. After consultation, we agreed on five in total: two with snotty looks standing at the front; two lying on their sides and watching us with curiosity; and the grey head of one old goat sticking out over the peak from the back of the rooftop. The roofing on which they lived had a thick green layer of sod. We joked and took pictures before venturing in to buy groceries. We had deliberately chosen the Alberni Highway route to visit the renowned Goats on the Roof.

Once inside, we marvelled at the bounty of food. The left side contained a bakery with fresh bread, pies and other deserts; the other, a deli with cold cuts, cheeses, meat pies and soups. It seemed you could find any meal you thought of here. Splitting up, we scurried around, each picking up whatever tempted their palate and returning to add it to our shopping cart.

"This is why they claim you should never shop on an empty stomach," I whispered in amusement as I gestured at our overflowing cart.

When we reached the cashier, Karen mentioned how much we enjoyed the goats, then enquired, "Don't they ever fall off?"

The plump middle-aged woman, who was probably a local farmer's wife, raised her eyes from the task of ringing up items and smiled. "Well, the old one gets mad now and then and pushes a younger goat off. But we just put them up again, and they're fine."

Karen chuckled as she took her change, and we carried the groceries out into the bright sunshine.

*

Before starting the ignition, I checked my Blackberry. Still no reception. I hadn't realized how mountainous the island was. In fact, as soon as we departed from Victoria, it began to resemble one big mountain range. The lack of reception didn't bother me though. I enjoyed the opportunity to disconnect from the office. But our daughters complained regularly on the drive because the places where we stayed had no free Wi-Fi. Eric, on the other hand, seemed content to gaze out the window at the passing scenery.

Karen furrowed her brow while she studied the map. "Okay, we continue along here; it's not very far. Cathedral Grove lies within MacMillan Provincial Park."

She planned a stopover at this old-growth forest because it lays claim to some of the biggest Douglas Firs on earth; up to 250 feet high and over 800 years old. As we started down the trail, the kids ran ahead, leaving us to hold hands and gape upwards at the tall canopy of the rainforest. Parts of the *Star Wars* and the *Twilight* movies were filmed here, and you could understand why. Gigantic roots twisted up and along the ground, and thick trunks covered in gnarly bark stretched up to the sky. The trees had an ethereal beauty, giving one the impression of having journeyed back in time to a mysterious land. And it felt very soothing; the air smelled of pine needles and the earthy aromas of wet soil and decomposing matter.

"Let's get a picture of everyone there," Meggy cried, pointing to the base of a giant tree.

We hesitated, not wishing to disturb our reposeful mood. Karen opened her mouth to protest, but I stopped her. Meggy had developed into a budding photographer with an expert eye for framing a shot, and I wanted to encourage her. So, while the others gathered in front of the tree trunk, with Meggy in front because she was the shortest, I set up the tripod. Once in position, I engaged the timer and ran over to join them. And she was right. Of all the pictures taken on the trip, this would be the one we'd mail out at Christmas. A stunning shot that exemplified our western holiday perfectly by capturing the ancient beauty of the land.

As we shuffled back to the parking lot, a quiet descended. Everyone looked bone-weary. We'd accomplished a lot today but still had a fair ride to our lodgings. The kids slumped down in the SUV, and I resumed my position in the driver's seat.

*

After an hour, the winding highway narrowed and became more challenging, with frequent hairpin turns that twisted around the mountainside. I squinted against the sunlight and pulled the visor down to block the piercing rays. The sun had moved lower in the sky, and its light streaked through the greenwood so that sunglasses alone weren't sufficient. A disturbing thought crossed my mind; I might have to navigate these twisting curves in the dark if we didn't make faster progress. The road followed a river and passed by a lake, and I glimpsed the sharp drop-off on the right.

"Oh, baby, look at that!" Karen shrieked.

The whole car groaned. This had become her favourite catch phrase of late. In many ways, she behaved like a kid herself, and although it occasionally grew tiresome, I'd be the first to admit that her excitement made our travels more enjoyable.

Meggy grabbed the camera to take shots out the window. The highway rose up the side of the mountain, and I glanced in the mirror. Despite the magnificent terrain, the kids appeared tired of sitting in the car. Eric's large frame slouched in the rear in a grey T-shirt and black shorts while his legs extended between the middle seats. He passively studied the landscape clipping by, while Meggy busied herself with photos, and her blonde sister reclined in her chair, eyes closed.

Jackie turned her head, stretched and yawned. "Ewww, where are we going, and will there be any cell reception there?"

"We're going to Tofino!" Karen responded enthusiastically.

I looked in the mirror again. "For the cell reception question, the answer is ... maybe." This, of course, is parent speak for no chance in hell, but luckily, she was too tired to challenge me.

*

Ewww had become her favourite expression recently, and I teased her about it. The other morning, I was standing by the kitchen window when she sauntered sleepily out of her bedroom in matching pyjama top and shorts. I turned to her with a grin. "Oooh, good morning, and how are you?"

Karen sat at the table and giggled over her coffee.

"OMG, it's not ooh, Dad. Its ewww! You don't even know how to say it," she snapped and plopped down in a chair by the table and rolled her eyes.

I snickered at her rudeness. Who did she think she was talking to? Why, I've mastered much more complex tasks than this. But I wanted to get it right to repeat it correctly to our friends, so I tried again.

Looking intently, I concentrated and drawled, "Ooooh."

"That's not it. Its ewww!"

"Is it like the French verb *bu*? As in *j'ai bu*? You know ... buuuu." I dragged out the word to emphasize the nasal sound.

Jackie said nothing, just shook her head with a superior smile. But the exchange caused Karen to double over with laughter. Then she straightened up and attempted it herself. She did no better.

I grinned broadly. "Perhaps it's like the whistle that only dogs can hear, but this is a sound only crabby teenagers can make." I chortled at my own cleverness.

A smile crept across her face, and she quickly turned away to hide it. "So annoying," she muttered.

"Hey, what good's a vacation if a dad can't bug his kids?"

*

Although it was fun to recall the incident, its enjoyment had been fleeting. Her attitude was a challenge on this vacation. At each new scenic spot, everyone's features lit up, except Jackie's. Usually upbeat and game for anything, she had traded it all in for a constant, sullen expression. Sometimes I tried to take a candid photo, thinking if she saw how sour she looked, she'd snap out of it. But that turned out to be more difficult than expected. Either something would get in the way, or she'd catch me in the process and cover her face. The best picture would be captured years later by a government agent who renewed her health card. The tall grey-haired man tried his best as Jackie waited impatiently.

After he finished, he beckoned Karen over and whispered, "You've *got* to see this."

When I got home that evening, she showed it to me. "He snickered when he handed it to me. He must have teenagers, too."

I studied the photo. There it was: that spoiled adolescent look. She sat upright on a stool and her face stared at the camera, as if to say — *why are you wasting my time, peasant?*

"Classic Jackie pout," I declared. "It's perfect,"

We'd keep that card for years as a memento, but that was in the future. For now, I continued my attempts in vain.

*

Strangely enough, she might have been enjoying this trip. Well, as much as any fourteen-year-old can. She just didn't show it. These thoughts were running through my mind when, all at once, the road opened up and became flatter. Soon, I spotted the ocean in the distance. I breathed easier because it meant we'd arrive before nightfall. Twenty minutes later, we entered the Pacific Rim National Park Reserve and passed a few sandy beaches on the left. Karen pointed out one we should visit.

When we pulled into the Crystal Cove resort outside Tofino, my eyes widened. It looked very picturesque; dotted with attractive wooden cabins, the extensive property ran down to the seashore. Before unloading, we rushed to glimpse the beach before the sun completely vanished. High waves crashed against big rocks at the shoreline, spraying salt water high into the air, as we scrambled on top for a better view.

Standing beside me with the ocean wind whipping us, Karen reached her arms out towards the disappearing red ball of sun. "Isn't it gorgeous? It's so wild and captivating."

I nodded and breathed in the invigorating air. "Be careful on the rocks, girls!" I yelled as they climbed over the boulders.

We headed to the van to unload. When I unlocked the cabin door, the girls pushed by me, ladened down with enormous suitcases. My eyes swept the large room; new pine panelling, a clean bright kitchen and wide windows. The word cozy came to mind. I stood for a moment, taking it in, and then carried my bags into the largest bedroom. Karen burst through the door moments later with two heavy travel bags.

"What do you think, dear?" she asked while her eyes eagerly searched my face.

"Well done, honey. It's wonderful, and I'm impressed at what you've been able to find in our price range," I said nodding vigorously. "This cabin looks brand new, and it's nicely furnished."

She beamed. Karen had put a lot of effort into planning this vacation, and it paid off.

"Thank you for a wonderful holiday," she said, putting her arms around me.

"And thank you for planning it," I replied, hugging her back. "You always plan the best vacations."

EWWW!

"To an adolescent, there is nothing in the world more embarrassing than a parent." - designpress.com

THE FOLLOWING DAY, everyone rose early for an excursion out of Tofino Harbour.

Karen leaned back from the breakfast table and described it to us. "We drive to this pier. I have the directions written down and cross Clayoquot Sound by boat to these hot springs."

Karen had done a superb job with the itinerary so far, and everyone beamed happily. We were getting into the holiday mode —even Jackie! An hour later, we pulled up to a marina where a plain and uninviting boat lay docked. I gave a crewman our tickets, and he directed us below.

The journey took over an hour, and the loud drone of the engines made it too difficult to talk. Even worse, as the boat chugged across the sound, it sprayed water over the few small windows that existed, thwarting any effort to look at the scenery. There was absolutely nothing to do. Karen tried to keep our spirits up, but her efforts met with such muted responses that she stopped and remained quiet. I stared in boredom at the meagre table we huddled around. It had become an endurance test. Not an impressive beginning to our adventure.

Finally, the vessel stopped, and people lined up at the stairway to disembark. We waited until the line depleted before getting up and following. Groggy from the tedious voyage, I stepped onto the dock and looked around. There were no beaches and no other boats in the bay. The line of passengers was plodding up the sandy beach and disappearing into the woods. It reminded me of a low-budget horror movie. The only thing missing was someone yelling, 'Don't go into the woods!'

I turned to Karen. "Is this where they murder us? Where are we going?"

A wide-brimmed white hat was perched on her head to block the sun, and she motioned with one hand holding a bag. "We go up there and walk to the springs." Karen said this with conviction as if it were obvious. But when we reached the end of the dock, she faltered and questioned a deckhand stationed to assist people stepping off the pier or to stop those who tried to escape their heinous trap.

"So, we just walk along here?"

"Yes, ma'am, you follow the trail," he said, jerking his head towards the shore. "It takes you to the springs and change rooms." He took her hand to help her step onto the sand. "You have four hours to enjoy yourselves, then come back. We'll be waiting here."

"Okay, thank you," Karen said and stared at the forest entrance. "Come on, kids. Follow the group."

*

After entering the woods, we encountered a boardwalk.

"We're actually walking through a temperate rain forest," Karen announced, and her eyes shone with excitement.

The other passengers were nowhere in sight, so we had the wilderness to ourselves. At the edges of the walkway stood massive timbers with enormous roots that wrapped around and stretched out in all directions. I wouldn't have been surprised if Bilbo Baggins had jumped out from behind one. There were Spruce, Western Hemlock, Red Cedar and Douglas Fir, but much more massive than the trees in Ontario. The kids sped ahead while Karen and I meandered, breathing in the cool air and gazing through the trees.

"Whenever I'm in nature like this, I feel close to God," Karen said, taking my hand.

"Me, too. This is wonderful. Boy, they undersell this excursion. The walk alone is an experience."

"I know, right?" Karen said, and her face glowed.

*

We continued walking across the damp timber planks and climbing up and down sets of stairs now and then. About forty-five minutes later, we emerged in front of a wooden bridge that spanned a little canyon. On the other side stood wooden huts, presumably the change rooms, and below to the right, people lounged in small pools scattered and hidden between large boulders. After donning our bathing suits, we waited beside the first pool until some visitors left and made room for us. Steam rose from the water.

"Ouch, it's hot!" Jackie squealed.

"Don't worry. You'll get used to it," Karen said encouragingly.

We immersed our bodies in stages to adjust to the hot temperature before fully descending. Only a trace of the characteristic sulphur odour was noticeable.

A narrow stone ledge jutted out from above on one side with steaming water cascading over it, making a mini waterfall. Eric and the girls took turns ducking under it and then floated happily back to us.

"Well, kids, what do you think?" Karen queried, gesturing at the surrounding rock cliffs and forest above them.

"Definitely worth it, Mum," Eric responded with a contented smile.

The girls nodded, and Jackie chimed in, "Beautiful. I like it."

Karen recalled her research. "This is natural hot water that pours out of the rocks and down this gorge into Clayoquot Sound. Apparently, they've been here for thousands of years."

I leaned back against the rock wall and let my legs float. "Amazing. I love Banff's hot springs, but this is so much better because it's out in the wilderness."

"Absolutely," Karen said and closed her eyelids with a sigh.

*

The kids moved on to another pool, but we stayed there, enjoying the scenery. Other visitors left, and new ones arrived; it was a busy place. I pointed at a crowd heading back to the boardwalk. "The plan must be to drop a boatload off, have them spend a few hours, and then leave as another arrives."

Her lips formed a smile. "Don't worry; there's no rush. We have plenty of time."

And we did. We moved through different pools and talked to other tourists. Karen struck up a conversation with a plump woman about her age named Janice. She was travelling with her twenty-year-old son, who occupied another pool.

"You don't have teenage girls?" Karen asked and rolled her eyes theatrically. "Lucky you!"

The lady seemed startled and momentarily at a loss for words, but she laughed. Janice had blonde, shoulder-length hair and an easy smile. Now that Karen had broken the ice, we shared stories and recommended sites to each other. She clearly enjoyed having adult company.

"The forest we walked through is ancient; many trees are over five hundred years old," Janice said, sitting beside us on a rock shelf that lay under the surface. "This tour I took a few days ago, called the Big Tree Trail, leads to a massive Western red cedar called the Hanging Garden Tree." She leaned forward. "It's said to be at least 1600 years old, making it one of the oldest on earth."

"That's amazing," Karen said. "I want to see that, but it'll have to be another trip because we're heading to Kelowna tomorrow. So, they call it the Hanging Garden Tree?"

"Yes, because other plants and trees live in it. It's incredible," Janice explained as she floated on her back.

Karen looked at her earnestly. "Goats on the Roof — don't miss it on your drive back."

Her eyes opened, and she sat up. "Really? I've never heard of it."

This brought forth an animated description and directions from Karen. Janice knitted her brow in concentration as she listened, but Karen reassured her. "The store's easy to find as long as you take the Alberni Highway."

Moments later, Karen and I realized it was time to get out of the pool to avoid overheating, so we wished her well and said goodbye.

*

We perched on top of a boulder in the warm sunshine and surveyed our section of the canyon. Chalk white cliffs stood on both sides, and a small stream of thermal runoff flowed through the middle.

I lay down, put my arms across my chest, and inclined my head towards Karen. "This is amazing and all natural, except for the stairs and change rooms. A truly unique experience."

She smiled and nodded. I had no compulsion to hurry. Time had slowed down, and me with it. There was peace here, and the combination of water, sunshine, rugged scenery and fresh air had a calming effect that soothed us.

Suddenly, Karen straightened up and peered down the gorge. "There're the girls," she said, pointing.

Lifting my head, I spotted them in the distance, making their way through the crevice. Meggy, in a red bikini, led the way, adeptly picking out a path by the stream. Jackie followed a few lengths behind, her blonde hair tied into a ponytail.

"But I don't see Eric," Karen continued, twisting her neck to look behind. "Where is he?"

"Don't upset yourself. He's nearby," I said nonchalantly. "He's a big boy; give him some space."

Karen stood up with an air of annoyance. "Well, I'm going to look for him. This spring runs into the ocean, you know."

"Alright, if you must," I said but stayed where I was, enjoying the sun and this wonder of nature. The girls reached me shortly, and I motioned for them to sit. "Wait here till Mother comes back. She's gone to find Eric."

After a while, the girls left to change out of their bathing suits, and I remained alone. No buzzer or alarm sounded to alert passengers to head back to the boat; they assumed everybody would keep an eye on the time. I sat up and wrapped my arms around my knees. Why hadn't Karen returned? I straightened up and went to put my clothes on. When I finished, they still weren't back, so I climbed the tallest boulder for a better view. They were nowhere to be seen. I had just decided to begin a search when I saw them progressing slowly through the crevice. What a relief.

As soon as they arrived, I blurted out, "I'm glad you're back. I was getting concerned."

"Oh, we're fine," Karen said serenely.

I looked at my watch. "You should change. I think we better head back to the dock."

Eric left, and Karen whispered, "That little ass. I found him farther downstream, sitting and looking out at the ocean. I said to him, 'I was afraid you got washed out to sea!'"

"What did he say?"

"He grinned and said, 'Oh, Mom, it's so beautiful, I just sat here staring at the ocean.' So, I plopped down and joined him."

"Good for you," I said. "What a wonderful opportunity to be alone with him."

*

When Karen came out of the change room, only Eric and I were waiting.

"The girls insisted on going ahead to the path," I said, anticipating her question.

"That's nice, but we should catch up to them." She started walking towards the bridge.

As we entered the woods, we spotted them sitting on a rock at the side of the footpath. They jumped up and ran to us.

Jackie gasped, "Mother... what did you say to that lady? Mother?"

Meggy arrived a second behind. "Yeah, what did you say about us?"

We stared blankly. "What lady? What are you talking about?"

Jackie grabbed Karen's arm and scrutinized her face. "You were talking about us, weren't you?"

Often, we do, so we must have appeared guilty because Meggy broke into a laugh. "Yeah, you were!"

"I don't know who you're talking about," Karen replied as we reached the boardwalk.

But Jackie marched alongside, holding her arm, and speaking in a low conspiratorial tone, she said, "A lady came by, looked at us, said 'Ewww!', then walked away."

"What?"

Karen and I exchanged glances, laughed, and continued hiking.

"What did you say to her?" Jackie persisted.

"Oh, we talked to a woman in the pool about how *fun* it is to travel with teenage girls," she snickered. "We told her your favourite word is *Ewww*."

"I knew it!" Jackie declared triumphantly and marched off, but she yelled back over her shoulder, "And you're *still* not saying it right!"

*

The next day we left Tofino, crossed at Nanaimo to the mainland, and worked our way east. As we reached the outskirts of Vancouver, my phone began buzzing like crazy. Connected again, the emails poured in. Karen took over driving, so I could check for anything important. I watched the landscape out the window and listened to three voicemails, all marked urgent.

All were from Suzanne, pleading for me to call as soon as possible. The first message, from three days ago, advised me of the critical need to initiate a drug recall. My heart started racing; I had let my team down, leaving them to cope with one of the most stressful situations in our industry. But after listening to the third, my mood became more upbeat. She had contacted the government and provided all the information needed at present. That was key. Authorities show no mercy if you delay informing them of a serious quality issue. And my department handles this, as well as ensuring our drugs meet all quality and compliance standards before being released to market.

Karen pulled over on the side of the highway so I could call Suzanne.

I immediately apologized. "It's the mountains. They're everywhere, and we had no reception until now. I just received your messages; I'm so sorry."

Her voice sounded calmer than on the voicemails, which reassured me. Then, as she provided an update on the events, I felt proud of her. She had assisted before but never led a recall herself.

"You've done magnificently, Suzanne; I certainly appreciate how you stepped up to the challenge. The fact you already have it underway is a huge load off my mind."

Recalls involve strategy and planning with many departments, and a conference call with the president and his leadership team was scheduled for tomorrow. She gave me the number and password so I could join.

As we resumed the drive, I slouched in my seat and filled Karen in. "Being cut off from the office can be a good thing. Your staff learns how to handle situations without you."

She kept her eyes on the road but nodded vigorously. "You need a break! They must understand you're on vacation."

"That's not how it works anymore, dear," I said with a shrug. "Companies expect you to be on call 24/7. But in this case, with no cell reception, they'll understand, especially since it worked out well."

I made a mental note to include this exemplary work in Suzanne's next performance review; she had earned a high rating.

*

We finished the four-hour drive to Kelowna and then navigated our way downtown to the rented condo.

"Turn it up. I love this song!" Jackie shouted from the back, and I obeyed.

Singing with a big smile and her ponytail dancing from side to side, we watched in amusement. "Your lipstick stains on the front lobe of my left side brains..."

Jackie played it a lot at home, so we knew the chorus and joined in, "Hey, soul sister, ain't that mister mister on the radio, stereo. The way you move ain't fair, you know." When it finished, we all laughed.

We carried our bags into the condo building and, within an hour, found ourselves at a patio restaurant in a vineyard overlooking Okanagan Lake. Karen had read about this winery and suggested having dinner before we even unpacked. We began with a glass of local sparkling wine and then ordered a three-course meal. It wasn't cheap but tasted fantastic. A breathtaking view of the lake and surrounding mountains lay before us, and the air stayed pleasantly warm during the evening, which suited our T-shirts and shorts. We stayed there after dinner, sipping coffee, and chatting about our experiences while the sun melted into the horizon but not before sending its crimson colours dancing across the water. It's incredible how your worries dissolve when you watch the natural world unfold in front of you. Even Jackie's scowl disappeared as she eagerly engaged in a discussion of holiday highlights.

"We've really enjoyed having you kids along on this trip," Karen gushed, and all three beamed. "Let's try to remember how well we all got along after we're home."

*

The next day, we got out of bed early for a scheduled bike ride across the Myra Canyon train trestles. Theses wooden trestles, which once supported long-abandoned tracks through the valley, were turned into a bike trail. They were destroyed a few years ago by a wildfire that made the news in Toronto. However, as a testament to the human spirit, the small population rallied, raised over a million dollars, and rebuilt them.

At ten o'clock, a van full of bikes duly appeared in front of our condo to take us up the mountain. The driver, a tall, bearded, fair-haired man in his thirties, advised us it was a two-and-a-half-hour ride to the end and back and that he would wait for us.

Jackie was the fastest and sped ahead with her siblings in pursuit. Karen and I followed, pedalling leisurely while gazing at the valley below. Although we worried the fire might have destroyed the view, the vistas were actually more spectacular because the loss of woodland opened up the panoramic view. Passing by wide tracts of black charcoal remnants, we noted that several trees had survived, and new saplings already sprung forth.

"Nicely done, dear," I said when we stopped to study a breathtaking scene. "This is definitely another highlight. How did you hear about it?"

"I phoned the local tourist office and asked them, 'If you only had a day to spend here, what would be the one thing you had to see?' The young woman thought for a moment, then said, 'The Myra Canyon Trestles, for sure.' She helped me book it."

"Good for you, honey. This should be on everyone's bucket list."

Often, I'm in awe of the fearless way Karen draws information from people. Her warm personality makes them want to help, but make no mistake — she's no pushover. I pity the poor soul who behaves rudely because she will give it back and more. Yet, she can do it in a way that, by the end of the conversation, there are no hard feelings. I don't understand how she does this, but it's a gift.

"You could be a travel agent if you wanted."

"Yes, but I'd rather be a tourist," she said, breaking into a grin.

Without question, she planned the best holidays, and this one now topped the list. However, every holiday includes at least one harrowing experience, as I was about to find out.

6
THE RIDE FROM HELL

"I believe that if life gives you lemons, you should make lemonade... And try to find somebody whose life has given them vodka, and have a party." - Ron White

I T WAS LATE morning by the time we left the Okanagan Valley for the town of Revelstoke. Upon arrival, we unloaded at our lodgings and headed right away to the national park, which had been a special experience on an earlier trip. Our enjoyment of the holiday was in full swing, and everyone was in the vacation groove. Even Jackie was buoyant, and she relished the wonderful natural vistas laid out on the horizon before us.

As I paid the entrance fee, I noticed a small sign beside the ranger station. "Look, Karen, they close at 7 p.m."

"That's okay. We have plenty of time," she replied, unconcerned.

The park ranger, a tall, dark-haired man in his late forties, stood ramrod straight while counting my change. He looked like someone suited to the outdoors and waved at us as we headed up the winding Meadow in the Sky Parkway. We didn't rush; we wanted to enjoy this ascent more than the last time when we had to hurry because of a late start. As I crawled through hairpin turns, I managed to catch the odd glimpse of the marvellous views below.

We rode up to the summit, stopping occasionally for a photo op, parked and did a brief walk about to reacquaint ourselves. This is the only mountain in the national park system where you can go all the way to the top, which amazes me. The cool air was invigorating, and we walked by subalpine firs and spruce, many of which were only ten to twenty feet high. Their youthful appearance is deceptive; in reality, they're over three hundred years old, stunted by the short growing season. The mysterious element of dwarf trees added to the allure of the landscape. Shortly after, we perched on a small stone wall at the mountain's edge to eat our sandwiches and gazed across the valley at snow-capped peaks layered one after another, like dominoes as far as the eye could see. Down below, a blue river snaked its path through the canyon and appeared so small, it felt as if we were observing it from an eagle's nest.

*

Refreshed, we were ready to tackle a trail. A large board displayed various routes and hiking times, and we found a couple that looked reasonable. Karen was keen on a three-hour route of moderate difficulty that led through gently rolling terrain to a high elevation lake. Everybody was enthusiastic except Jacquelyn, who, although keen to hike, didn't want to trek that far.

"We don't have to go all the way," I reassured her and paused for a moment, calculating. "I'm not sure there's enough time to reach the lake anyway. Let's hike until we've had enough and then turn around."

Everyone agreed, so off we marched. The trail dipped into a small valley and rose again on the other side. We passed through woods with pleasant aromas of cedar and hemlock. The going was slow because tree roots crisscrossed the path, making us concentrate on our foot placement, but we still tripped every so often. After an hour, the path cut through an alpine meadow bursting with sunshine and wildflowers, and all of it was surrounded by the quiet beauty of mountain peaks. Sweat trickled down from under my Tilley hat, and I wiped my brow as we trekked past yellow, red and purple flowers. The burst of bright colours brought moans of admiration and pleasure. We re-entered the woods and continued for half an hour when Jackie, who was in the lead, stopped and swung around to face us.

"Let's go back. I'm tired."

Everyone halted, and I dropped the backpack on the ground. "Let's stop for a break."

We squatted on the ground and discussed our options.

"But it's so beautiful. I want to continue," Karen protested.

Meggy and Eric also voted to keep hiking, but Jackie looked worn out as she leaned against a tree trunk. She was the youngest, so her tiredness was understandable.

I shrugged. "It's alright. She's tired. I'll head back with her."

This brought a smile to her lips.

Karen frowned, but I insisted. "I'm hot, anyway. We'll wait for you in the van." I looked at my watch and then fixed my gaze on her. "But remember, they close the gate, so you need to meet us by six at the latest."

"Okay, don't worry. We will," she replied with an air of certainty.

Eric stood adjusting the straps on his backpack, and I caught his eye. "Did you hear me about the time?"

"Yeah, I got it, Poppo — be back at six."

That made me feel better because Karen had a propensity to be late, and whenever we hiked, she never wanted to stop. She's an 'all in' kind of person who never does things half-heartedly. When we'd try to turn back, she'd keep saying, "just a little further," until she coaxed us to the end. But Eric was more cautious, like me, and I knew I could count on him to adhere to the parameters and reign her in. Jackie and I sat cross-legged on the sparse grass as we watched them leave. Even Meggy appeared full of verve, her black ponytail swinging side to side from the back of her baseball cap.

"Thank you for coming back with me, Dad," Jackie said as we straightened up.

"It's really no problem. I know you're tired." But I was pleased to hear appreciation in her voice, and I smiled. "Don't feel bad. You hiked well. I hope you enjoyed it."

"Yes, I did, but now I'm beat."

*

When we arrived at the parking lot, our black SUV was easy to spot because most of the vehicles had departed. We sat inside and surveyed the scenery. After a few minutes, I grew restless and glanced at her. "Why don't we run into town and get groceries for dinner? We should be able to make it if we don't dawdle."

"Yeah, I could do that."

Since we weren't stopping at scenic lookouts, I didn`t think the descent would take long, but it did, mostly because of the constant need to slow down for blind turns.

"Wow, it's farther than I thought," I said, staring at the dashboard clock. "It's taken half an hour so far!"

Although surprised, I wasn't worried; we could always abort the mission if needed. Soon we reached the bottom, where I could speed faster on the flat ground.

The bridge over the Columbia River afforded a pleasant view of the quaint little town on the other side. Old-fashioned buildings with coloured awnings that stretched out over sidewalks lined the main street. The thoroughfare led to a grocery store where we picked up chicken breasts and vegetables. Jackie and I moved through the aisles efficiently, getting in and out fast, which made me happy. Neither of us was fond of shopping.

We put the meat in the cooler with the ice packs we had used to store our lunch and climbed into the SUV.

*

On route to the park, I spied a hamburger stand. "Want to grab a milkshake?"

My mood was upbeat; we had accomplished the goal and would return to the summit in good time.

Jackie, too, was happier than on the hike, and I was glad we were having fun together. When we reached the entrance booth, although I had my pass displayed, I stopped to confirm the closing time.

The same fellow leaned out the window and smiled. "We close at seven."

I waved my hand in thanks and accelerated away.

"These milkshakes are pretty tasty," I said, sipping on my straw as I followed the winding road upwards.

"Yeah, they're not bad."

I fretted that the others would be waiting, but I shouldn't have. When we reached the top, they were nowhere to be seen. The parking lot was practically deserted, so they would easily spot our car when they arrived. We got out and scouted the nearby area in case they had found a pretty spot to wait but had no luck. Returning to our vehicle, we lounged inside with the doors and windows open to let the breeze cool us. *They should be back any minute.* A bird was singing nearby, and I watched the sunshine dance on the treetops. I was wonderfully satisfied and relaxed.

"What a perfect day, Jackie," I said happily. "Think of all the gorgeous scenery we saw today."

She smiled and nodded.

I waited excitedly and thought how surprised they would be to learn we made it to town and back. We waited and waited, and still, the others did not appear.

A rising feeling of apprehension crept over me, and I glanced at my wristwatch. "Where the heck are they? I told your mother to be back by now," I sputtered in exasperation. Jackie said nothing.

I looked around; no other vehicles remained. Suppressing the urge to bang my head on the steering wheel in frustration, I fumed silently. Karen had done it to me again. The woman has no sense of time. I'd even told her when to be back. If I gave a deadline at work, everyone met it, so why couldn't she? More time ticked by, and I rubbed my hand at the knots in my stomach. Finally, after what seemed like an eternity, there was a noise in the distance. It was them, and they were singing. Down the trail they strutted, belting out a tune all the way. Not wishing to ruin the bliss that shone on their faces, I stifled my annoyance and greeted them cheerfully.

"We had so much fun!" Karen exclaimed as she handed me her backpack and walking stick. "I'm sorry you couldn't come. The lake was beautiful."

I put her things in the trunk.

"You made it to the end?"

"Yes, and it was lovely."

"Listen, we need to hurry," I said, shutting the rear door. "You can tell me about it on the way down."

I envied their contentment; Karen practically glowed. After climbing in, she twisted around in her seat towards Meggy and Eric. "You had fun. Didn't you?"

Both grunted affirmatively. Then she motioned to our son with her head. "He went swimming, the little ass!"

"What? You went in?" I glanced in the rear-view mirror. "But you didn't have a bathing suit."

A smile flashed across his face.

"Oh, I just went in with my underwear. It was cold but very nice."

"I can see you enjoyed yourselves. That's great," I pulled out of the parking lot. "Jackie and I went to town and picked up something for dinner."

*

They were all chatting at once, each wanting to describe their experience. I touched Karen's leg and spoke in a hushed voice so the kids wouldn't hear. "It's six-thirty, and I don't know if we'll make it before the gate closes."

She slumped in the seat, unperturbed. "Don't have kittens, dear. We'll be fine. You'll see."

I do tend to be a worrier; it's been the secret of my success. Worry about failing a course at school or deadline at work often drove me to stay up late and excel. But at this moment, I had good cause to be. I whispered again, more anxiously, "We only have thirty minutes, and the descent to town took us forty-five. I timed it."

That made her sit up and take notice. Meggy said something to me as I entered a sharp turn, and Karen twisted her head around and barked, "Leave your father alone. He has to get to the exit before it closes."

A brief moment of silence followed, and then Eric's calm voice resonated from the rear, "When does it close, Dad?"

I answered, and silence descended once more. No doubt this was a downer compared to the fun day they experienced. Due to the high elevation, the sun was already setting, and the fading light hampered my speed.

"Be careful, Andrew. Animals come out at night."

The thought of hitting a beast and veering off the road gave me the chills.

Coming out of another turn, I had to slam on the brakes. A party had spilled out from a set of cabins onto the road. They must have booked them for the night and arranged an outdoor social event. From the stares we garnered, it was obvious they hadn`t expected someone to be driving at this hour. I crawled through the merrymakers. A pretty young woman with long brown hair, a glass of wine in her hand and not a care in the world, smiled at me. How I wished I was having a drink with them instead of racing down the mountain.

Karen looked back at the crowd after we passed. "They rent cabins, and they're not expensive. Maybe we should rent one if the gate's closed?"

I smiled wryly as I put the hammer down to race off once more. "Yes, dear, but I think you have to make those arrangements earlier, before the ranger leaves."

She swallowed and stared ahead. A heartbeat later, my eternal optimist said, "Oh well, so we have to sleep in the car then."

"Yes, but it gets pretty cold at this altitude overnight. Temperatures can fall to zero Celsius," I answered, keeping my eyes fixed intently on the small bit of pavement illuminated ahead by the headlights.

*

The kids began to shout encouragement.

"You can do it, Faja," Eric shouted from the back. They didn't seem too worried, but then I was the poor slob speeding down Mount Revelstoke, not them.

I went as fast as I could, but it was tough. I'd go straight for twenty seconds, then put on the brakes for a hairpin turn. And because of the steep grade, the SUV rapidly gained speed on the straightaways, making me pump the brakes every few seconds to keep from flying off the road. The clock moved to 6:50 p.m.

The sun had set now, and it was completely dark. I didn't see anything but the stretch of road ahead in the headlights as I threw the SUV down the narrow, twisting roadway, not even the trees whipping past the windshield. My entire focus was on each dark turn illuminated in segments by my lights. A horrible picture formed in my mind of arriving before a locked gate.

"Faster, Father, faster." Meggy and Jackie had joined the effort to cheer me on.

We weaved in and out of hairpin bends, our bodies shifting sideways with each motion, while I gripped the wheel like a kid on his first ride on a roller coaster. I felt the black SUV thrust forward as the heavy weight of the vehicle along with our five bodies quickly gathered speed and hurled itself downward. The brakes groaned as I slowed into the curves and raced out as soon as possible. A sense of desperation came over me. Steering out of another bend, I saw the dashboard clock hit 6:55 p.m.

Then, miraculously, the ground levelled off, and we could see the gatehouse in the dim light ahead, like a beacon, waiting for us.

Karen smiled and visibly relaxed in her seat. "Here we are. You did it!"

But I froze as I stared through the windshield. The barrier was halfway across, and fifty feet farther on, a car idled at the side. Its headlights formed the silhouette of a person walking towards the exit.

"He's closing the gate," I yelled, and my body tensed, as I pressed sharply down on the gas pedal. We roared up to the gate, then quickly slowed down to pass safely through. Standing just fifteen feet from the barrier, the ranger watched us with a look of astonishment as we glided by, giving him a weak wave. A surge of relief flowed over me.

"You did it, Faja. Good job!" Eric cried, and the girls yelled, "hurray."

"Aaugh! That was *soo* stressful," I gasped as the vehicle coasted to a stop. "My heart's pounding. Twenty seconds later would have been too late."

"You did great, Andrew," Karen said. "You can relax now."

I slumped forward with my head on the steering wheel. I swear I could even feel the SUV shudder.

"This is ridiculous. I'm driving down a mountain like a madman while my family's shouting, 'Faster, Daddy, faster.' Sooner or later, I swear I'll have a heart attack."

With my fingers still clenching the steering wheel, I muttered to the floorboard, "If I die and they ask me about my life, this is what I'll remember — always racing for something before it's too late."

Karen gave a quick laugh, thinking I was being funny. But then, a look of concern crossed her face.

"Oh, I'm sorry," she said, and her voice became soothing. "My poor honey, how I stress you out." She massaged my shoulder. "I'm sorry, dear, but we all got lost in the moment and lost track of time. Listen, when we get to the chalet, you just take it easy, and I'll do the dinner."

My heart rate began to decrease. "Thank you," I said and slowly resumed driving. "But it's true. Remember when we went on that ski trip to Tremblant and almost missed the bus? We had to run in front and flag it down before it left the car park."

"That's not fair," she answered, getting her hackles up. "It wasn't my fault the taxi came late."

"Okay, that's true ..." I shrugged, "but you're not on time for anything. Admit it."

She admitted it, and by that, I mean, she stared out the window without another word.

*

Twenty minutes later, I sat on the porch steps of our two-story log cabin. Exposed beams supported the overhang of the high peaked roof that provided protection from the elements. I heard pots banging around, and I glanced up. Karen and the kids were busy cooking dinner in the kitchen, emitting aromas and light through the small window. The interior had knotty pine panelling on the walls and ceiling throughout. The cabin lay in a valley of the Kootenay Rockies, and I felt like an early pioneer as I sipped my beer and contemplated the dark mountain ranges in the distance. Majestic under a cloudless ink blue sky, the Selkirk mountains stood on one side and Monashee on the other. I leaned back on my elbows, grinned with pleasure and inhaled the cool evening air. Karen had done it again and scored another excellent accommodation with breathtaking vistas. This was unquestionably the climactic moment of the trip, and I shivered at the recollection of trees flashing by during the dash in the dark. Funny, my job at work is to ensure that everything functions in a state of control, but at home, I can't control events like this or even my own family. I thought to myself — *who needs a thrill ride at an amusement park? Not me, that's for sure. With my family, every day is as scary as hell.*

7
CELL PHONE MANIA

"I just spotted some ducks practicing their teenage girl faces." - designpress.com

AFTER BOARDING THE plane, I looked at my family sitting around me, tired and contented in their seats, and smiled. This trip had generated many memorable moments. And Jackie didn't even say 'Ewww' once today. Everyone was relaxed from the holiday, and it had been a great bonding time for us. It's essential for families to get away together, especially during the teenage years.

I closed my eyes, leaned back in the seat, and prayed that the closeness and positive feelings we had shared would continue at home. They did but much too briefly for my liking.

*

When we entered the front door, Milo greeted us loudly. I petted him and rubbed his light brown floppy ears between my fingers. It always amazed me how soft they were.

"Thank you for staying here and taking care of the animals, Ma," Karen said, giving Anna a hug.

"You're welcome. Did you have a good time?"

"Wonderful."

Everybody embraced Anna and chatted about the trip. Meggy lifted Moochie onto her lap, and we pulled out the souvenirs we bought for Anna. While it must have been a pleasant change from her rental in Fort Erie, we were grateful for her willingness to house sit. She never hesitated to come and watch the pets or kids, which was a great consolation when we travelled. But now came the hardest part of a vacation: returning to our work and school routines. Oh well, in a few weeks, everyone would be used to it once more.

The IT department upgraded my Blackberry, so after her siblings both declined the offer, Jackie received the old one. When I presented it, she lifted her eyebrows, and her face lit up.

"For me? Thank you, Poppa!" she chirped merrily and examined it as one might a precious stone.

Then she bolted out of the room and raced upstairs to tell her BFFs. The suddenness of her departure was startling.

"Is there a burglar behind me with a gun, or is the house on fire?" I asked Meggy, who was sitting at the kitchen table.

"You're funny, Dad," she cackled, and her blue eyes danced.

When she was a child, I used to call Jackie "Tigger" because she practically bounced around like the Winnie the Pooh character.

As a teenager, Jackie leapt out of chairs and ran up and down the stairs, often skipping the last three steps, where the banister curves at the bottom, to jump from the landing to the floor. I cringed every time I heard the thud as she hit the ground, half expecting a scream to follow, announcing a broken leg.

Of course, her excitement in this case was understandable; possession of a Blackberry was the ultimate status symbol among her peers. It felt good to see her happy, and my spirits rose with optimism. Fall was shaping up to be a great season at the McKinney household.

*

It may be hard to believe today, but teens had just started to get mobile phones back then. Our daughters had their first a couple of years earlier — flip phones that could only text and call. They'd borrow my Blackberry to create fifteen-second videos. Sitting on the swing at the cottage, hair hanging down over their faces, they'd make scary clips reminiscent of *The Ring*. And they'd do this over and over for hours on end. Or they'd take a thousand photos of themselves making cute, funny and even ugly faces.

"What do you think of this?" Meggy asked, thrusting her phone in front of me.

Two faces stared out from the camera, lower lips pushed up over the upper ones and ears pinned back with their hands.

I studied the photo. "That's a face only a mother could love, and even she'd scream now and then."

Meggy smirked as she grabbed it out of my hands. Girls seemed to have a stronger need for cell phones than boys. Perhaps it feeds their hunger for collaboration and communication. Eric didn't acquire his first until university, after we insisted he carry one for safety reasons.

Another thing about girls and cellular phones is that they tend to destroy them. I don't understand it, but they either drop them on the floor until the screens break or drown them in the bathroom.

At dinner on Wednesday evening, Karen announced that Jackie had ruined the latest model.

"It got wet," our blonde daughter said sheepishly.

"That's never happened to me, but it's the second time you've done that," I said, stabbing a piece of meat on my plate. "How do you do it?"

She sighed and chewed a mouthful of food before answering. "When I go to the bathroom at school and then get up, it falls out of my back pocket into the toilet."

"That's ridiculous. Don't put it in the back pocket."

She squirmed in her chair. "We all do. That's how girls carry them. The same thing happened to Katie last month."

"Well, you're crazy. You need a better system."

"Don't worry about it," Karen interjected. "She pays for the phone, so if she destroys it, that's her problem. She'll have to learn the hard way."

"Okay, okay," I moaned.

When mistakes occur during manufacturing, my department ensured that procedures were put in place to prevent a reoccurrence. Therefore, it was frustrating for me to watch my kids repeat the same errors. But I dropped the subject. I just wanted to enjoy my dinner, and we seemed to be having too many disagreements as of late.

*

In the morning, Karen and I were fighting. I'm not sure why but probably over how much money we were spending. I ate breakfast in silence and hurried to the office without saying goodbye. To my surprise, she called that afternoon. When I saw the number, I figured she had phoned to apologize. After an awkward exchange of pleasantries, she informed me that she was stuck at a coffee shop and needed help. After meeting Vicky, a BFF from prenatal classes, Karen had accidentally flushed her car keys down the toilet. I was silent, not fully comprehending what Karen said, so I asked her to repeat it, and she described what happened. She placed her purse on the back of the toilet and the key chain on top of it. When she stood up, she flushed and grabbed her handbag. The keys fell off and into the toilet, disappearing into that great swooshing sound that belongs to powerful industrial units. She needed me to go home, get the spare car key and bring it to her.

I checked the computer calendar on my laptop; it was clear for the next two hours.

"Alright," I groaned. "I'll do it."

"Thank you, dear," she said before hanging up, and her voice dripped with sweetness.

Grabbing my fall jacket, I hurried past my administrative assistant's desk.

"I have to run out for a while, "I said, trying to act nonchalant. "If anyone calls, I'll be back in an hour."

Brenda looked startled. Her eyes blinked below the dyed blonde hair, and she sat up straight. In her forties, she had worked with me for years, including time at my previous company, and I saw in her eyes the expectation of more information. It was not my habit to dash out suddenly, and she knew there were no meetings or conference calls in my schedule.

So, I paused and added as if it were a regular everyday occurrence, "Karen flushed her car keys down the toilet at Tim Horton's, so I have to bring her the spare."

Her hand went to her mouth, and she giggled impulsively. Perhaps she thought I was pulling her leg. I provided more details and, before running off, added, "What can I say, Brenda? My life's a sitcom."

I could hear her laughter as I rushed to the elevator. The insanity of the moment wasn't lost on either of us.

*

When I approached the coffee shop, Karen was standing in the front, waiting nervously in a black car coat. "I'm so sorry to bother you at work, but there was nothing else I could do." Beneath her light brown hair, her eyes were pleading.

I shrugged, "That's okay, dear. These things happen. But I can't believe the toilet sucked them away. They're heavy."

"I know, but they're gone," she sighed.

Seconds later, she perked up. "It was funny, though. Vicky was waiting outside the door, and when I told her what happened, she said she heard a strange noise and thought to herself — *that doesn't sound good.*"

It was amusing, especially the way Karen imitated Vicky's voice. After making sure her car started, I hurried back to work and contacted the dealer for another key. That was my second surprise. A replacement cost three hundred dollars. I made a gasping sound, and the service agent attempted to make me feel better by explaining the fee included labour to reprogram the fob to match the car's receiver. It didn't.

When I came home, I told Karen the price.

"I'm sorry, dear," she murmured and her expression was contrite. "I didn't want to call you because we'd been fighting, and I know how busy you are. But I must admit, you were very good about it."

She seized me in a bear hug, which made me grin with embarrassment.

"It was an accident; I had to help. What else could you do?"

She kissed my cheek, and I wondered if women in general, not just teenage girls, had problems with toilets. Oh well, at least it wasn't her cell phone.

*

The times were a changing. Teenagers made all their plans by text, and parents no longer knew who they hung out with or who called them. Not like in my day — *Andy, there's a girl on the phone for you!* Boy, was that embarrassing.

When Eric first moved into his house, he shared a landline phone with his roommates. But soon, he requested we text first before calling to avoid having someone take a message if he wasn't there. Next, he asked us to only call his cell, so we could keep in touch without anyone being aware he was talking to his mommy and daddy.

Battles with our daughters still flared up over losing their cells before bed. The greatest protests came from Jackie, who became quite angry. But one night, she stopped fighting and willingly shut it down before handing it over.

"How did it go?" Karen asked, sitting in bed with a book. "Did they fight with you?

"Not tonight," I replied, trying not to appear too smug. I went into the bathroom to brush my teeth and then stuck my head out the door. "You should work at being more consistent with them too; we might have fewer problems."

"Hmmph," she muttered and resumed reading.

I couldn't help smiling as I climbed into bed and pulled the covers up. After all, I had been a director for many years and learned a thing or two about managing people. How satisfying it felt to be able to demonstrate this with our children.

*

It took me a while to realize she was slipping me a dummy. At some point, I tried to turn the phone on, and when it failed to do so, I knocked on her door. Hearing no answer, I slowly opened it. Jackie lay in bed staring at a phone. She jumped up in surprise and pulled out her earphones as I entered.

"What's going on, Jackie?" I demanded, holding the dead device towards her. "It doesn't turn on."

"Ha-ha-ha, that's a dummy I handed you," she replied, chortling.

"What?"

I looked closer at the Blackberry I was holding; it looked just like hers.

"Where did you get this?"

"That's Harry's old BB. It doesn't work." She smirked.

She created amusing nicknames for her BFFs, who I believe tolerated them because of her winning personality. Katie was Kat, sometimes Kit-Kat; Rachel was Roach; and much to her chagrin, poor Hayley was Harry Potter, often abbreviated to Harry.

"Why, you little sneak!" I cried.

She handed me her actual one proudly. "You've been collecting it for a month, ha-ha-ha!"

I couldn't help smiling; she really enjoyed putting one over on me. I watched her climb back under the covers, said goodnight, and went to my room, where Karen was already asleep.

My youngest was a con artist, and apparently, she had a real flair for it. She tried the dummy trick many more times but never with the same success. Her girlfriends ardently assisted by supplying her with broken units or older ones replaced by upgrades. Over the next six months, I confiscated five more, all of which shared quarters with my socks and underwear in my bedroom dresser.

*

Of all the irritating habits that teens have, their constant obsession with cells bugged me the most. Of course, these phones provided us with a sense of security when the kids went out by themselves. In November, Karen had dropped them off at the cinema to see the second *Twilight* movie, *New Moon,* with their friends, and we were comforted by the knowledge that they could contact Karen if there was a problem. But, in my opinion, this advantage was vastly outweighed by the negative effects of these phones.

Our girls spent hours staring at them, taking selfies and texting. And it wasn't just our girls; this phenomenon seemed ubiquitous. They are addictive, hence the nickname, Crackberry. To avoid constant conflict, I searched for ways to limit their use. An article on the internet caught my attention. A teacher used a device that jammed reception so his students wouldn't be distracted in class. *Brilliant, just brilliant.* Instead of disconnecting the internet or fighting for their phones at night, I could simply block them.

I imagined myself calmly answering their questions with a confused look on my face. *What? No reception? Hmm, must be an outage in the area. Don't worry. If it's not fixed by tomorrow, I'll speak to the technical support.*

How marvellous it would be. Why, I could dupe them for days or weeks even before admitting the truth. After more searching, I found such a device online and ordered it. Joyfully, I anticipated its arrival. But I waited, and I waited. An entire month went by, so I followed up by email. A Chinese company responded to advise me it had arrived in Vancouver but was held in Canada Customs. They suggested I contact the customs office to speed up clearance. Wading through the government bureaucracy seemed too formidable a task, so I held out a bit longer, then gave up and requested a refund. This annoyed me, but after some reflection, the issue became clear. A criminal or terrorist could use the device to block cell reception, making it easier to do their dirty work and escape. While I appreciated our federal officials being on top of these things, I was disappointed to lose what could have been a game-changer in the war on teenagers.

However, taking away their cells remained the best punishment in the parental arsenal.

*

In December, I spent a week in Windsor inspecting two of our third-party manufacturers. The town was prettier than I expected, and my hotel room faced the River Walk, a pathway along the Detroit River, which flows from Lake St. Clair to Lake Erie. Every morning I gazed out the window and saw people walking or jogging along it. The view across the river was scenic as well; new skyscrapers graced the horizon. The General Motors Renaissance Centre rose above the pack, with one graceful round tower standing tallest and flanked by four attractive hexagonal buildings. My days were very hectic, visiting different soft gel plants and writing reports at night, but it was an enjoyable change from the normal routine.

When I arrived home, Karen broke the news that Jackie wanted out of her school. Wearing an attractive orange top and beige slacks, Karen sat on the love seat with her feet stretched across it.

"She wants me to get her into Hillside."

My stomach lurched at the idea of changing schools, but a glance at Jackie evoked my empathy. She sat slouched in an adjacent armchair, looking despondent.

As I caught her eye, she pulled herself up and said with agitation, "Yeah, I hate that ratchet school."

The use of foul language always irritated me, and I gave her a stern look. "Honey, I understand you don't like it, but there's no need to say rat shit. Don't use those words — find another way to say it."

Her eyes opened wide, and she snickered, "Not rat shit, Dad — ratchet! You know, it means crazy, nasty."

I laughed awkwardly. "Ah, young people's language, eh?"

At least I'd gotten a laugh out of her.

*

Although we suspected she was being bullied, Jackie denied it. Nevertheless, she implored her mother's help. We weren't prepared to leave her at this high school if she was miserable, so Karen spoke to the Hillside principal and requested a meeting. She does this better than anyone else. Despite the soft, friendly appearance, Karen has a tough core that ensures she gets her way, but without harsh feelings. First, she explained the situation and then summarized Jackie's excellent dance credentials, including the fact she'd auditioned previously and been accepted before choosing the other institution. Both my daughters did competitive dance for years, and their studio team won many trophies. To be honest, I was happy when they stopped. Watching them perform aerial cartwheels with no hands for support gave me the willies. I lived in constant fear they'd land on their heads and sustain a spinal injury. No, it wasn't a sad day at all for me when they decided not to continue. Nor was it for Eric because dinner was bad on studio nights.

He often came home from school, realized it was a Tuesday, and said, "Oh, dance night. That means another crap dinner for us, Dad."

*

The principal listened as Karen presented her case. While sympathetic, he couldn't let her join in the middle of the year or his teachers would revolt. She'd have to audition for September, which was disappointing but understandable. However, having inherited the impatient gene (it must be from Karen's side of the family), Jackie was not pleased. She sulked for days, and that one always wore her heart on her sleeve. Whenever she was unhappy, everyone was unhappy. One day, she suggested we sell our house and move within the school boundaries so she'd be able to attend immediately. We told her this wouldn't happen.

The next thing we knew, she had spoken to a real estate agent about condo rentals and presented us with a list of prices. I was flabbergasted.

"Did you say you were enquiring on behalf of your father?" I asked.

"No. I just said I wanted a three-bedroom condo within these boundaries. And he keeps texting me to come and view them. It's so annoying."

The image of an agent talking earnestly to our daughter, unaware she was only fourteen, cracked me up.

We told Jackie firmly that the answer was still no. Kids understand very little about money. We couldn't afford it, and even if we could — why would we do it? But I admired her gumption. She'd go far one day if she didn't end up in jail first. And I took pity on her; she was obviously desperate. But having exhausted all alternatives, she finally accepted reality.

"Alright, alright," she announced, squaring her shoulders, "I'll audition again."

*

Karen wasn't taking any chances. She arranged for a former instructor to choreograph a lyrical dance routine and provide space to practice. Meggy and I watched a video of the finished routine at home in January. Gliding across the screen with graceful sweeping movements to a popular song, Jackie's elegance and beauty were impressive. She was very talented; they just had to accept her. The auditions would be held in two weeks.

These experiences taught me a few things. First, as much as I desire to control things, it's impossible, so try to relax and go with the flow. Second, never underestimate your child's creativity and drive for a goal they really want. They will astound you as Jackie did us. The ideas to move within the boundaries or rent a condo were genius, given her age. One could only hope that when she grew older, she'd use this talent for good and not evil.

TEMPERS  RISING

"My kid is turning out just like me. Well played, karma. Well played." - Betsy Farrell

IN FEBRUARY, WE learned that Jackie's audition was a success, and she could start in September. We were all thrilled but none more than Jackie. She bounced through the house with her old zip as if a weight had been lifted off her. Some of her closest friends were at Hillside, and she missed them.

Karen and I sat in the living room on Saturday afternoon, reading the paper and talking about it.

I love this room. Karen had tastefully decorated it. Behind the couch I was sitting on, light poured in from the five-tier white aluminum bay window with gold muntins and an oak trim and oak laminated head and seat board, which was filled by large green plants: a money tree, desert rose, hibiscus, and palm tree. The eye-catching green foliage filled a third of the windowpanes, drawing compliments from visitors who approached the front door. From under the built-in valence, flowing sheer curtains fell to the floor and were pulled back and tied at each side. The walls were a light brownish colour.

"It's called Gold Digger Yellow!" Karen laughed whenever friends asked the colour. "Which is funny because Andrew always says that I spend all his money."

That aside, I like the colour. When it was redecorated, we had the thick wall-to-wall carpet removed, and the oak floor beneath re-stained to display the beautiful hardwood that had been hidden by the previous owners. French provincial side tables held lamps on my left and both sides of the opposite love seat where Karen sat and cast soft light in the evening. A long matching coffee table in front of me was placed on a large taupe rug that was centred in the room and conveniently held teacups, books and glasses. Above us was a white stucco ceiling that had been the fashion back in the '70s when the house was built. I watched proudly as guests cast their eyes about and quickly registered the room as warm and cozy.

I started to speak, but suddenly Karen held her hand up. "Just a minute." After listening, she added, "Milo's howling."

"I'll get him," I said, jumping off the couch and hurrying to the patio door. The baying changed to barking as I opened it. "Shut up, Milo!" I bellowed.

The beagle stopped in his tracks and stood there looking at me with his body still facing the fence. Perhaps he saw a squirrel; they loved to tease him by running back and forth along the top.

I made a rapid motion with my hand. "Come in, Milo."

He trotted in, tail wagging, and I slid the door closed. The way he pranced in, as though he had an agenda, made me laugh. Moochie lay lifeless in her bed as he strolled by and flopped on the carpet. The sun streamed in from the bay window and bathed them in its warmth. I sat down again on the couch but left my paper on the coffee table while I admired them. The animals epitomized a lazy Saturday afternoon, and their contentment was contagious.

*

When Eric was young, he called them the tuxedo pets because their white chests against the dark fur reminded him of a tux. Milo lay on his side, and his brown eyes flicked sideways towards me. He sensed me studying him, and his eyes watched me anxiously. They're set in a brown and white face, capped off by a light brown head and floppy ears. His stomach, face and paws are white, and the rest of his fur is brown and black.

I turned my attention to Moochie and saw the sun's rays catch the brown highlights in her black fur. She rolled on her back, twisting her head to the side and displaying her white belly and white markings on her face, paws and tail. Sticking all four legs out in the most enviable stretch, she pawed the air and finally succumbed to the biggest yawn imaginable. The gaping mouth revealed the sharp teeth I'd come to know too well. All at once, I felt jealous. Oh, to be a lazy cat. Then the mouth snapped closed, and she blinked as if to say — *that felt good*. She looked at me expectantly, as if she thought I might feed her. With coal-black noses against white faces, both pets are very attractive. Friends said we should put them in commercials. And they'd be perfect performers if they were in pet food ads that allowed them to claw and fight their way to the bowls. Needless to say, we never pursued it; the risk of a lawsuit for biting someone on set appeared too great.

*

Like all hounds, Milo loved to howl, and we'd race to quiet him when he did. Otherwise, our neighbours, Kurt and Sharon Turnbull, would complain. When the kids were little and ran around the back yard squealing with their pals, Sharon called over the fence, "Is everything alright over there?"

"Yes, Sharon, they're just being kids and having fun. Don't

worry about it," Karen shouted back. She told me afterwards, "I'm not going to tell my kids to be quiet. She'll have to get used to it or move."

"Yeah, to a retirement home if they're smart," I joked. They never had children, and their lack of tolerance for kids was disconcerting, particularly since he'd been a teacher, and she, a principal, and had worked with children for their entire careers. Recently retired, they hadn't mellowed a bit. If we didn't stop the barking right away, Sharon phoned us. The first time she did this, we ignored her. Then she rang the doorbell.

A steely eyed glare from an overweight figure greeted me at our door.

"I thought your dog might be in distress," she said in a deadpan voice.

"No, Susan," I replied with an exasperated sigh, "he's fine. Don't worry. We've brought him in."

*

A week later, a letter arrived from the city claiming our dog had violated the noise bylaw. I called the bylaw officer to explain the situation.

"Honestly, he doesn't bark much, but when he does, we make him stop. In fact, I worry the poor beast thinks his name is really *Shut up, Milo* because that's what we yell as soon as he lets out so much as a little woof."

The voice at the end of the line snickered. "Well, make sure you quiet him when he does," he said congenially.

Although we tried to be extra zealous to keep Milo quiet, it wasn't always possible. Take the incident a few weeks ago.

"Milo's barking — will you let him in, please?" Karen hollered from the basement.

"I'm in the bathroom," I shouted. More barking ensued. "For Pete's sake, Milo, will you shut up!" I yelled at the small window above in frustration with the faint hope he might hear me. He didn't. By the time I reached the door, the telephone was already ringing. I ignored it.

"Arrgh! Milo, come in here."

Karen came upstairs and looked at me. "Who was it?"

I glanced at the phone. "Sharon, of course, but who cares? He's inside now."

*

It's difficult having next-door neighbours with unreasonable expectations, but we did our best to keep things friendly. The Turnbulls grumbled about petty things. Last summer, we took our wind chimes down because they whined it kept them awake. While we try to brush it off, the constant complaints were annoying. Let's face it; they themselves were weird. Kurt told Karen once that he bought his marijuana from a former student. It didn't surprise me at all. And his last job before retirement? Guidance counsellor. I pity the poor youths he must have screwed up.

Kurt also enjoyed parading around his pool naked. Since our street has two-story buildings, his fence did nothing to hide his manhood. One day, I gazed out the upper window and accidentally caught the full Monty. It was very upsetting. Kurt is not a handsome specimen. Short, stocky, with long hair and a moustache, he strutted across the yard with the air of someone with a high opinion of himself. It was all I could do to keep my lunch down.

When I told Karen, I got no sympathy. She thought it was funny. "Sometimes, when my girlfriends are over, we peek out the upstairs window and have a laugh."

I tried to shake the image out of my head. "The things you see when you don't have a gun."

One time, worried the girls might see him, I complained to the police, but they said since he was in his own back yard, they couldn't do anything. As my thoughts returned to the present, I looked outside. At least it was winter; Kurt wouldn't risk frostbite. Thank goodness for that.

*

Karen's mother, Anna, came to visit for a week, which was a special treat. She enjoyed spending time with the kids, and we could be carefree for a night, knowing Anna would keep an eye on things. We left for dinner and a play with Iris and Rod, who lived across the street and provided much-welcomed banter over drinks beforehand. By the time we got home, their friends were long gone, but we listened solemnly, still slightly aglow from the fun and alcohol, to Anna report they'd been smoking marijuana in the basement rec room. Shorter than us at five foot-seven, she had grey hair laced with patches of white, but she was still sharp as a wit. Although we suspected they experimented with weed, she had given us the first hard evidence.

Karen and I exchanged uneasy glances. "Thank you for watching them, Ma," she said and giggled. "They probably didn't think you knew what it smelled like."

That was an inside joke; when Karen was a teenager, Anna found marijuana in her room and flushed it down the toilet. "I think it was a nickel bag," she said dryly, in the vernacular she learned from her murder mystery shows.

It cost a lot more than that — Karen thought but said nothing. Instead, she went to the bathroom to check it out. The green proof lay around the lip of the bowl. Truth be told, teenage Karen had been quite a handful. Once when her parents were at the movies, she and her friends broke into the locked bedroom where they hid the liquor. When they returned, she claimed someone had burglarized it. Karen's parents listened in silence. Although they didn't challenge her story, she suspected they knew what really happened.

Every Friday night with her best friend, Maria, she crossed the bridge to Buffalo, where the bars stayed open longer. Maria drove because she had a licence but often navigated her way home drunker than Karen. It's amazing they were never arrested or in an accident.

*

When asked about Anna's claim, our daughters readily confessed.

"We heard Grandma upstairs ..." Meggy said sheepishly, and her eyes darted from Karen to me.

"Yeah," Jackie interjected, "she yelled — smells like something evil here!" Adding a rasp to her voice to sound like Anna, she made us laugh.

"We panicked when we heard her," Meggy continued.

"Katie and Hannah panicked, so we put out the joints and opened the basement windows," Jackie concluded.

No harm had been done, so we didn't get mad. But from then on, whenever Anna came, they knew Grandma was on the lookout.

*

The following week Meggy was invited to a party, so Karen arranged for her friend Hannah's mother to drop them off and for us to pick them up. On Saturday night at midnight, according to plan, I pulled into the designated driveway. There had been a decent snowfall earlier that day, and the tires made the soft compacting noise I love as they turned over the fresh-fallen snow.

Karen was already texting Meggy before I came to a full stop. I turned the ignition off. "Well, what did she say?"

She lifted her head from the phone. "She hasn't answered. Probably hasn't noticed the message yet."

We sat in the dark and listened to the music blaring from the house. White billows hung from the eves, and big fluffy snowbanks lined both sides of the driveway, making it feel like we were sitting in a snow tunnel.

Moments later, Karen said, "I'll call her." She was usually ready when we arrived, so the wait was unexpected.

"Hi, we're here, honey..." She paused, then blurted out, "Okay,"

She hung up and turned to me. "She's getting ready now, Andrew, so relax."

"Oh, I'm relaxed," I said with irritation as I shifted in my seat. Her telling me to relax seemed ironic. After all, Karen's the hyper one in the family. Oh, I admit I'm impatient when she and the girls are dressing to go somewhere, but with three women in the household, is it any wonder? I'm always waiting an eternity for one or more of them.

The icy cold crept in and chilled our legs, so I started the engine again to warm up. Twenty minutes had passed since we'd first pulled in.

Looking up at the house, I sighed. "I wish we'd dropped off instead of picking up."

"I know," Karen nodded, "but we can't always do that. Let me text her again."

Most parents hate picking up on the weekend; they'd rather relax, have a few glasses of wine and not have to drive when they're half in the bag. The parents of one friend always said, "Sorry, we can't. We're going out." After a few times, we knew it was a ruse. But we couldn't pull that stunt; it was only right to take our turn.

After a few minutes, Meggy reappeared at Karen's door. She leaned down and put her hands on the window. "I can't find my Ugghs."

Karen's face was cross. "Your expensive boots? I told you not to wear them to a party."

An awkward pause followed, and I leaned over. "You have to look again. Go through all the boots."

"I did," she wailed, but off she trotted to try again.

"What's she wearing if she couldn't locate them?" I asked, confused.

"I don't know, but she'll figure it out."

*

Twenty more minutes passed, and I began to get annoyed. It was late, and I wanted to go to bed. "Where did she disappear to? Did she rejoin the party? Is she drinking in there?" I asked in rapid succession.

Karen picked up her cell. "Let me call her again."

As she dialled, a vehicle in the rear-view mirror caught my eye. Drifting past, it turned around and stopped on the other side. "Police," I said, studying them. "Maybe somebody complained about the noise."

I started working on an explanation as to why we were here, in case they knocked on my window, but before I could finish, the house exploded with kids. There had to be over fifty, streaming out every door like ants and running in all directions. Someone inside must have sounded the alarm. We scanned the departing hordes for our daughter, but she was nowhere to be seen.

A shadowy figure beside the car made me jump. It was Meggy.

She bent down with a solemn face and wailed, "I still can't find my boots, and I've looked everywhere. Somebody stole them."

In the darkness, I could make out the lower half of another person; Hannah was standing by her side.

"All right, get in," Karen spoke with an edge to her voice. "You'll have to go home in your socks."

The girls scrambled into the van, and I glanced in the mirror. I felt sorry for Meggy; she didn't give us half the trouble her sister did.

"It's not my fault somebody stole them," she wailed.

"Well, I'm not buying you another pair. They cost over a hundred dollars," Karen snapped. "Maybe now you'll learn not to wear expensive boots to a party."

A loud moan emanated from the rear as I backed onto the street. I crept parallel to the police car and managed a small smile before crawling away. Impressive. They didn't even have to get out and knock on the door; they accomplished their mission simply by being seen.

*

Parties add another level of stress to parenting because of the potential bad influence by peers. Jackie received many invitations, but when another occurred in March, we didn't let her go. I forget why, but there was a good reason. In response, she hollered and slammed her bedroom door.

"I'll check on her," Karen said, getting up from the dinner table. She returned visibly upset.

"Don't blow a fuse," she said, fixing her gaze on me, "but she's kicked a hole in the wall."

"What do you mean — a hole in the wall?"

"She kicked a hole in the hallway upstairs," Karen said louder as if I were hard of hearing. "Her emotions are out of control at this age, so don't be furious. She's hiding in her room."

"Okay," I said gruffly, "but she'll help me patch it."

I ventured upstairs to examine the damage. An area about twice the size of her foot was smashed in, leaving a two-by-four stud exposed, and I ran my finger along the edge of the broken drywall. Fortunately, this timber stopped the destruction from getting any bigger. I straightened up and clenched my fists. I didn't need an unnecessary chore like this.

Karen studied me closely when I returned. She said, "If it makes you feel better, my friend Sue's oldest daughter kicked her bedroom door and put a cavity in it. Phil was mad because he had to patch it."

That was unfortunate, but strangely enough, it did improve my mood. Karen had met Sue when their kids were in public school. An inch shorter than Karen, but slim with an oval face and brown hair, Sue hit it off with Karen, and they have been friends ever since. I found her husband, Phil, to be agreeable, too, although more reserved. Their oldest daughter, Julie, was a year older than Eric, tall and beautiful with platinum blonde hair.

Julie and her sister always appeared well-behaved and mature whenever we met. But now that I think about it, our friends often described our girls that way, too. And they are, whenever they're out in public. Appearances are deceiving, and apparently, Julie also gave her parents nerve-racking moments.

The following weekend, I collected my tools and told Jackie to come with me. She followed obediently and sat on the hall carpet, watching. First, I cut a piece of drywall a little smaller than the hole, screwed one end to the stud, then covered over the gaps with drywall filler. Jackie said nothing but handed me the materials meekly when asked.

"So, we let it dry, and tomorrow sand it," I told her as I gathered up the equipment. "You can help by cleaning up the mess on the floor."

The next day, I showed her how to sand it smooth until there was no bumpy sensation when your fingers ran over it.

"Clean it off with this rag, and we'll paint it," I said, handing her a damp cloth.

"Sorry, Daddy, I really didn't think it would make a hole when I kicked it," she said, looking remorseful.

Nodding sadly, I felt the tension leave my body. That was believable; teenagers have no concept of how a house is constructed. After touching up her paint job, I got to my feet slowly, stretched my back and examined the job.

"Pretty good, if I do say so myself. You can't even tell it was damaged."

"Thank you, Daddy," she said with a smile.

*

Karen believed it was important to start each day fresh and forget about earlier fights. I had more trouble doing this than she did. But even though it was hard, I tried not to hold grudges or lose my temper. Shouting matches could be avoided by removing phones for a few days, which we did to Jackie for damaging the hallway. Unfortunately, Karen often reinstated them before the end of the punishment period. She called me at work on Tuesday to forewarn me.

"You gave it back? But she lost it for three days."

"She got the message. It's been long enough."

"One day. Are you kidding me?" I cried incredulously.

"I think it's okay. Besides, girls need their social time, and they use it to stay in touch. You don't know because you never had sisters."

That was true, and because of that, I relied on Karen's perspective, but she often caved.

*

Karen's brother was nineteen when he died, making her an only child. The trauma aged her parents twenty years, and they were still shattered when I met them two years after. Anna wouldn't celebrate Christmas, and Fred never spoke his son's name; his eyes would well up with tears whenever someone did.

Karen responded differently. She started living for two, quitting her job in Toronto and going to university. In all likelihood, his untimely death left her with a deep-rooted fear of losing people. Perhaps that's why she was soft on our daughters.

Whenever they threatened to run away or kill themselves, she'd panic. I've talked to her about it because I believe a parent needs to be firm. If kids misbehave, you punish them. It's that simple. However, when I broached the subject that evening, Karen shut me down.

"Just because you go to work each day and tell people what to do, you think you can do the same here," she said with a glare. "But that doesn't work here."

Maybe not, but life would be much easier if it did. At work, my department ran like a well-oiled machine, and if she'd listened to me, the house could, too. After all, as the head of quality, my job was similar to that of a police officer, making the company and contractors follow the rules and regulations.

"Everyone gets along when you're away on business," she insisted.

While that bothered me to some extent, I suspected it was because they got away with murder. But I held my tongue.

"Your trips aren't just a pleasant break for you but for us, as well," she added with a sarcastic laugh to ensure she had the last word.

*

Nevertheless, I was proud I hadn't lost my temper when Jackie damaged the wall. Her demure manner and subsequent apology convinced me our girls just needed firmness and discipline. Now all I had to do was persuade Karen, but that could be the hardest part of all.

TRAVEL HELL

"A husband is a man who wishes he had as much fun when he goes on business trips as his wife thinks he does." - Ann Landers

MY PLANE TOUCHED down in Zurich at 9 a.m. Sunday morning, a day before the corporate meeting for regional quality heads. After dropping my luggage at the hotel, I ventured out to reacquaint myself with the old section of the city. I ambled down the white cobblestone street of Niederdorfstrasse, with its art galleries, shops and cafes. Passing by a bakery, delicious aromas of coffee, chocolate, fresh bread and pastries wafted out. I stopped to gaze wistfully through the window, debating whether to treat myself or not. I decided against it and carried on. Some buildings were hundreds of years old; one five-storey with dormers was striking. Tall and narrow, with a series of ornate paintings along the bottom panels of a bay window that jutted out over the sidewalk. Magnificent. You don't see anything like that back home.

I continued my journey along the Limmat River towards the lake, walking past the famous Grossmunster cathedral with its distinctive double towers. Sweat trickled down my forehead, and when I finally reached the water, I welcomed the light breeze coming off it. At the lake's edge, a set of wide concrete steps led down into the blue-coloured water for easy access. No one was swimming today, but couples and individuals sat scattered across the steps gazing at the lake. I found a spot away from others and studied my surroundings. People were lunching in outdoor cafes and restaurants facing the water. Europeans seem to enjoy life better than North Americans, often gathering at outdoor patios with friends or coworkers for a drink or coffee after work before going home for supper.

After a while, I strolled both sides of the lake, returning each time to the steps for a rest. What a peaceful way to spend an afternoon. I sat and enjoyed the scenery for another hour before deciding to head back into the heart of the old town to find a place to eat.

*

As I crossed the road, my cell phone rang. I glanced at the number — Ken, a colleague, originally from England. Perhaps he was inviting me for a drink.

"Hello, Ken."

"Hi, Andrew." He sounded merry as usual, but his tone soon became serious as he started asking questions about a contractor's production issues.

Disappointed, I answered him, nonetheless. When he finished, I said, "You're working from home on a Sunday afternoon, Ken? I assumed you'd be sitting outside with a few cool ones enjoying the sunshine."

"Well, in truth, I'm in the office tying up a few loose ends."

We chatted a bit more before hanging up. Another myth shattered. I guess Europeans don't have it any easier after all!

Following a narrow side street up the hill behind Fraumunster church, I stumbled upon a cobblestone square with a steep slope. A restaurant sat perched at the top, kitty-corner to where I stood. I hiked up, took an outside table, and ordered a beer. The server poured a tall, frosty glass of local brew and put it on the slanted table. I had to laugh. The table tilted so much that I feared the bottle would fall over, drop off the table and roll down the hill to the other side.

But the cold liquid satiated the dryness in my throat. Below me, the square appeared deserted save for the odd person scurrying across on their way to a family meal. Sundays feel particularly lonely when travelling, and suddenly, this pleasant break from the constant commotion at home wasn't as enjoyable as before. The solitude weighed on me, and I longed for the sound of a familiar voice. As I ate my meal, I thought of the quiet evening ahead in my small hotel room. When I got in, I called the family right away and felt cheered by the sound of them on the other end. The girls missed me already, which was a pleasant surprise.

*

The next morning when I went down for breakfast, I discovered some colleagues in the modest eating area. They greeted me eagerly, and the camaraderie lifted my heart. I signalled to one of the waitresses working the room; she nodded and returned shortly to place a small carafe of coffee beside me. The breakfast area was done in various tones of brown — dark brown tables, leather-clad wooden chairs and a lighter checkered floor. A bookcase built into one wall caught my eye; uncluttered with lots of spaces, it contained books stacked horizontally and vertically (some of which stood open to display pictures), ceramic figurines and one attractive vase in the centre. The overall effect was sombre and elegant. Each table had a white tablecloth laid across the middle that hung down to the knees, with its own unique arrangement of orange and yellow flowers in a vase. I ate quickly as I caught up on events with my coworkers from different regions.

Then we walked en masse to the Marketplatz and rode the tram together to the meeting site each day and back. We ate supper together and had drinks on the patio. What a difference companionship makes. The days seemed to click by. On Thursday, my global manager arrived at the conference room to collect me for dinner.

Paul Schmidt joined the company a few years ago, possessed a good sense of humour and was very agreeable to work with. Tall, fit, and in his fifties, he had only a trace of his native South African accent. His appearance and accent reminded me of the singer Roger Whittaker when he was younger. At his suggestion, we took the tram to a promenade area with an excellent selection of outdoor restaurants. We studied a few menus and decided on one with a red awning and potted shrubs around the perimeter, which added to the ambiance.

The waiter brought our beer, and Paul raised his glass in a toast. "Here's to your visit to Zurich!"

"Cheers and thank you for inviting me out."

"Not a problem. It's nice to have a guest. By the way, there is an asparagus festival here," he said, perusing the menu.

I looked at the prices — thirty Euros for an appetizer that had five of these precious gems with hollandaise sauce and thirty-five for a main course with sides! I swallowed hard and looked at Paul.

"Why do the Swiss have a festival for asparagus?"

"By law, they're only allowed to sell it for six weeks, so that makes it special."

I nodded and made no comment. In Canada, we can buy the vegetable year-round for four dollars a pound. Obviously, the government intended to block imported products until the local crop came in season. But what a price they paid for this protectionism. I decided on a plate of pork schnitzel and vegetables instead.

As we talked, I described my sightseeing on Sunday, and Paul looked envious. The head office drove them hard, and I had the distinct impression that he didn't have many lazy days like that. The waiter reappeared with our orders, placing them on the table in front of us with a flourish.

After he retreated to the kitchen, Paul said, "I must say, Andy, I'm impressed with your knowledge of quality issues and production processes."

The compliment caught me off guard. "Well, I've been in this business over thirty years, most of those at production sites."

"It shows," he added between mouthfuls. "And it's not just me who's observed it. Klaus also mentioned to me how you provided some valuable insights during the breakout workshops."

My heart sped up and made me pause before responding. "Thank you very much for the kind words, Paul. That means a lot to me."

Klaus was a senior person in the organization, and his opinion carried weight. Paul also wasn't prone to insincere flattery, so his feedback resonated with me.

My meal tasted delicious, and we ordered more beer. The conversation flowed easily; Paul was great company. And while we talked about other subjects, I caught myself grinning needlessly every now and then. I fairly floated with pride through the rest of the evening. Afterwards, he left me to head back to his apartment while I strode off in the other direction to my accommodation.

After entering the room, I kicked off my shoes, lay on the bed, and phoned home.

Karen answered brightly, and I greeted her with equal enthusiasm, "Hello, dear, how are you?"

"Andrew?" I heard her speak to someone else in the background. Seconds later, she said, "Meggy wants to say hello."

"Sure, put her on."

"Hi, Meggy. How are you?"

"Hi, Dad, I'm fine. How is it going?" Her normally calm voice was full of excitement, which thrilled me.

"It's going well, Meggy."

I told her what I had been doing this week and afterwards asked for Jackie, repeating the same conversation to her. I always worried one would be jealous of the other if I didn't talk to both. Eric was working at his summer job, so he wouldn't be slighted. Jackie talked about her homies and slipped in some other youthful slang. Her favourite catchphrase lately was 'do-rag.' I had to look it up — *the head cover like a bandana, worn by young African Americans.* I doubted she ever saw many people with a do-rag. How this became her favourite phrase was a mystery, but I suspected it had a lot to do with liking the sound of it. She slipped it in as a sentence filler, often saying 'where's ma do-rag?' or 'you know, the guy with the do-rag.' She made me laugh.

Karen came back on the line.

"Now I forgot what I was going to say!" I gasped.

She giggled, "I know, but they miss you."

"I miss all of you, too."

"How are the meetings?"

"They're good, but I'm glad we finish tomorrow. I'm looking forward to getting back."

I reminded her of my arrival time. Instead of flying out Saturday morning and changing planes in Frankfurt, I planned to take the train there Friday after work and fly directly from there the next day. After hearing how inexpensive and convenient trains were from my colleagues, I was keen to try them. Besides, the connection through Frankfurt was so brief that my bags often didn't make it on the plane. This new strategy promised less hassle.

Karen's voice took on a worried tone. "I hope there's no problem with the train."

"There shouldn't be," I answered, shrugging off the concern. "Although I have to run right after the meeting, once I'm on, it's direct to the airport, or Fluuug-hoff-in as they call it here," I said, exaggerating the sound and chuckling at the German name. Flughafen, what a word! "Besides, it doesn't matter if it is delayed, since I'm spending the night there."

I heard her voice soften. "I miss you, honey. Oh, and you'll be happy to hear this — I think this will be the last summer for the trampoline."

"Why? Is it breaking down?"

"No, the girls just don't seem interested in it anymore. You know what they say, *there's a season for everything*. Well, it's time to move on, but I don't regret buying it. They've had a lot of fun.

"They sure did."

"Okay, have a good flight, dear. Where are you staying?"

"I forget the name, but it's very convenient, right in the terminal. Then tomorrow, I catch the noon flight to Toronto. I'll call you from there tomorrow. "

"Love you."

"Love you, too, honey. Goodnight."

*

Even though we kept in contact by texting, it was wonderful to hear their cheerful voices. As I climbed into bed, I reflected on the trampoline. I felt sad that the kids didn't use it anymore; it was as if a chapter in our life had closed. When Karen first purchased it, I was mad because we hadn't talked about it beforehand. She had bought it on impulse, which was something she frequently did. She'd spot something in a store and be able to imagine the kids having fun with it. A neighbour brought it home for her in his truck, and she was so excited when she showed it to me. But I regarded the new acquisition with skepticism. It wasn't a normal size trampoline; it was humongous. Sixteen feet in diameter and without screened sides for safety, it appeared to be a professional unit rather than a toy.

"Are they joining a circus?" I asked sarcastically, while reading the description.

"Stop it. The kids will have a ball with it. You'll see."

What bothered me most was I didn't believe they'd get enough use out of it. I figured after bouncing a few times, they'd be bored. Boy, was I wrong. Sure, Eric didn't use it a lot, but the girls? They loved it. They bounced high in the air, touched their toes, and did the somersaults they'd learned in gymnastic dance. Despite my fears, they never bounced off and hurt themselves, thank goodness.

What was unexpected, though, was its use as a platform for socializing. The girls would sit or lie on the trampoline with friends after school and talk for hours until dusk. Six or eight adolescent girls spread out, heads to centre and feet to the edge, sometimes touching hands, talking, laughing and gazing at the sky. I watched from the kitchen window in amazement. Karen didn't seem surprised at all, but I was damn well mystified. Karen had been right; I was glad we bought it.

*

On Friday, our meeting ended late, so I had to run to catch my train. Smartly dressed patrons in cafes looked up in surprise and curiosity as I raced down sidewalks, constantly glancing at my watch. When I entered the station, I grabbed a sandwich and pop and found the platform. The train arrived minutes later.

I lifted my luggage into the overhead compartment and settled into my first-class seat. Now, I could relax, eat and do emails. My pulse slowed down, and my breathing became more even. A porter came by pushing a trolley ladened with sandwiches and drinks, but I waved him off. I had my snack and would arrive in Frankfurt early enough for a fine dinner.

I reviewed my itinerary. Although I didn't recognize the hotel, it would be luxurious because the ones inside terminals always were. Stretching out my legs, I gazed at the countryside rolling by. The train made a clickety-clackety noise as it rocked gently sideways and moved leisurely through farmland. This was the way to travel. I'd sleep in tomorrow morning and then meander down to the check-in desk in front of the hotel lobby. No 6 a.m. rising and rushing by taxi for me. The plan was brilliant, and I smiled with satisfaction.

When we pulled into Frankfurt, I stepped down with other passengers and ambled off the platform. Strange, I couldn't find my hotel. I stopped at an information desk where a middle-aged man with thin hair, a black moustache and a disgruntled look busied himself with papers. When he glanced up, I asked for directions.

Without a smile, he pointed. "The Sheraton's down there and to the left. See the sign?"

I shook my head. "No, not the Sheraton, here ..." I unfolded the piece of paper and handed it to him.

He frowned. "I see, but that's not inside the airport."

"Really? The agency said it was. Are you sure?"

He read the address again. "Yes, it's about fifteen minutes by cab." Then he handed it back and resumed his activity.

"Uh, okay. Thank you."

I turned away, confused and annoyed. But continuing through the terminal, I spotted the taxi zone and exited. The driver nodded when I showed him the name and address, so I got in. Our company had recently engaged a cheaper travel agency, and they must have screwed up. Oh well, it wasn't the end of the world. I'd just have to wake up earlier than expected.

*

Twenty minutes later, the taxi was crawling down a side street when the heavy traffic came to a complete stop.

The driver waved his hand in frustration. "It's a one-way street, so I have to go down here, then turn left and work my way back."

I leaned forward and pointed. "You mean this is the road here?"

He nodded, so I said, "That's no problem. I only have a bag and a single suitcase. Let me out and I'll walk."

I gave him a generous tip. As he handed me my suitcase, he appeared uneasy. His eyes darted down a narrow alley. "Uh ... don't wander around here, sir. This is the red-light district."

He jumped back in the car and drove off. I watched him leave in stunned silence while standing on the sidewalk clutching my bag. I glanced again at the name on the paper and then at the sign in the distance. This seemed to be it. So, I straightened up, slung the laptop bag over my shoulder and pulled my suitcase conspicuously behind me.

Inside, the lobby was small but clean, with a solitary desk that appeared to function as a combined reception and bar, judging by the large display of bottles. My heart sank.

A large, burly receptionist/bartender, sporting a buzz cut and wearing a crisp dress shirt and tie, turned to me with a welcoming smile. "Can I help you?"

I sized him up. Maybe he was a bouncer/receptionist/bartender. Shifting my feet, I mentioned uneasily that I had a reservation. He turned to his computer.

"I'm sorry, sir, but nothing has been reserved. Would you like me to book you a room?"

I was struck speechless. The agency had sent me to a bordello, didn't make a reservation, yet listed it on my itinerary — what kind of morons did they employ?

Clearing my throat, I sputtered, "I need to talk to my travel agent. They must have made a mistake." I spoke calmly and professionally, trying to keep the dark pull of anger at bay.

As I dialled their number, I noticed an older guy with grey stubble studying me with great interest. He sat on a barstool, elbows on the counter, looking bored and smoking a cigarette. This was probably the highlight of his day. Finally, after what seemed to be an eternity, someone picked up.

I turned my back to the reception desk and, in hushed tones, berated him, "... and you put me in the *red-light area* ... and even then, *they don't have a reservation for me!*"

"Just a moment, sir," the curt voice said and put me on hold.

I stood fuming. A slight smile crept over the bearded guy's face, and he took a drag from his cigarette. Out of the corner of my eye, I could see the receptionist/bartender motioning me over. He looked like an enormous football player calling me into a huddle. I smiled weakly as he pushed a piece of paper across the countertop.

"Sir," he said excitedly, "I can offer you this suite today for the special price of only 60 Euros!"

I recoiled in horror. The normal rate was four times that amount, and I was tempted to ask if it was by the hour. Instead, I inhaled deeply and declined the proposition. "I'm sorry, but my travel agency made the mistake, so they have to fix it."

His face fell, and he turned away.

Now, the agent was back, talking rapidly in a monotone. "I apologize for the inconvenience, but I've booked another hotel, and it's only a few kilometres away."

I went nuts, but quietly, so that any nearby pimps or disreputable characters wouldn't hear me. "Are you kidding me? I don't want a place near here. Look... I want to stay ... at the airport. I think there's a Sheraton there. Do you understand me?" I sensed my voice rising. "You've got me in a hotel with prostitutes! Now get me the hell out of here and into the terminal!"

"Hold, please," and with that, the agent cut off my tirade.

I spun around with the phone to my ear and grinned feebly at the receptionist/bartender.

The agent was on the line again, still talking fast. "The Sheraton is actually out of the recommended price range ...." I felt a rage forming inside, "but because of the inconvenience we've caused, I've managed to secure approval."

The last part of the sentence stopped the ballistic assault I had been preparing to deliver after hearing the words *'out of the price range.'*

The air flowed out of my lungs like a deflating balloon. "Okay, very good," I said and hung up without even saying goodbye.

Stifling my anger, I approached the receptionist once more under the watchful gaze of Mr. Grey Beard. I explained that they had found me another hotel and asked him to call me a taxi. When it came, I gave a quick wave to him and the barfly and hurried out.

*

Shortly afterwards, I strolled into the plush lobby of the Sheraton. This was more like it. A team stood by to greet me, as if I was someone important. Minutes later, I sat at the bar, looking morose and consoling myself over the nightmare I had endured. The dining area lay to the side, and I could smell the emanating aroma of fine cuisine, which I no longer desired. Towards the entrance stood a tall glass structure with vertical racks of wine.

After ordering a burger, I complimented the bartender on the height of the wine unit. I wasn't sure what to call it; wine cellar didn't seem appropriate. He grinned and told me that they used aerial ballet artists with wires attached to select bottles. Then I spotted two attractive young women, dressed in white ballet outfits with wings attached to resemble fairies, standing between the racks. It didn't take long before an order arrived. Up in the air ascended one fairy, twirling in aerobatic movements, then stopping high above to gracefully select a bottle before descending back to the floor in spins and somersaults. It was fascinating. A few more bottles were ordered, and I was able to observe both at once. Whenever I thought about my ordeal, I shuddered, ordered another drink and observed their performance. It was like candy after a bitter pill, and I went to bed a happy man that night, knowing I had resumed my proper place in the world.

10
GIRLS ARE NUTS!

"How do you write women so well?" Receptionist.
"I think of a man, and I take away reason and
accountability." - Jack Nicholson in As Good as It Gets

AS THE TAXI pulled onto Maple Street, I felt a familiar disorientation resurface; everything seemed surreal. Not only because of the time difference between Europe and Canada, but also from the shift between my professional and personal life. All the noise and chaos at home kept me off balance, but it was a different story at work. There, I felt completely in control. Paul's words resounded in my mind and made me smile. I was at the top of my game, and the respect conveyed to me at company or industry meetings both surprised and gratified me. As I got out of the taxi, I realized I was leaving behind a world where everyone listened to me, to enter one where nobody did except maybe the dog, but I even had my doubts about him.

After unpacking and changing, I sat with the family to catch up on events of the past week. I regaled them with the story of my hotel disaster and the wine fairies. Meggy recounted a recent trip to the vet where Milo peed on a potted plant in the lobby.

"It was so embarrassing!" Meggy cried with a big grin. She wore a T-shirt and shorts, and her face shone under her black hair.

Karen shrugged, "Oh well, I'm sure he's not the first to do that. Although the receptionist did look horrified, come to think of it. But she was very nice and told us not to worry about it."

Milo stretched out in front of me on the rug, while Moochie purred contently in Meggy's lap.

A whistling sound came from the kitchen, and Karen glanced at me, "That's the kettle."

I leaped off the couch and hurried to make my tea.

When I returned, Jackie glanced up from her phone and squealed, "Oh, Dad, you tucked your shirt into the pants ha-ha-ha. Nobody wears it like that."

"What do you mean?" I asked, looking down at my T-shirt. "I've always worn it this way; everyone does."

"Nobody does that anymore," Meggy sighed. "You have to get with the times."

Jackie jumped up, walked over and pulled the shirt out with a smirk, "There, that's better. You really don't know how to dress, do you?"

"You should've seen him when I met him. Woof woof!" Karen cried and broke into peals of laughter.

"Oh, Faja," Eric said solemnly. Even he had thrown me under the bus.

Meggy shook her head, and all four of them started cackling. As annoying as it was, I couldn't argue with her. Karen had improved my wardrobe when I met her. With three men in the family, mother had little sway with our clothes, and it wasn't until my twenties that I learned my father was colour blind. Perhaps listening to his opinion hadn't been so wise after all.

Karen appeared to rally to my defence. "Now children, your father is a very kind and smart man," she said in a reproachful voice, "but let's face it you can't be good at everything!" More laughter ensued.

They certainly kept me humble, and I grinned sheepishly while tucking the shirt back in, "I like it this way."

I found it shocking how quickly a child's perception of their father can change. From supreme, wise leader when they're small, to the guy who dresses like a clown when they're in their teens.

*

Fortunately, the conversation shifted to another topic, "How are things at the house, Eric? How are your roommates?" Karen asked. Our son was sitting in an armchair with his feet stretched out.

"It's good. They're fine, the only thing is … nobody does the dishes."

"Why not?" Karen asked. "You've got a dishwasher, for heaven's sake."

"I know, but the thing is, no one empties it and then the dishes pile up. So, what we do now is, when someone finds the last clean plate or fork, they lick it in front of the others. They'll say, 'look, this is mine because I licked it,'" he smirked.

"That's so bad, Eric." Karen didn't share his amusement.

"That's pretty disgusting, I agree," and I looked at Karen, "but I guess it's what you'd expect from a bunch of guys."

Karen ignored me and peppered him with more questions. "What about your laundry, are you changing your bed sheets every week like I told you? Cause you're not bringing much laundry home. I don't mind doing it you know."

"Oh, I don't change the sheets every week, Mom. I just rotate them," he said and grinned in deep satisfaction. "I figure they get dirtiest where my face is, so I rotate the sheets around until the face part is where the feet were. Then after two weeks, I wash them."

"That's so gross!" Karen said.

"Ewww!" Meggy moaned as well.

"You know it makes sense to me," I said, mulling it over. "Maybe it's a guy thing, but I think it's quite clever."

Eric closed his eyes and threw his head back in a crazy laugh. He obviously enjoyed the freedom of being out from under his mother's watchful eye.

*

The talk turned to a party that Jackie wanted to go to with Kat, whom she'd known since kindergarten. We liked Katie, but the usual inquisition still took place.

"Okay, who's having it?" Karen probed.

Sprawled on the couch in a T-shirt and faded jeans, our daughter's blue eyes stared absently, "You don't know them. It's a friend at school, but I'm with Kat so it's okay." Then she added the magic words, "And you don't have to drive or pick us up, because her mom will do both ways."

We exchanged glances, and Karen asked, "Where is it?"

A loud exasperated sigh broke out, and Jackie rolled her head from side to side, "OMG ...it's not far, okay? Don't worry about it."

Karen met my gaze and said hesitantly, "I guess it's okay, if Diane is driving the girls and picking them up."

I said nothing, and in that silent language families have, they understood this to be consent.

Karen turned back to Jackie, "Okay, but I want the parents' land number, just in case."

"Oh ... my... God...I don't have it!" she groaned. "You can call me on my cell, okay?"

We looked at each other again, then Karen said in frustration, "Alright, alright."

*

That evening Jackie busied herself in her room getting ready. Her plan was to walk to Kat's and depart from there. Around six o'clock, she trotted downstairs wearing blue jean shorts and a white top. As she set her purse down on the floor to get her jacket, it clinked.

"Check it, Andrew," Karen directed with her eyes fixed firmly on the bag.

Jackie watched in alarm as I picked it up.

"Wow, it's heavy!" Then, I slowly pulled out five bottles. "Isn't this my beer?"

"I need it for the party. It's on the parents' lawn, and they let kids drink. Not everyone's as uptight as you two." She spoke aggressively, but her face wore a guilty look.

"No way. You're too young." I said.

In response, she bolted back upstairs.

She had turned fifteen two weeks ago but remained four years below the legal drinking age. I studied the bottles in my hand and pondered the situation.

"I don't like it," I said after a minute. "This party's beginning to sound weird. Who has one on their lawn? There must expect a swarm of teenagers."

Karen said nothing, but I could see worry in her face. We were experiencing the discomfort that arises when your kid's story changes.

*

Shortly afterwards, Jackie reappeared to say she'd be leaving later, because Kat was running late. Karen started dinner while I went into the living room with a drink to read the newspaper. A few minutes later, I heard my name and looked up. Karen stood at the entrance, brooding. Something was on her mind.

"Jackie slipped into the backyard and then came back in," she said tersely. "You'd better check it out."

I groaned and set my paper down, "Okay, okay."

I stepped out the side door and opened the back gate. There it was. Half a dozen coolers and bottles of beer lay in view under a bush. I picked them up; they were the same bottles I'd confiscated earlier. She was persistent.

We called her downstairs, showed her the booty and asked for an explanation. At first, she denied knowing anything about them, but then realizing it was fruitless to lie, she confessed. The scheme was for Katie to collect them before leaving for the party. At a loss for words, I just stared at her in bewilderment. Foiled again, she ran to her room while I took the bottles to the basement.

Twenty minutes later, she bounced happily down the staircase and announced she was leaving. I stopped her with her hand on the front doorknob. Her coat appeared bloated, and I felt the pockets — they were stuffed with bottles.

I waved my arm, "That's enough, Jackie. Now, you're not going at all!"

A look of terror came over her face, and she became hysterical, falling to her knees and crying. But I held my ground. "No Jackie, three strikes and you're out. There's no party for you tonight. You had your chance, and you blew it. How many times do we have to catch you before you realize this is unacceptable?"

She wailed as she clutched my pant leg, "Pleeease, I beg of you. Let me go."

Unnerved, I glanced at Karen. Her features were twisted in anguish as she struggled with the emotional turmoil. I knew she was waffling.

Before she could relent, I shouted, "Enough is enough. The fact she keeps stealing our booze and trying to sneak it out after being caught twice already, shows you she's out of control!"

The sobbing continued, becoming more desperate, and she sat upright, "No, no, don't do that! I won't do it again." Tears rolled down her cheeks.

"I'm sorry, Jackie," I said, softening my tone, "but you've lost it."

She ran up the stairs screaming, "Noooooo!"

Karen yelled after her, "Maybe you'll learn a lesson from this!"

*

Meggy descended the staircase, and her was brow furrowed. She sat down on the love seat.

"She's on the roof, Dad. She says she's going to kill herself." Her blue eyes looked earnestly at me.

"Go and see, Andrew," Karen said tensely.

I walked onto the driveway and turned around to look at the house. There she was alright, hunched over on the garage roof, arms around her knees and head turned away from me. Our bedroom window was open, showing her mode of access. It reminded me of an incident when the kids were small, and Michael and Stephanie Robinson came over to play. The doorbell rang, and when Karen opened the door, she found a small boy brushing off his pants.

"Good thing the bushes broke my fall," he muttered before running upstairs.

"What the heck?" Karen thought.

She watched the vanishing legs for a moment before rushing after him. Michael was halfway out the window, in the process of rejoining the others, when she stopped him. She brought them all inside, told them off, and closed the window.

When his mother arrived to collect them, she promptly smacked him on the arm.

"Michael! You could have broken her shrubs!"

"Donna was more worried about my bushes than Michael," Karen laughed when she recounted the story to me. I chuckled too at the thought of a ten-year-old boy hanging from the eavestrough before dropping into our garden.

Of course, they're older now, but still, my youngest was up there sulking. Without a word, I went back inside to the others who were waiting in the living room.

*

I reported my findings, "She's fine. She's on the garage, and she won't hurt herself badly jumping from there. Also, she can't climb higher from there either, so the situation's not dangerous." Having delivered a logical and accurate assessment, I sat down.

They didn't seem reassured. Perhaps, because they'd never been a boy and jumped from such a height, they doubted me.

Karen crossed her arms, "Well, we can't leave her up there, Andrew. We need to bring her down."

"Yeah, Dad, I don't want her to hurt herself. Why don't we call Sue?"

Sue was younger than Karen, and therefore much cooler in the eyes of our girls. When they were younger, our daughters took dance lessons at the same studio as hers, and Sue did their makeup before competitions. She seemed to have a special rapport with young people.

Although she was a friend, I dismissed the idea, "Jackie's fine. Leave her alone and she'll come in on her own. Let's not make a mountain out of a molehill."

Karen paused, then said, "I agree with Meggy. I'm calling Sue."

*

I resigned myself to the fact they needed to reach out to someone. And despite the fact it was Saturday night, and she had her own family to take care of, she came over right away. I watched Karen open the front door and Sue rush in, talking as she did. Petite and attractive with long brown hair and a big smile, she gave me a wave and then conferred with Karen briefly before scurrying upstairs. She returned with Jackie in tow and announced they were going out for coffee.

When they left, we all breathed a sigh of relief; quiet had returned to the household. Over the next hour, I occasionally glanced at my watch, wondering what Sue could be saying. Soon they returned, and we gathered at the entrance. Talking calmly, she reminded Jackie that we loved her and wanted to keep her safe. Jackie nodded silently. Sue beamed at everyone, gave big hugs, and then with a quick wave of her hand was gone. Jackie appeared drained and trudged up the stairs to bed.

Meggy sat across from me on the love seat beside Karen. The transformation that had occurred was stunning, from hysterical to calm within an hour.

"That Sue is an angel," Karen said warmly, "She has a lot on her plate, yet she comes right over to help."

"Aren't you glad we called her, Dad?"

"Yes, I have to admit you were right. And she is an angel; this felt like a miracle."

Like most men, I didn't want to ask for help. My father wouldn't have. He'd leave me there to cool my heels, and I would have slunk back inside, ashamed and powerless. Even now I believe that approach would have succeeded, but maybe it works better with boys. I don't know. However, there was no point in second guessing them, what was most important was that the crisis was over. Besides, I was clearly outnumbered by the women's point of view; Meggy had been especially vocal and adamant. I carried the beer downstairs to put back in the spare fridge, hiding them in the vegetable bin with the onions. But as I started to close the door, I paused, reached back and grabbed two. Walking into the former family room, I opened one and placed the other on the coffee table. I turned the radio on low, lit the gas fireplace and sat on the old sofa in the semidarkness, just beyond the light shining down from the hallway above. Worn out, I needed some quiet to recharge. All the arguing had been stressful, and my stomach was in knots. I listened to the soft music and tried to relax.

*

Why was there so much fighting, particularly with Jackie? She was a drama queen, that's for sure. Before her audition, Karen said if she wasn't accepted for dance, she'd be a shoo-in for drama. Teenage years can be difficult, but we had no trouble with Eric. Maybe he spoiled us. I wished he was here now. We almost never had to discipline him, much to the annoyance of his sisters.

"Why couldn't you have misbehaved when you were our age?" Jackie accused him one time when he was home.

"Yeah, you make us look bad!" Meggy agreed.

He raised his eyebrows and stared at them, not knowing what to say.

The sound of voices made me glance towards the top of the stairs.

Karen's voice rang out above the murmurs, "Leave him alone, Meggy, he's in his cave."

She was right, I guess. I needed some solitude, and that's a good expression for it. This phrase first came to my attention in a book of hers, *Men are From Mars, Women Are From Venus*. A lady on the plane spied it on the empty seat beside me and cast a knowing smile. Hearing Karen say it made me chuckle, because while I had read the book, she never did. Yet she used that expression frequently, ever since she heard me quote it. The book provided me with an understanding of her need to talk about everything. The management training I'd undergone also gave me insights into people and different communication styles. My goal in these sessions was not only to become a better manager, but a better human being. Although it didn't seem to have helped much with my daughters, I was determined to keep trying. I leaned back and tried to figure out today's behaviour. Sometimes having a scientific mind is a curse, it often keeps me awake at night working to solve problems.

At the office, I met situations head on and brought them to resolution. But at home with all these women, I felt ineffective. Boys are easy; I know how to raise boys. To my brother and me, girls always seemed to be mysterious creatures, and this remained true even after I was married and had daughters. Sometimes I think that despite all my efforts, I'll never understand women, not even if I live to be a hundred.

*

A sudden noise caused me to glance to the top of the stairs again. Milo came padding down the steps with his tail was wagging. I stuck my hand out to pet him.

"Good old, faithful Milo. You understand me, don't you boy?"

He nuzzled my hand before dropping to the floor with a thump and lying across my feet. I opened the other bottle while listening for further sounds above. All was quiet. Then an idea popped into my head. I got up, went in the other room, gathered up all the beer and wine and placed them in the antique steamer chest my grandparents had brought over from Europe. I found a small lock and put it on. That would thwart the little darlings.

As I climbed up the stairs to go to bed, I realized that life had just got a little bit crazier. The bedtime routine would now be: collect the cell phones; put the cat and dog in their beds; and make sure the liquor chest was locked. If only this strategy would work.

MILO – FEARLESS DOG AND NOBLE BEAST

"Dogs feel very strongly that they should always go with you in the car, in case the need should arise for them to bark violently in your ear!" - Dave Barry

IMUST CONFESS THAT I often lost my temper during the teen years. It's not easy to admit because I've always regarded myself as a patient man: a calm man, not quick to anger. Sadly, my family doesn't agree. Take the other week, for example. After we had finished eating a delicious crackling pork roast dinner, I leaned back in my chair, put my arm across the top in an obviously relaxed posture and posed the question, "Kids, who do you think is more patient — me or your mother?"

There was a pause before Meaghan spoke up. "Well, neither

of you, to be honest." She smiled, and her blue eyes darted around the table.

That answer didn't satisfy me; it seemed ambiguous. So, I looked to the others. "What does everyone else think?"

"Yeah, you're the same," Jacquelyn agreed, nodding.

"I'd say you're about the same, too," Eric said, with a gleam in his eye. "You both have your moments."

My jaw dropped. "Really — you wouldn't say I'm better?"

"Oh no," Jackie snorted. "You're not a patient man, ha-ha."

Meggy chuckled, then clenched her fist, grimaced and imitated a rant of mine, "Bloody Hell. Bloody... ***bloody hell!***"

They all joined in the laughter and group ridicule. I sat flabbergasted; I was certain they'd pick me. Even Eric had let me down.

*

When I walked Milo around the block later, I reflected on the discussion of patience. Probably what upset me most was their unanimous opinion. Karen is a hyperactive person, and by consequence, impatient. When I asked the question, I expected the kids to compare us and conclude that I was more tolerant than they realized. But that didn't happen.

Getting the women to leave the house on time is extremely stressful for me, an experience similar to herding cats — completely uncooperative. No doubt, this was the reason for the impression of irritability on my part. As I moved up management levels in my career, I had to become organized and punctual. A boss sets the tone for his department, and punctuality is the cornerstone of efficiency and success. I'm also very goal orientated, which was something I learned in leadership training I've received over the years. Given a deadline, I will beat it, meet it or die trying. Employers value this trait. Therefore, it's only natural that I grow frustrated at delays, particularly when my family is the cause.

*

Be that as it may, I believe things riled me much less before I got married. Before all the stress took its toll. When I first met Karen, she was late for everything — and I don't mean by minutes but an hour or more. And this was before children. It drove me nuts. My parents had instilled in me the discipline to always be on time for an event or appointment.

First, I endeavoured to trick Karen by telling her a party started thirty minutes or even an hour earlier than it really did and going so far as to write the false time on the calendar. Unfortunately, when she noticed I wasn't as upset as usual, she figured it out. Next, I tried explaining how our lateness disturbed me and how our relatives would conclude we were bad-mannered. This helped marginally; we were tardy by only thirty to sixty minutes from then on.

Once we had kids, even worse — girls, I might as well have abandoned all hope.

Earlier that summer, I vented to my buddy, Steven Fisher, when I spent a weekend at his cottage — just us guys. The cottage is perched above one of the many small wilderness lakes in the Muskoka region and built on a steep slope with a porch supported by twenty-foot wooden posts fastened into concrete piers. The view of the surrounding treetops and lake below is superb. We'd been friends forever and caught up on each other's lives while relaxing on the porch before dinner. I sipped a cold beer, gazed through the trees at the water and inhaled the comforting aroma of the spruce forest. Squirrels scurried back and forth, fought in the trees and, strangely enough, reminded me of my family dynamics.

I grumbled about the agony I endured in my attempts to make the women punctual. Much shorter than me, with black hair and a moustache, Steven had had the good sense never to marry. His dark beady eyes didn't move as he listened in fascination to my description of a recent hair-raising incident. When I finished, he gazed down at the lake. "I like to be on time, too," he mumbled. Then cocking his head to the side, he grinned. "I'm actually amazed I'm not visiting you once a month in the loony bin where you spend your days pushing pins into female dolls."

"You're right," I said with a deep sigh. "Sometimes, I think I'm halfway there already."

*

Things had levelled off at work in July, so I booked two days of vacation before the weekend to go camping at Pinery Provincial Park on Lake Huron. It's a beautiful spot with an oak savannah and sand dunes situated on the second-longest freshwater beach in the world. An enormous lake which, together with the four other Great Lakes of Ontario, contains twenty percent of the world's supply of freshwater. This water eventually thunders over Niagara Falls and spills down the St. Lawrence Seaway into the ocean.

Karen and I both loved the outdoors and wanted our children to enjoy it, too. Eric did. In fact, he couldn't join us because he was doing a canoe trip in Algonquin Park with his chums. As I loaded up some of our gear Wednesday night, my neighbour Rod stopped by to investigate. He stands six feet two, with a grey moustache and greying hair. When I mentioned our destination, he seemed envious.

"You have a lot of stuff there," he said, peering into the van and at the rooftop carrier.

"And this is only the camping gear. Karen and the girls need to pack, but we plan to hit the road by eleven."

His mouth twisted into an amused smile. "Eleven o'clock. Are you sure? The women have to get ready, and that can take forever." He had three older daughters and understood the challenge I faced. Besides, he'd observed our delayed departures before.

But I nodded in response. "We talked about it. We plan to leave by eleven to arrive early enough to pitch the tent and still hit the beach."

His eyebrows raised, and he gave me a skeptical look but wished me well and headed home. The next morning, we all woke early and started packing. Hours ticked by. It seemed to take forever. And squeezing baggage into the vehicle began to require bigger and bigger acts of magic.

Once most items were loaded, I stopped and stretched. Now I was stuck. The big coolers and boxes needed to be packed next so I could pile the rest on top of their flat surfaces, but they weren't ready. I looked at my watch; it was already one o'clock.

Stepping inside to hurry Karen up, I groaned in exasperation. "This is why we should start packing earlier."

"That's not any help," she snapped. "Do you want to do the food?" and she gestured to three half-filled cardboard boxes and two coolers. I stared at them. It was impossible to know what had been packed and what hadn't. She must have read my mind because she barked again, "No, you don't, do you? So, why don't you take Milo, the flatulating dog, for a walk instead of hassling me?"

"He hardly farts since we changed his kibbles," I protested, as I grabbed the leash and made a hasty exit with my hound.

*

As I passed Rod's house, I heard him shout. He was sitting on his porch. I waved, and he came over.

"I thought you'd have left by now."

"No, we're not ready yet," I replied briskly.

For a second, he was distracted by Milo. "Looks as if he has a hard time."

I examined my beagle's attempt to pee. "Yeah, he's usually fast, but not today."

Returning his attention to me, Rod said wickedly, "Wow, the way you talked yesterday, I half expected to look out my window this morning and see you blowing your whistle like Colonel von

Trapp, while the whole family marched out single file and got in the van."

What an ass, I thought, but he made me laugh. "That would be the dream, wouldn't it? But unfortunately, that's not how it works."

Finally, at three o'clock, still in time to at least catch the sunset, we left. Karen volunteered to drive as compensation for her tardiness.

"Slow down when we pass by Rod's house," I instructed as she crawled out of the driveway.

"Why?"

"You'll see. Stop here!" I lowered my window, pulled out a whistle and blew it loudly. "Okay, you can continue now," I snickered.

*

As I stood in the men's line for showers the next morning, I realized that camping is the great equalizer. It doesn't matter if you're rich and staying in a big, fancy trailer or middle class in a humble tent like us; everybody lines up together with their bag of toiletries. I scanned the queue and tried to guess who might be leaders of industry or average Joes, but it was impossible. They all had the same sluggish, scruffy appearance of fellow campers waking up.

Afterwards, I returned to the campsite to start breakfast on the propane stove. The others soon returned, refreshed and cheerful from their showers.

"You have to show me how to make the coffee," Karen exclaimed as she watched me fry the bacon. "I don't want to wait until you shower every day to have a cup."

I showed her the measurement of grounds and water. "You have to fill it to the bottom of the meniscus," I said, pouring a bit off.

"What's that?"

"You know, the curve across the surface of the water."

She dutifully looked at the measuring cup. "Okay, I see. But why do you call it a meniscus?"

"I guess it's a scientific term, now that I think about it, but it's how we make an accurate measurement in the laboratory. When you put water in a glass, the surface makes a concave shape due to the surface tension of the liquid."

After eating and brushing our teeth, we went to the beach. We swam and lay on the beautiful sand for a few hours before walking back between the dunes for lunch. I had made hamburgers before we left and stored them in the cooler. After building a fire, we settled in camp chairs and waited for them to cook. At one point, Jackie jumped up and grabbed the flipper.

"I'm turning mine over," she said, fixing her eye on one.

I watched closely. "Be careful it doesn't ..."

The words weren't all out of my mouth before the burger she rotated slowly onto its side slid through the grill and into the fire. I jumped up, pulled it out with a fork and placed it on a plate.

She looked at it distastefully. "I won't eat that. I'll get another."

I sighed reluctantly. "Well, there's only one each because extras won't keep long in a cooler. So, if you don't want it, then you'll have to find something else or be hungry."

She was quiet for a minute, contemplating this. Then she lifted the burger up and dusted the ashes off with her hand. "It's not so bad. I think it'll be okay."

At first, I said nothing as she munched away. But once we had finished and sat with our tea, I turned towards her. "I'm proud of you, Jackie, for not being a baby and for eating that burger. Good for you."

Her lips curled into a small smile as she stared at the fire.

"You know, a person can never be a real camper unless they're prepared to handle a little dirt because it's everywhere out here. I lifted my cup of tea. "Look at my cup. Stuff from the trees fell in, but I simply blew it out before pouring my tea." She glanced at the mug, and I continued. "Like Yoda would say, if you wish to be a true camper, you must first become one with the dirt. Today, you became a true camper!" I wrapped my arm around her, and Karen laughed.

*

But despite the beauty of the park and the fun we were having, after a few days, the girls complained.

"There are only old men on the beach," Jackie moaned, looking woefully at me.

"What do you mean by old men?"

Meggy glanced at me. "You know, guys in their thirties."

"Oh, now that's *old,*" I said, rolling my eyes.

Karen jumped in. "Listen, let's take them to Grand Bend tomorrow. Sue and her daughters went there last year and told me our girls would love it." She beamed happily. "It's our last day; we can enjoy the town and the beach and head out from there."

The girls weren't enthusiastic at first, but as we cruised down the main street towards the waterfront, they became excited. This was more like it — a happening place, with lots of young people, restaurants and boutiques. The sand beach resembled the California ones on TV, with attractive lifeguards stationed every hundred feet.

"Keep your eyes in your head, dear," Karen chided as we walked between bikini-clad sunbathers to the wide blue water. Dropping the towels, she glanced around approvingly. "See, girls. Lots of hunky young men here. I'll help you look, ha-ha-ha."

"Ewww!" Jackie whined. Throwing her towel down, she ran with Meggy to where the waves were rolling in.

We spent the day on the beach and roaming through the boutiques before heading off to hit a restaurant on the way home.

Once the waitress took our orders, we chatted about how great Grand Bend was. Jackie also talked about her last two years in middle school. "Want to know something? I never learned to play the clarinet."

I studied her from across the table. "But Mr. Kirkpatrick's an excellent teacher." The performances by his bands always impressed me, especially since most students had never held an instrument before.

She sipped her pop and gazed at the table. "Uh-huh, but I didn't like the clarinet, so I just faked it."

"How could you do that?"

"Just put it in my mouth and pretended. He never caught on, ha-ha. Oh, but one day, he was so mean to me and Kat."

"What did he do?" Karen asked, leaning forward.

"Well, we missed band practice. He scheduled it over lunch, and like, we're not going to miss our lunch! Besides, we thought he wouldn't notice. But afterwards, he told everyone to play what they rehearsed, and we didn't know what to do. He got angry and yelled at us."

"Seriously?" Karen sat up straight: her large eyes bigger than usual. She'd never seen this gentle teacher do anything but smile ingratiatingly.

"Yeah, he made Katie cry."

I glanced at Karen; Jackie's anecdote seemed incredulous.

"Yes, but then he felt so bad, it was funny," she giggled. "I told him we missed it because I felt sick, and Katie had to give me a cookie to make me feel better. He looked surprised, said he was sorry and called us his angels. He brought out some cake, saying, 'This is for my little angels!', and he acted extra nice for the rest of the class ha-ha-ha." Her face lit up with joy at the memory of her trickery.

"Angels with horns," I joked.

"You must have scared him," Karen said. "He figured he'd get in trouble."

Jackie threw back her head, her body shook with laughter, and she said between gasps. "He gave me an A in the course... and ... I can't even play the instrument...boo ha-ha-ha! And those kids that really tried to learn didn't get an A, but *I* did." She had a gift for storytelling and made us all laugh.

When we had settled down, I said, "An A. So, you scammed him."

"Yep," Jackie replied, "and last year he posted a picture of Katie and me on the wall of my social media account with the caption, 'two of my sweetest students!'"

And there it was. She had fooled her teacher and been rewarded. As we drove back on the highway, I thought of Mr. Kirkpatrick; the poor fellow never did know he'd been duped by his angels.

*

As nice as it was to have Eric in the house for the summer, we'd forgotten how much he ate. When we finished dinner, he leaned back in his chair and stretched lazily.

Karen proudly observed him. "He's your son alright. He lives to eat. He's like Gordy the Gut!"

Eric gave us a perplexed look.

Karen grinned. "Gordy is a relative of your dad's aunt Kathleen and a bit of a bum. He stayed at her place once while job hunting and liked to go drinking with his pals and sleep in late. She told us this story when we went to her place for lunch." I recalled how Kathleen had strode purposefully across the kitchen, with her dark brown, shoulder-length hair and Irish confidence as Karen continued. "Kathleen described how she rummaged through the fridge the week before. 'Where's the white wine I put in here the other day? It has to be somewhere,' she mumbled as she moved things to uncover the elusive bottle. Gordie was parked in the kitchen with a coffee. He stroked his reddish beard and cleared his throat. 'Ah yes, that was a fine wine, Kathleen. My buddy and me came home last night and sampled it.' Sampled, in Gordie talk, meant they'd finished it."

"She was livid," I added, "and christened him with the new nickname. Aware his welcome had worn thin, he moved out afterwards. It's a wonderful expression, though, to describe someone with an enormous appetite, which all of us have in this family."

The story made me smile and reminded me of the time when Kathleen came to our house for dinner. Karen and I were fighting because I wanted us to start cooking, but she wanted to continue socializing. After observing our debate for a moment, Kathleen commented in her Belfast accent, "I get a kick out of you two. You're hilarious. But Andy, you have to think about this — do you eat to live or live to eat?"

Before I could finish pondering the question, Karen squealed, "Oh, he lives to eat. That's for sure!"

"Who are you kidding?" I smiled at her. "You gobble up food pretty well yourself, dear."

Kathleen was right, of course. We should be eating to live, but our family often behaved as if we lived to eat.

*

The following week, Karen took Milo to the veterinarian, who delivered horrible news. He had found an inoperable tumour that impeded the dog's urination, and he had to be put down. Fourteen was a decent lifespan for a dog but still too short for our liking. The vet gave Karen some painkillers so she could bring him home for one last night to say goodbye.

When I came home, I stroked my pet, who lay quietly in his bed. "Good dog, Milo. Fearless dog and noble beast." His tail thumped against the floor.

Karen took him back the next day after I had left for work, and I preferred it that way. It was too sad, and I'd rather remember him as the youthful and healthy dog he'd been. But I would miss him. He loved me so much that whenever I stepped out of the van, he'd bark like crazy and drive everybody mad. The memory of this cheered me up. Good old faithful Milo.

When I walked into the house after work, Moochie lay in the dog's customary place on the top step of the stairs.

Karen's eyes watered, and she pointed, "Isn't that cute? She misses him."

"She doesn't miss him," I said, staring in amazement. "Remember? You told me Milo bullied her from that exact spot. Well, she's taken the high ground now and looks really pleased about it, too."

A look of surprise came over Karen's face. "I guess you're right. She's the boss now."

On behalf of my beloved beagle, I prodded Moochie with my foot. "Come on, Mufasa, get to your bed." She sauntered off but not before throwing me a nasty glance.

*

Milo's absence was noticed in many ways.

"He was a canine vacuum cleaner," Karen declared at dinner after spotting crumbs under the table. "I always saw him going over the floor with his nose after we ate, but I had no idea how much stuff he cleaned up."

We reminisced about our dog, which helped deal with his passing. While there were many funny stories, the sausage incident garnered the most hysterics. The kids were quite young, Eric would have been eight, and we all had gathered in the living room. Milo sat on the loveseat facing the window and Karen in an adjacent chair. On an impulse, she shot her finger out at him and yelled with a scowl, "Sausage!"

The reaction was hilarious. He stared straight ahead in fear but watched Karen from the corner of his eye. Then he started barking without turning his head. He didn't understand what she said, but he knew he didn't like it. She repeated this over and over, with the same reaction each time. We howled without restraint, and he was known as Sausage Dog for quite a while after.

"And remember how he dug a hole in the winter to find a bone he'd buried in the fall?" Karen giggled. "The dumb beast came inside with a bloody nose from pushing it into the ice. We kept an eye on him all winter because he'd try to dig whenever he ran out. You'd think he'd realize the ground was frozen and hurt him, but he never did."

*

The week after Milo died, I took down the swimming pool because we weren't using it anymore. The kids had outgrown it. Sixteen feet wide and three feet deep, it hadn't been easy to erect. I had to remove the grass, level the lawn and lay a plastic sheet down before assembling the pool on top. Levelling the ground alone took days to complete. Now I worked in reverse order, cutting up the plastic sides and throwing them in the recycle bin. As I rolled up the groundsheet, a horrible stench assaulted me. The odour was so strong that I stopped and took a step backwards. I didn't understand it. I had painstakingly removed all the grass below so it wouldn't rot.

Then I spotted a slight mound near the middle. Digging under, I discovered an old rawhide bone. The little jerk must have buried it right before I laid the sheet. Boy, had it ever decomposed. Holding my nose with one hand, I picked up the offending object with a rag and threw it into the trash can. Okay, Milo, you got the last laugh, even from heaven. Looking up at the sky, I could imagine him smiling down at me.

12
JACKIE HAS A PROJECT

"The quickest way for a parent to get a child's attention is to sit down and look comfortable." - Lane Olinghouse

ALTHOUGH THE DAYS were still bright and warm, nights became cooler as the calendar flipped into early September. Jackie started at Hillside, Meggy entered her last year of high school, and Eric began the third year of his engineering program.

After a few weeks, we grew accustomed to the school routine, and daily life began to be less hectic. Summer was fleeting, but we would still manage a month of barbecues before it became too cold. When we sold the cottage and started using our back yard more, Karen devoted more time to her flowers, and they bloomed magnificently. But while I loved the floral displays, they also depicted the bittersweetness of fall since the colourful splendour reaches its zenith just before the frost kills them.

These thoughts ran through my mind as I stood on our patio

and cleaned off the barbeque in preparation for guests. To the right of me, on the brick wall under the awning, hung a wooden sign carved with the words *McKinney's Bistro,* which Karen had made to highlight the outdoor dining area. And while the overall ambiance was very pleasing, she had acquired a collection of the most unique and bizarre yard ornaments and plaques I'd ever seen. There were gnomes of various sizes and colours and two large metal frogs playing instruments. One of these was a trumpet that reminded us of Eric's music days. Scattered on the ground and trellises were various ceramic flowers, lizards and animals. And frogs. A lot of frogs, actually, displayed below Karen's plants and bushes, on the fence or beside other ceramic creatures. A small green frog, with his arms behind his head and a lazy smile on his face, slept in a miniature hammock hung from the purple lilac bush beside the patio. At the base of a shrub to its right sat a fat bullfrog, a rabbit and several psychedelic-coloured mushrooms. Groovy, man.

After dinner, Marie and Gary Dryden gazed around the yard while we enjoyed coffee and dessert. Karen had met Marie, a fetching and petite brunette, in one of her psychology classes at university. After Gary entered Marie's life, we hit it off and have been great pals ever since.

Gary and I chatted while Marie and Karen caught up on each other's activities. I overheard the last part of Karen's sentence.

"...that was the summer that I worked at the Clarke Institute of Psychiatry."

"Oh, yes, that's what we *told* her," I said with a wink, "that she was *working* there for the summer."

Karen flinched. "Ha-ha, very funny."

Marie laughed and then surveyed our back yard. "I can't get over how beautiful your flowerbeds are!"

"Thank you, Marie. But I won't take any credit. Karen created all of this." I gestured at the array of colours surrounding us, and Karen beamed with pride. "But she may have gone overboard with the knickknacks. Sometimes, when we sit in the fading evening light and I see all these weird mushrooms and creatures in the shadows, I can imagine what a bad drug trip must be like — *Bring me down, man... bring me down!*"

Marie chuckled, and her dark eyes sparkled, but Karen shot me an irritated look. "Oh, stop it. I like them." She half-whispered to Marie, "Andrew has a problem with garden decorations."

I nodded vigorously. "Yes, I do. I mean, just look at those magic mushrooms and that sleeping frog over there." I pointed at the ground and her shrubbery. "Now, don't tell me that's normal."

Karen shook her head with exasperation and sipped her coffee. "Never mind, I'm keeping them. Besides, my friends gave me quite a few."

"Well, people are going to think your friends are druggies."

"You two make me laugh, the way you banter," Marie said, and her green eyes crinkled at the corners. "It's so funny."

Karen shifted in her seat and sighed. "Well, he's going to drive me crazy one day, Marie."

"Oh, come on now, dear. It's not really a drive — it's more of a short walk."

Gary couldn't restrain himself anymore. He leaned forward, and his tall body shook with laughter. "You're a funny guy, Andy."

Karen tried to glare at me but couldn't resist smiling.

*

Perhaps deep down, I hoped my teasing might persuade Karen to give some away, but that never happened. I complained to my pal Steven about her obsessive nature — how she went overboard on things, and the ornaments were just one example.

He listened to my complaints and then said, with the confidence and satisfaction only a man who never married can possess, "But all women are obsessive. Didn't you know that?" He said this as if it were an absolute fact and followed it with a list of women he knew and their guilty obsessions.

Perhaps he's right, but I still think that Karen leads the pack. She placed a candle in the living room five years ago, and I have to admit, I enjoyed the way it softened the light. Then she added more candles: tall ones and short ones; fat ones and thin ones; aromatic ones and smelly ones. And she added more on the patio, in the kitchen and even in the bathroom. Some nights when I got home late and an army of burning wicks greeted me, I was afraid the neighbours would think we joined a cult. Maybe these obsessions were a stress outlet. I'm not sure, but I learned not to discuss candles and ornaments with Karen anymore.

*

During the following week, we took away Jackie's cell phone for three days as punishment for rude and angry behaviour. Yet when I walked through the door the next night, there sat my blonde daughter on the sofa with the phone in her hands.

I put my jacket away and scowled. "You stole your phone back, Jackie! Now you'll lose it longer."

Unruffled, she didn't even bother looking up. "No, I didn't. Mother gave it to me."

I stared in confusion, then turned on my heels. A dark cloud hung over me as I strode up the staircase; this had happened before. Karen would agree to a discipline — then go behind my back and reverse it. We'd talked about her need to change this pattern but, obviously, with no impact. Karen was sitting on our bed sorting laundry and smiled when I entered.

"I'm mad at you," I said, confronting her. "You gave Jackie her Blackberry. Are you crazy?"

She paused while folding a towel and appeared embarrassed. "I know, but these were special circumstances."

The blood had rushed to my face, so I sat on the bed and moaned, "What's so special?"

"Well, she hasn't many friends at Hillside, and without her cell phone, she can't connect with them to meet for lunch."

"Are you kidding me? She has lots. Natalie, Vicky and Katie all go there."

"Let me explain," she said and set the laundry down and looked at me compassionately. "Natalie joined the 'cool girls' clique and doesn't bother with her. But I'll tell you something. I saw her once when I drove Jackie to school, and she's not a member — just a hang-er-on. Although Natalie desperately wants to be part of the group, they weren't very nice to her. I felt sorry for her."

That caught me by surprise, and I began to relax. She brushed her light brown hair away from her face and continued. "I remember a group of snobby girls in Fort Erie we called the 'Untouchables'. They thought they were so incredible and were mean to everyone else. It left an impression on me. Even today, I could name each girl in that group."

I'd never even witnessed this behaviour. The closest I came to the experience was watching the movie *Mean Girls*. But I do recall Eric saying there were distinct groups at the school: he had been in the music group; there was a smokers' group that gathered at the front of the school and two other cliques that didn't interest him. He was lucky; he had a nice circle of pals who were also academic and have remained close friends to this day.

But this news touched me, and I empathized with Jackie's predic-ament. "What about Vicky?"

"She has a boyfriend and doesn't bother with her," Karen said and giggled. "Jackie complained to me after the first week that she saw Vicky kissing her boyfriend in the hall, and he was butt ugly!"

I smiled. I could picture her saying that.

Karen went on. "Even so, the couple's inseparable, and Jackie's on the out."

I started to speak, but she put her hand on mine to silence me. "Her other best friends, Haley and Sue, go to the crime-ridden local school that we wouldn't let her attend. That only leaves Katie, and she isn't in any of her classes. So, she's trying to make new friends, but she needs her cell to connect, or she'll be an outcast."

Faced with this reality, I felt my anger deflate, and I stared at the floor. I only had a few pals at her age, but I was fine and got through unscarred. However, Jackie had a stronger need for social engagement than I did, and this tugged at my heart. Even though she had four BFFs at the school, because she joined them a year later, most had moved on and connected with others.

"Alright," I said at length, exhaling loudly. "I understand."

"Just try to act nice and be understanding," she said, and there was tenderness in those light blue eyes. "She needs our support now more than ever."

"Okay, don't worry. I will."

*

The next month, Jackie announced she had an assignment on Zeppelins.

"That's a great topic," I said enthusiastically. As a boy, I loved disaster stories. "The most famous Zeppelin was the Hindenburg," I said, warming to the subject. "It exploded during a live radio broadcast and was captured on newsreel. 'Oh, the humanity!' the reporter cried, and his words became famous."

"Father can help you with this," Karen said and cast a glance sideways at me. "It's boring, but he likes that stuff."

Not quite the motivating speech I hoped for. Feeling disparaged, despite the faint compliment at the end, I replied weakly, "Sure, if she wants me to."

Jackie looked hopeful. "Yes, Daddy. I can't find anything on it."

Honestly, at first, I hoped she'd say no, but then I realized this might be an opportunity to bond and impress her with my project skills. Perhaps after we finished, she'd view me as a helper instead of an adversary. We also owed her our support and attention. Jackie picked things up exceptionally fast in her younger years. Of the three kids, she needed the least assistance with homework.

I had helped Eric with science and Meggy with math, so it was no small relief when Jackie turned out to be more independent. But when she hit the teen years, our prize student changed. Last year, she had asked me to check a quiz she had completed, and her sloppiness horrified me. Squinting, I struggled to read the crude scrawls in light pencil. Some answers climbed the page diagonally, making me wonder if she wrote it while riding in the van. I looked at her and back at the paper. "Don't you want to rewrite this neater?"

She squeezed up beside me and gave the sheet a quick once-over. "Nah, that's good enough," she snickered.

I realized my mouth was hanging open and closed it. It would only have taken five minutes to redo the fill-in-the-blank answers neatly, but she had declined. Her approach was certainly different than mine; I may not have gotten the best marks, but I made a splendid effort. Yet, she seemed happy to drift by with acceptable but not astounding marks.

*

Yes, perhaps this project was a blessing and would bring us closer. At the office, I searched the internet and discovered that the Germans used Zeppelins during WWI to drop bombs by hand on fearful British citizens. This new technology appeared to be impervious to attacks by the air force, which couldn't halt their raids, leaving the British inhabitants in constant fear of this menace from the sky. That is, until a young British pilot followed one and, in a last futile attempt, sprayed a burst of bullets from behind. They hit an undiscovered weak spot where the hydrogen was stored, causing the vessel to burst into flames and crash in front of thousands of cheering Londoners.

Jackie will love this, I thought. *It's fascinating.* The aviator became an overnight hero, and others were able to repeat his attack angle and bring down more. With no ability to correct the deficiency, their military use had to be discontinued. The propaganda value was enormous. Until then, British subjects had been terrorized to an extent that would never be equalled until the German air blitz in WWII.

I eagerly presented the material when I arrived home, along with an exciting synopsis of the episode. While Jackie seemed pleased at the amount of information, she wasn't as enthralled by the story as I expected. Nor was Karen, who I insisted listen while I described it. I guess not everyone is a war fan. Nevertheless, Jackie had all the facts she needed and prepared a draft of the essay. I reviewed it, made many corrections and suggestions and had her add a drawing. *She should get a decent mark,* I thought, and I waited expectantly for the teacher's evaluation. A decent grade might be the spark to ignite her passion for academic excellence. But the result turned out to be not quite what I expected.

*

The following week, Jackie told us at dinner that the teacher had marked their assignments. "I got an A," she said matter-of-factly.

"That's wonderful!" I exclaimed, feeling pleased with myself. And yet, the pretty blonde girl sitting across the table didn't exhibit the exuberance you'd expect from a person who had obtained such an outstanding grade. "What's the matter, Jackie? Is something wrong?"

She looked sheepish, "Well, he gave me an A, but then made a little speech to the entire class about how I received the highest mark. It was *sooo* embarrassing because you wrote it for me."

"That's not true," I countered. "You earned it. I didn't write it, Jackie. I edited it."

She brushed me off. "It doesn't matter. I have no interest in Zeppelins, and I learned nothing from the assignment." She ate another mouthful from her plate, before resuming. "And then after class, these nerdy kids, who never talked to me before, came up and asked me how I did it. They wanted to learn my technique! Ha-ha-ha. I didn't know what to say, because I don't have one. Then, they asked if I wanted to study with them for the upcoming test."

"What did you tell them?"

"I said sure, but seriously, Dad — are they joking?" she chortled, and her eyes bulged. "The test is two weeks away. I won't be studying until the day before, ha-ha-ha. They're studying now."

My dream of rekindled ambition was dashed, and the teacher's, too, if the intent of his speech was to motivate Jackie, as I suspected it was. Her encounter with the academic kids didn't have an impact either; they never talked anymore after that first conversation. Well, at least she got to feel like a nerd for a day.

*

On Friday, Jackie and Katie were having a sleepover at her friend Maddy's house, so Karen took her right after school. Maddy, or Mariana as her parents referred to her, was a cute girl with long black hair. Jackie had met her last year. Maddy was academic, and her greatest passion, an uncommon one these days, was horses.

After dinner, Karen called Jackie to confirm the expected pickup time the next day.

"Hello... hello, Jackie?" She turned to me with a confused look and said, "The reception's terrible! It sounds like she's walking or driving down a road. I'm calling again."

"Hello... Jackie?" she yelled once more into the phone. "Where are you?" The call ended again.

"All I heard was a garbled response, and then the line disconnected," she said in frustration. The third time, our daughter didn't even pick up.

"This is ridiculous," Karen vented. "Okay, now I'm calling Katie."

I watched her bolt out of the chair and grab her phone book. Seconds later, she had her on the line. Shocked at receiving a call on her cell from Karen, Katie readily admitted that they'd gone to a

Rib Fest in the local park and were walking home. Karen texted our daughter but received nebulous responses. So, she texted Maddy's mother, Sharon.

"She says Mariana is spending the night at Katie's," Karen said, looking up from her phone.

Our radars went to full alert, and Karen focused like a laser beam to uncover the hidden truth. She was incredible to watch: a well-oiled machine in action. I admired her efficiency as she flipped the pages to Katie's mother, Diane.

"She's not home!" Karen exclaimed. "Diane's spending the weekend at her boyfriend's and was surprised by my text. Katie said she was staying overnight at *our* house. Let's get the car and go over to her place." Karen marched to the closet for her jacket.

"I'll come, too," Meggy chirped in. Her sister's antics never failed to provide entertainment for her.

An unfamiliar black car stood in the driveway when we arrived. I walked past it to ring the bell. When Katie opened the door, I told her I needed to speak to Jackie. She turned and climbed the four steps of the backsplit to the living room. Looking up the stairs after her, I could see a boy's legs sticking out from an armchair.

Jackie scurried down the stairs. "What's up, Dad?" she asked innocently,

I frowned. "You lied to us, so you're coming home."

She protested, but when I said her mother was in the car, she capitulated. She knew she was busted. As she got her boots on and exited, the boy came down the steps.

"Hi, I'm James," he said, thrusting a hand out. I shook it and explained that Jackie had to come home.

Tall, dark-haired and good-looking, he flashed a big smile. "That's okay, I should be leaving, too. I have to work in the morning."

I fixed him with a death stare and said nothing. I knew how to intimidate young men.

So, he continued a little awkwardly. "Yeah, I have a job at the grocery store." And he mentioned a local supermarket.

"Okay." I gave him a nod. "Goodnight."

He was smooth, too smooth in fact. Never trust a boy this confident, especially if he has his own car. And if he thought he was impressing me with his industriousness, he was wrong. I wasn't going to have the wool pulled over my eyes by a slick charmer. Jackie grimaced with her arms crossed in the rear seat beside Meggy. I couldn't help smiling. Jackie had attempted the three-way con, a scheme hatched by generations of teenagers over the years to keep their watchful parents at bay. Executed flawlessly, only a chance phone call had tripped them up.

"How did you find the number for Kat and Maddy's mother?" she demanded after a few minutes.

"Oh, whenever I get one for your friends or their parents, I write it in my book," Karen answered, with a smug glance sideways to me "so we have it in case of an emergency."

We spent the rest of the ride in silence.

The next morning, I meandered downstairs while the others were still sleeping. I'd have about an hour to myself before I needed to start breakfast, which on Saturdays is my famous over-easy eggs, bacon and fried potatoes. All cooked in a single pan, flavourful, simplistic, and with few dishes to clean up after.

But something caught my eye when I entered the kitchen. Karen's phone book lay on the table, open and empty. I discovered the pages in the small garbage can under the sink, ripped into pieces. The anger inherent in tearing up the book was palpable. The empire had struck back and without mercy. No distinction had been made between phone numbers for her friends and our contacts; there were no survivors.

"This is appalling!" Karen shouted as she sifted through the debris on the counter.

"That's Jackie's handiwork," I said conclusively.

"That little brat. I need those numbers, and some are important."
She surveyed the shreds. "This will take hours to tape together."

"If I were you, I'd make her do it — to teach her a lesson."

*

Although she directed Jackie to repair it, Karen ended up doing it herself, because she couldn't wait for our daughter to get around to it. Then she hid the phone book and did this so well, even I had trouble finding it.

Raising kids is like a chess game; you have to stay one move ahead of them. Karen and I had succeeded this week, but I knew we wouldn't always be so lucky. For as hard as you try to rule your teenager, sometimes they reduce you to king, while they take over as queen — with all the moves!

13
PASSAGES

"To everything there is a season and a time to every purpose, under heaven. A time to be born, a time to die, a time to plant, a time to reap, a time to kill, a time to heal, a time to laugh, a time to weep." - The Book of Ecclesiastes (3:18) The Bible, King James Version; incorporated in the song "Turn! Turn! Turn!" and recorded by The Byrds.

"WHAT A BEAUTIFUL day!" I cried as sunshine shone down on the highway and streamed through the windshield. I glanced at Karen. "I hope your mother has packed a lot in boxes."

"She should have. Every time I've talked to her, she said she's been taking things to the dumpster when she walks at night and getting ready."

We were on our way to Fort Erie to bring Anna back to a house near us that we helped her purchase in the summer. I was driving one van with Steven's trailer attached, and Eric drove the other. Karen worried about her mother living alone in another town, and

Anna had the annoying habit of knocking her telephone off the hook, which didn't help. Almost every month, Karen had to ask a neighbour to check on her because she hadn't been able to contact Anna for three days.

I often heard Karen yell into the phone, "Ma, you left the phone off the hook again. I was worried about you!"

"I'm okay."

"You need to be more careful, Ma. If I can't reach you, I get anxious."

"Hmmmm..."

Even louder, "Are you watching TV, Ma?"

There was a pause on the other end. "There's a good murder mystery on ...." Anna provided a brief summary of the plot. She loved TV murder mysteries as much as romance novels.

*

She had lived happily in Fort Erie ever since she got married, but Fred had passed away years ago, and the time had come to say goodbye to that stage of her life and move closer so we could assist her.

"It's a nice little town," I said as I turned down the familiar street with a park on the other side.

"Not for a teenager," Karen replied. She had felt very stifled when she was an adolescent and couldn't wait to leave. "Growing up in small town, everyone knows your business. You sneeze and it makes the local paper. Funny, you always thought it would be nice to live in a small town until you met me."

I nodded, and an amusing memory surfaced of a recruiter who tried to get me to take a job at a fledging pharmaceutical company some years earlier.

"They would do handsprings to get you," he stated on the phone and tried to sell me on the position and company. Little did he know, as he touted the benefits of the opportunity, and the reduced stress to be reaped by moving to a small town, that my wife came from that very same town and was vehemently opposed to the idea.

Over my dead body," she declared with an air of finality.

I had turned him down, and things had actually worked out better for me after I passed on the offer. I ended up at an even better company in Toronto.

*

Karen embraced Anna, who greeted us at the door. "Hello, Ma."

Anna smiled. When I hugged her in turn, I wondered where Karen got her height from since both her parents had been five foot-seven.

"I see you still have a lot of books, Anna." My eyes surveyed the room. The walls were lined with tall bookcases bursting with paperbacks and extra volumes were piled on top to the ceiling.

She nodded her head, a mixture of grey and white hair. "I get them from the library. They sell me the old ones for a buck or less."

"Didn't you say she'd been clearing things out?" I whispered to Karen. Although partially deaf, Anna often heard what she shouldn't.

Karen's head turned to me and nodded. Then she squared her shoulders. "It is what it is. Don't worry. We'll manage."

She kept the novels she enjoyed the most to read over, cataloguing them on small bits of paper scattered amongst the informal library. Lurid potboilers: each one complete with a sexy cover. And she read these voraciously: one, sometimes two a day. I never understood how they captivated her. The plots followed a basic formula; only the characters changed. You could literally fill in the blanks; the _____ (cowboy, pirate, virile tycoon, handsome bachelor, etc.), and the _____ (city girl, lonely princess, sexy secretary, country girl, etc.).

"Great," I muttered, "we're hauling a thousand paperbacks home that are worth pennies each."

"We can't leave them," Karen insisted. "Reading is her only

hobby, and these," she gestured at a mass of softcovers, "for all intents and purposes, are her friends."

And she was right. These novels meant the world to Anna.

*

Nothing had been packed. I spied a solitary box lying in the middle of the floor with a few items in it. Opening a closet, I discovered it was filled from top to bottom with boxes of cereal and other items. If Anna couldn't leave the house for three months, she wouldn't starve. Elsewhere, we uncovered thirty bottles of dish detergent, a mountain of paper towels, and so many clothes that the drawers of her dressers and the doors on her closets wouldn't shut. In preparation for the move, I figured two vans and the trailer were sufficient, but I was wrong. Anna was a perpetual hoarder, and I had underestimated her badly. She bought multiples of an item on sale to store for future use, which never came. Many still in the original packaging with price stickers from stores that went out of business decades ago.

Eric and I emptied the contents of the cupboards into boxes and carried them to my van. Meanwhile, Karen bustled back and forth, putting things in her van and running them to the dump or a local charity. Jackie and Meggy were amazing; they hauled bags and boxes up from the basement and put them on the lawn for us to pack. We worked all day long for three days, racing both vans to Streetsville and back.

And like a squirrel, Anna hid her treasure in the most unusual places. When we took apart the bed, we uncovered boxes of books underneath. They were hiding everywhere: under furniture and in cupboards, in place of food. Evil books.

Old drawers reclaimed from someone's trash and packed with paperbacks were scattered throughout the musty basement. In the dim light, I spied a soft cooler we gave her to carry food home after visiting us. I grabbed it, expecting it to be empty, but it didn't budge. Afraid of finding rotten food, I unzipped it gingerly only to discover ... more books. Things were getting absurd. Towards the end, I no longer cared. I threw out several boxes when Anna wasn't looking.

It was exhausting, but we finally finished and took the last load home. Jolted awake one night later that week, I was filled with a sense of dread. The vividness of a nightmare dissipated, but not before images of novels flying around the house and falling from shelves flashed through my mind. I got up for a glass of water, and my heart rate began to drop. Anna's move must have been more traumatic than I realized. But although hard on me, the reduction in Karen's stress was worth it. Every afternoon, she went to help her mother unpack and settle in, and worried much less. Whenever Anna failed to answer the phone, we simply strolled over and made sure everything was alright.

*

The girls had been real troupers during the move, which made us realize that not every week was a struggle. And we still hiked and played board games together. Stress from teenagers is intermittent, comparable to patches of fog creeping across a lake. Now and then, there'll be spots of clarity, but then the mist reappears to obscure it. And like patchy fog, the stress can make you forget there are more bright spots hidden behind.

Ed and Greta Larsen, friends since university, came over for dinner one night and reminded us of this with our own kids. They live far away, and we're both busy, so we don't see each other as frequently as we wish. Three of their children are older than ours and were otherwise engaged, but their youngest accompanied them. The girls took Matt, three years younger than Jackie, downstairs to watch TV while we had a drink and caught up on each other's lives. Karen and I took turns checking on the meal we were cooking together. At one point, we were both in the kitchen dishing the dinner out into bowls when Greta came in.

Appearing slightly embarrassed, she blurted out, "You know your girls are gorgeous, right?"

We stopped in bewilderment for a moment before Karen stammered, "Uh, yes, they are. Thank you."

"I haven't seen them for a long time, and they're so grown up. They're young ladies now and stunning."

"Yes," I said, and my mouth curved into a slight smile, "they have their moments."

After our company left, we viewed the girls with fresh eyes. They were both indeed very attractive: slim and blue-eyed with delicate features; one with lovely blonde hair to her shoulders; and the other with jet-black hair cut in a cute bob cut below her chin. Yet with all the fighting and stress, it had escaped our attention. Karen and I agreed to focus more on the positives with our kids going forward.

*

For a period, a pleasant peace descended on the McKinney household. There was an unexpected lull in stressful events, and it was calming. Perhaps it was the aftermath of the team effort in moving Grandma or maybe my helping Jackie with her assignment. I don't know. But for whatever reason, there was nary a raised voice or angry word for the past two weeks.

Consequently, it was in an upbeat mood that I journeyed to Fort Lauderdale for organized meetings with the regional quality heads. Florida was chosen for the benefit of our South American colleagues, mostly women, who loved to shop in the States. It made no difference to me. My approach to shopping is best described as — get the hell in, get what you need, and get the hell out again. The outcome of which is that none of my family wants me along shopping with them. But that's okay. I'm just as happy.

On the first morning, we gathered around a large, horseshoe shaped table, which is a format that promotes discussion. Paul, country manager for all directors in the Americas, stood tall at the front of the room and kicked it off by highlighting the fact Thursday was American Thanksgiving. This brought knowing smiles and nods from the women.

Julieta, a tall, comely, dark-haired woman from Peru, grinned beside me and whispered, "Meednight Madness." Her soft dark eyes were perpetually smiling, but at this moment, they were especially lit up. Seeing my confused expression, she explained, "Zee stores are open all night, with special deals after meednight!"

I smiled. They picked the right name for it, in my opinion. If I took part, there's no doubt I'd be mad by midnight. Paul confirmed we'd still meet on Thursday, since only one person lived in the US and would sacrifice the holiday for the group. After that, we could depart Friday morning or do additional shopping if one were masochistic enough.

The meetings progressed well: presentations with discussion, planning objectives and reviewing inspections performed at our company's own sites and at third parties around the world. An informal dinner was scheduled for Thursday, and as I waited with Paul in the lobby, Julieta and a blonde-haired colleague breezed by with hands full of shopping bags. They'd started early.

Julieta glanced over her shoulder and lifted both arms. "Wee'll join you een a meeneet. We're jest droppeeng theese een our rooms."

Paul made a face. Clearly, he had no love for shopping either. The next morning, as I checked out, I noticed a hotel employee decorating something in the vestibule. On closer examination, I realized the object of attention was a Christmas tree. This had to be a record. The morning after Thanksgiving, and they were putting up the tree. I frowned. Yuletide was my favourite holiday season, but now, I felt like it was being pushed on me.

*

The return flight was uneventful and on schedule, but even short flights leave me tired, probably because of the lower oxygen levels on planes. A taxi dropped me off in the driveway, and I looked up at the house. But this time, there was no dog in the window; no excited barking greeted me when I walked through the door, and I missed it.

During dinner, Peter called to tell me Mom wasn't doing well, and may not last more than a day or two. She'd been in an old-age home ever since Dad died ten years ago. After several strokes, she couldn't speak and probably didn't even recognize us. In order to overcome the silence on my visits, I'd lift down the calendar we made each year with family photos for the grandparents. I'd slowly flip through the months and describe the people and location. Many were beautiful shots from our travels. Even though I had repeated this on every visit for the past two years, Mom listened as if hearing it for the first time.

Still, there was the occasional enjoyable visit. One time, Meggy came along, and Grandma squeezed her hand hard so she would feel the love she couldn't express with words.

And during another visitation, Karen gave my mother an affectionate hug and said, "I love you, Martha."

"I've always loved you, Karen," came the heartfelt response.

We were both stunned. It was a rare moment, as if someone had briefly pulled a curtain back and allowed us to see the person we knew and loved, before slipping it back into place again.

*

We drove to Richmond Hill that night to see her, and she passed away the next afternoon. Although my father's death had been upsetting, of course, in some ways it was even more poignant when Mom passed. While one parent is still alive, they keep the memory of the other present, but once they've both passed, the memories fade and the loss seems greater. I loved them deeply, of course, but I also admired and respected the good people that they were.

Then, the oddest thing happened. I heard an old song on the

radio called 'The Living Years' by Mike + The Mechanics, which was a favourite of Dad's. It hadn't played on the radio for ages, but after Mom passed, I heard it often, particularly during difficult periods with the family or work. It felt like my parents were sending me a message to keep going and not worry; everything would be alright.

This was the only spiritual story I had on my side of the family, but Karen's experienced several. One involved the antique clock in her brother's bedroom. The swinging pendulum that kept time stopped on the morning he died, and Karen and her family believe it happened at the moment of his death. Whenever we visited her parents and slept in this room, my eyes were drawn warily to the old clock with the frozen hands. To be honest, I was skeptical of her stories until I had my own. I began to hear this tune more and more frequently, and it gave me encouragement on the occasions I needed it most.

In the new year, I bought a new dark beer and left it outside the locked chest. It's an acquired taste that most girls don't like, so I figured if Jackie tried it, she'd hate it and wouldn't steal anymore. Friday afternoon, I brought a few upstairs to have before dinner.

As I opened one, Jackie sailed by and gave a derisive chuckle. "Dad, you've *got* to buy better beer. How can you drink that stuff?"

"Well, it's cheap and I like it, so why not?" I turned to look at her. At five foot ten, she stood eye to eye with Karen and me.

She stood steady by the counter and faced me. "You should try Molson's or a craft beer."

"I thought some were missing. You stole them, didn't you?" I waited for her to tell me it was awful.

"Yeah," she snorted, "I took it to a party to trade for something else, but they wouldn't do it. They said, 'What is this cheap ass beer? Get out of here.' See, it's sooo bad, nobody will take it."

"Hey, there's no need to be insulting. Tell your friends they don't know what fine beer tastes like."

As I walked out of the kitchen, her voice trailed behind, "Right, *they* have no taste. '*It's cheap ass,*' they said, ha-ha-ha."

Trading it, I hadn't figured on that. Well, at least my booze was safe as long as I kept drinking the 'economical' brand. I took a sip and studied the label. *Hmmm, maybe she's right. I should buy a better beer. But if I do, I'm locking that one up.*

*

Often, we had the impression our daughters were a tag team and took turns giving us stress. On the following Wednesday, Karen found a bottle of booze in Meggy's room.

"It's strawberry flavoured vodka," she said, putting a half full bottle in front of me.

As I picked it up, inspiration hit me. "Don't say anything to her. Let's pour it out and refill it with water. Then, they'll pass it around at a party and say, '*Hey, what is this? It tastes like water!*' That'll teach her a lesson."

She giggled, "You're bad...let's do it!"

A week later, with still no word from Meggy. I couldn't wait any longer. When she came strolling downstairs, I said to her straight-faced, "I've been meaning to ask you, Meggy. How was the strawberry vodka?"

A startled look appeared on her face. "What do you mean?"

"You know, the bottle under your bed."

She turned away and acted disinterested. "Yeah, okay. Why?"

"Because we found it and replaced it with water."

Her blue eyes glared at me. "You took my vodka? Give it back."

"We can't. We drank it with friends. Didn't you notice the difference, ha-ha?"

"No, I gave it to a friend to hold for me. You didn't really drink it, did you?"

"Oh yes," I chuckled, "and believe me, Meggy, the best tasting vodka is the *confiscated* vodka!"

She set her mouth in a pout. "That's not fair. It's mine."

"That's what happens when you hide booze in the house," I said and went upstairs to let her ruminate on this.

Come to think of it, I guess by doing our parenting duties, we give our children a lot of stress, too.

*

I had to commend Karen, though. She could let things go more than me. Jackie's bratty attitude resurfaced soon, and my first instinct was to squash it.

But Karen calmed me down. "She's being a teenager, and they're all a pain in the ass at this age." Then she told me about a conversation with a woman on the street behind ours. "Remember last summer, we walked on Mary Street and saw this two-story house with plywood nailed across the garage door?" I nodded, and she continued, "That's Kate Callaway's place. You remember her, the tall redhead. She's the guidance counsellor at Jackie's old school. Anyway, we were talking today, and it turns out you were right. Someone drove into the door. It was their *daughter*."

"I knew it," I said, proud of my deductive skills. "What happened?"

"Kate and her husband left for a holiday together and had just arrived at the airport when her daughter called to say she had an accident. She had been wearing flip-flops, and one got stuck under the gas pedal. Since she couldn't work the brake, the car smashed into the door. They had to phone a friend and ask him to cover it over with plywood. And the real kicker was — the car was brand new. They'd only picked it up a few hours earlier."

"Oh, my goodness."

"No kidding," Karen said, warming to the subject. "They needed a new garage door *and* a car repair. She said it was quite the way to start a vacation. And another time, Kate mentioned to me that she drives to work. I asked her why because it's only a few blocks away.

She said if she doesn't take the car, her daughter will take it without asking. And Kate's a student advisor, for goodness sake!"

"It must be very frustrating for her. At the school, the kids listen, but at home, she can't control them." As I spoke these words, they seemed to have a familiar ring to them. Then I realized it was because this was my predicament.

"Yes, even though they have the knowledge for the situation, their own kids won't listen or respect them," Karen said, drawing on her psychology background. "That's because they have an emotional involvement with their kids."

"I'm shocked she would be so frank and tell you about their family problems."

"*Everyone* has difficulty with teenagers, dear, not only us. And women tell each other these things because it helps us to get it off our chests." Karen leaned back against the couch with an air of satisfaction.

Strangely enough, hearing about the issues of other parents did bring me a degree of comfort. Maybe there was something to this notion of sharing problems with others.

14

UNDER PRESSURE

*"Behind every great man is a woman
rolling her eyes." - Jim Carrey*

I LAY THERE WITH my eyes open and stared at the alarm clock.
Three a.m. Rats. I knew I wouldn't fall asleep again once my mind
began thinking about work. Instead of lying in bed frustrated, I'd
developed the habit of getting up, having breakfast and either working on my laptop or going to the office. With this approach, even
though I had little sleep, at least I'd accomplish something to reduce
my workload. Surprisingly, I still managed to function at a high level
despite the lack of sleep.

Not to disturb Karen, I slipped out of bed and proceeded
downstairs.

"Mrrrrrrrawr!"

That cat doesn't miss a beat. She must lie awake in that laundry
room and listen for my footsteps. Once fed, she collapsed into a

lump in her bed. After eating, I crept upstairs, shaved and climbed quietly into the shower. Although I can't sleep, there's no reason the others shouldn't slumber on undisturbed. The hot water was soothing, and my body temperature warmed up as I lathered conditioner into my hair.

"Bam, bam, bam!"

What the hell? Somebody was banging on the door.

Karen shouted urgently on the other side, "Andrew... Andrew!"

I shut off the water, wrapped a towel around myself and, still dripping, yanked the door open.

An angry face confronted me. "Be quiet. The kids are sleeping. You'll wake them up!"

"I'm just having a shower," I sputtered, feeling confused.

"You're singing!" she yelled, and her eyes rolled in exasperation.

"Oh, okay, I'll stop."

Ashamed and reprimanded, I didn't do any encores as I finished. Although I had a habit of singing in the shower, who would have thought singing was so automatic that I wasn't even aware of it?

*

At work, I grabbed a coffee and sat down to talk to Carol, who started at six a.m. to avoid the heavy traffic on her lengthy commute. Only five-four, she was young and pretty, with sandy brown hair and an amiable face. When asked the reason for my crack of dawn arrival, I admitted to sleeping poorly. Normally, I avoid showing vulnerability to my staff, but I didn't want her to think I was checking up on her.

"We call them workmares," Carol said with an understanding smile.

"Really? You worry about work?"

"Every Sunday night, I wake up and think of all the things to do that week. Susanne and Sarah do as well."

That shocked me. I assumed I bore the brunt of pressure and

shielded them from it. When the others arrived, I enquired awkwardly about their sleep patterns, and they confirmed the Sunday night issue. But, instead of being viewed as weak, I had the distinct impression they considered me more favourably — as a boss who was transparent and authentic and could relate to their issues.

Throughout the day, my mind returned often to the cause of my insomnia. Balancing my job and family was a challenge, and I often raced home frustrated at the traffic, only to arrive tense when I walked through the front door.

Business expects too much from employees today, and the Swiss head office constantly pushed labour-intensive projects on us. New computer platforms, additional reporting requirements and more, always on short implementation dates. And we had no influence on the deadlines; they mandated these regardless of our other commitments.

A previous country manager once said, "Andrew, our company has a reputation for chewing people up and spitting them out."

Not very motivating words but honest. And the past six months had been especially gruelling. For the first time, I had to fire a person; a compliance issue arose with a contractor and required constant oversight; and my boss retired, so I needed to prove myself all over again to a new supervisor. I also travelled more on business, which, while a pleasant escape from domestic life, was tiring and required me to catch up on work when I returned to the office. Every month, I flew to Montreal for meetings with my boss and other departments. And even though it's only a one-hour flight, there is something about air travel that sucks your energy.

*

On Friday, Suzanne and I went there for the day. Brenda always booked my return flights for four o'clock, but since they have hourly departures, I could often catch an earlier one.

When we finished our meetings and climbed into the taxi to

leave, I turned to her. "If we hurry, we might make the three o'clock flight." Her jaw dropped, and I saw alarm flashed in her dark eyes. "Don't worry. I'm an expert on this," I assured her, as I handed the driver enough money to cover the fare and tip.

He wrote the receipt when we stopped for a red light. As soon as the taxi's wheels stopped turning, we hopped out and rushed through the departures' door.

"Go straight through security to the Air Canada desk and change the ticket there," I hollered over my shoulder to her. "There's never a lineup there." The kiosks were too risky. They stopped issuing boarding passes thirty minutes before a flight.

Waiting for my bag to emerge from the scanner, I spotted Suzanne in a neighbouring line.

"We won't make it," she cried.

"All we can do is try," I shouted back, and scooping up my bag, I sprinted to the airline desk.

Darn, someone was ahead of me. Suzanne arrived shortly but not before another passenger got in between us. The smiling blonde-haired attendant waved me up.

"I was hoping to catch the three o'clock, but I guess I'm too late," I said.

The attendant made no comment but called up my ticket on her computer.

While she typed, I looked at Suzanne and grinned. "We may be okay. The kiosk has a cut-off, but if you go straight here, they can often process it."

The attendant looked up. "Are you travelling together?"

"Yes."

She waved Suzanne up to join me. Startled and a bit embarrassed, she squeezed by the other passenger.

The attendant handed us new boarding cards with a smile and said, "You need to hurry. The plane leaves in fifteen minutes."

"Thank you!"

I turned to Suzanne and said, "Run!"

I took off, but once the gate came in sight, I slowed down. The boarding area was deserted, so I could have breezed through, but I had no desire to leave her behind. If we missed the flight, we could grab a bite together. I needn't have worried. She passed me on my left with a look of terror on her face. I sprinted ahead again to an amused attendant with my boarding pass and identification held out in front. Click, bzzz, my card zipped through the machine. Blood pounding in my ears, I stood by the ramp entrance and waited. Suzanne came through seconds later, and they closed the gate after her.

As we walked to the plane, I laughed. "Well done, Suzanne, and I'll be honest, I've never seen anyone run so fast in high heels."

She smiled and gave a throaty laugh.

We had succeeded, and I felt like dancing to my seat. I really had this regular Montreal-Toronto flight down to a fine art. As I fastened my seat belt and settled in, it occurred to me that my constant drive to excel also contributed to my tension. Maybe I shouldn't push myself so hard. No matter, my mood was buoyant. I'd return to the house earlier tonight, and Eric would join us on Saturday.

*

The mood in the house was always lighter with him around, and on this visit, he was bringing a girlfriend.

"This girl must mean a lot to Eric," Karen confided, "by the fact that he wants us to meet her."

On Saturday afternoon, we ensured a grand meal was underway and then waited excitedly. He was the first child to bring a date home for dinner.

"We're huggers," Karen declared when introduced and gave Gloria a hearty embrace that made her beam. The rest of us followed suit. Eric told us beforehand that her family had emigrated from China but had lived in Canada for more generations than ours. Pretty with delicate features, long black silky hair and warm dark eyes, she chatted nervously over dinner as we got to know each other.

At one point, I heard her whisper to Eric in a quivering voice, "What's she doing?"

I glanced down. The cat often prowled under the table, and I hardly noticed her, but tonight she was pawing softly at Gloria's leg.

"Moochie, get out of there!" I commanded, and then I smiled at Gloria. "Don't mind her. She won't hurt you. She's begging for food. Most people think it's cute."

But Gloria didn't think it was cute. In fact, she kept a wary eye out in case Moochie decided to eat her. That's just silly; I mean you'd have to be dead first.

"Do you have any pets?" Karen ventured with a smile.

Gloria shook her head. "My dad's allergic, so we never had them. But when we were older, we found out he only said that so we wouldn't get one."

I opened my eyes wide in admiration. "Brilliant. Just brilliant. What a simple way to avoid them."

Why hadn't I thought of that? Of course, I wanted a pet but not two or three if you count the hamster years.

We learned her family didn't take outdoor holidays. "We're more Disney people," Gloria laughed. "We've been there many times. I told Eric, he'd better like Disney ... or it's a deal-breaker!"

Karen passed the vegetables and chuckled. "We've never taken the kids. There's too many other exciting places to see." She looked around the table. "Besides, we enjoy outdoor activities and nature more than amusement parks. Our children may not have been to Disneyland, but they've snorkelled coral reefs and hiked the Rockies."

*

Once we served coffee and dessert, Eric leaned back and grinned from ear to ear. "Guess what? I've got a sixteen-month co-op position that starts in May."

"Wonderful, Eric!" Karen exclaimed. "So, you'll stay at home all that time?"

He shook his head. "No, it's in Hamilton, so I'll stay there."

His eyes sparkled and for good reason. In his first summer job, he watered flowers and killed weeds for Parks and Recreation. I shouldn't say killed; scared was more like it. With the city's ban of effective pesticides, they could only spray them with steam from a canister strapped over their shoulder. Two weeks later, the weeds rose again, and they repeated this futile operation all summer long.

"And when you drove by the park," I teased, "you'd think they'd painted the grass yellow because of the sea of dandelions."

He leaned forward and clasped his hands together on the table. "But the next summer was even worse. I had only about an hour of work each day. It was so boring, I took naps in the car. Dragan, the old guy on permanent staff, told me to slow down and not work so fast. How could I slow down? I didn't have anything to do." He threw his hands up at the memory.

"I remember, Sonny. It was bad."

His lips formed a rueful smile. "Then one day, I got to paint the curbs in the parking lot; I was so happy. These little kids came along and sat beside me to watch. They wanted to help, but I couldn't let them. I felt bad, but if I did, I'd have absolutely nothing else to do."

Now, he finally had a job to be excited about, and it was in his field. We moved into the living room, where Meggy and Jackie chatted with Gloria, who had a younger sister around their ages. All in all, meet the parents' night had been a great success.

*

On Tuesday, Karen was scheduled for surgery. Her bladder fell down, not an uncommon occurrence for middle-aged women, and needed a sling installed to hold it in place. Just the thought of it made her overwrought; she had a deep fear of needles, never mind operations. In public school, it took two nurses to hold her down for vaccinations.

But in this case, there was more reason to worry; it was a major operation with a general anesthetic. I tried to calm her down as I took her to the Pre-op Admission, and then I sat in the waiting room. After the operation, the surgeon came by to tell me everything had gone well. He described the details of the completed procedure and said she'd be in recovery for a few hours. Since she'd be sleeping that long, I drove away with a plan to return in the evening with the girls.

When we arrived, Karen seemed very disorientated and groggy from the morphine.

"I feel drugged and sick to my stomach," she moaned. A minute later, she asked for a bucket to vomit in. I left the girls with her and headed to the nursing station.

"The morphine is making her sick; you need to lower the dose or switch to another painkiller."

The middle-aged nurse's face showed no emotion as she listened. Her black hair was streaked with grey and tied in a ponytail, and she sat in a chair in front of a computer.

She studied her screen and nodded. "Alright, we'll notify the doctor."

When I returned, Karen was lying on the bed, looking like a truck had run her over. "Go home," she gasped. "I'm sorry, but I can't keep my eyes open."

"Okay, we'll come back tomorrow then."

Her eyelids had already shut when we kissed her goodnight. At the elevator, I glanced at my watch. We'd only been there ten minutes.

*

Our next visit was quite different. She was sitting up, more alert, and looking forward to being discharged on Thursday. "Oh, I'm much better since they switched my medicine. I never could tolerate morphine."

Afterwards, I dropped both girls at a friend's house and continued home. It'd been a stressful few days. Despite assurances to Karen, I had taken her to the hospital with a sense of foreboding: a feeling I couldn't shake that something was going to go wrong. Maybe Karen's worrying had rubbed off on me, but I breathed a sigh of relief now. Everything had turned out fine.

I prepared a cup of tea and lay on the couch, using throw pillows to prop myself up. Moochie lay in her bed eyeing me from the other side of the room. She got up and crept over — hobbled, actually, because of arthritis. It affected her gait but wasn't severe enough to prevent her from throwing her weight against the laundry room door during the night. If I didn't lock it, I'd wake up to find her on my chest, licking my forehead to let me know she was hungry.

She sat down, stared at me and emitted a musical sound followed by a quick forward motion of her head. This was her signal to be picked up; she couldn't jump up on her own anymore. The thought of her warm body purring happily on me was comforting, so I swung her up and planted her on my chest where she assumed the sphinx position. As I sipped my tea, we lay there with our faces inches apart. Occasionally, I'd stroke her, and she'd add a chirp or trill to her sounds. These were the same noises that were amplified to make the raptor sounds in *Jurassic Park,* and this recollection made me smile.

With the girls out for the evening, it was strangely calm. No running up and down the stairs, no fighting and no demands on me. A rare night indeed. Moochie lay and purred while my chest rose and fell. We were tea buddies, she and I, and I became sleepy. Every few minutes, I stirred to take a sip from my cup, and each movement startled her. Without exception, her eyes flickered open, gazed at me, then closed again.

It was very tranquil, but I began to feel her hind claws digging into me. So, I put the tea down and lifted her up to shift her position. Quick as a flash, she turned and sunk her teeth into my right wrist. I felt sharp, blinding pain.

Letting out a whoop, I attempted to pull my hand away. No success, and I began to get alarmed. The pressure on my wrist was equivalent to being squeezed in a vise. Ears laid back, eyes closed as if in some weird state of nirvana, she lay motionless with my wrist seized between her teeth. I tried to pry her off with my free hand, being careful not to tear the wound, but she had really locked on. I bet I could stand up, wave my arm around, and she'd still hang on in this death grip. Slowly, I worked my fingers under the upper teeth and lifted them off.

Then I jumped up and ran to the bathroom. After washing and patting it dry with a towel, I examined the damage. The top fangs had hit bone and left only a shallow pit and scratches, but there were two small holes in the underside. I put antibiotic cream on and bandaged it.

Back in the living room, the little assassin sat on the chesterfield awaiting my return with a confused expression.

"Bad cat! Bad!" I yelled. Then I pushed her off and smacked her bottom. "You little viper!"

She ran for her life.

*

The following evening found Karen savouring her first home-cooked meal in three days.

"The bill from the hospital totalled $25 dollars," she said. "Thank goodness for healthcare. My friend Kathy in Florida had the same thing done, but instead of a sling, they stitched the bladder to the wall. It's cheaper but not as effective. Yet it cost her 10,000 dollars!"

"Canadians don't appreciate our healthcare system. It's amazing. Can you imagine having to fork out that much money?" I said, shaking my head.

She appeared delighted to be in her own house, enjoying a tasty meal.

Suddenly, her face clouded over. "Why is your arm swollen?"

Looking at my two arms, I couldn't see the difference, but I told her the harrowing story of the death grip.

"Stupid cat. This is the second time she's done this to me."

"You better go to the walk-in clinic. It's infected."

I glanced at the clock on the wall. Nearly eight-thirty. The idea of sitting for an hour in a clinic at this time of night wasn't appealing, but I grabbed my coat and rushed out. Upon arrival, the receptionist advised me that they were closing in twenty minutes and weren't seeing any more patients. I looked desperately at the young woman behind the desk and explained the urgency.

She stared blankly for a moment. Probably a cat lover, I thought. Then she said, "Just a minute. I'll check." She jumped out of the chair and disappeared down the corridor. When she returned, she gestured towards one of the rooms. "Okay, have a seat in here. The doctor will see you."

A middle-aged Indian lady walked into the examination room, and I relaxed. You never know who will see you at a walk-in, but Dr. Francis was very knowledgeable. She inspected the wound, dressed it and handed me a prescription for powerful antibiotic tablets.

"Cat bites can be nasty and deep. Take two tablets tonight and then one a day until they're all gone."

I thanked her and hurried to the pharmacy. By the time I got to bed, it was already eleven.

The next day, Moochie sauntered over and waited beside the couch. She seemed to have no memory of her vicious attack. With an icy glare, I blared, "Bad cat, demon cat — go away!"

She waddled off but never gave up. Their brains are quite small after all. Every day, she reappeared and looked astonished when I shooed her off. Eventually, I relented, and she resumed her position. The punishment had been long enough, and it was time to let it go.

*

Teenagers can be hard on parents and a marriage. And pets add another level of stress. My sleep issues had worsened over the years from the pressures of work and the teenage girls. Most days, I felt as if I had reached my limit. However, there's an old saying, *it's going to get worse before it gets better,* and somehow, I'd have to rise to the occasion.

THE DOG NAZI

"No soup for you come back one year. Next!" - Soup Nazi to Elaine, Seinfeld 1995 Episode 116

KAREN HAD PESTERED me for a dog during the past few months. I listened but put her off. Then in February, she started up again.

"Why do we need another pet?" I asked. Moochie lay lifeless in her bed at the end of the room. "Honestly, I found it too stressful before with two pets."

"Because it's been more than a year now, and I think we should — a golden retriever or black lab this time. The kids are in their teens and often a pain in the ass." She looked forlorn. "I want it for company when I'm walking or in the car."

She had a valid point, and I empathized with her. "Those dogs are too big; I'd rather have one Milo's size."

"Not a beagle," she said flatly. "They run away all the time."

That was true. Milo would find a scent and disappear, oblivious to our calls. We'd circled the block a few times in search of him.

"Fine, but let's go slow and make sure we get the right one."

"A puppy!" Jackie exclaimed, somehow having overheard the conversation. She bounced into the room with her blonde hair tied in a braid.

"No," Karen corrected her, "puppies are too much work."

"But we want a puppy, not an old dog!"

"Yeah, we've always wanted a puppy," Meggy chimed in. "A golden retriever, like Haley's."

Jackie's friend Hayley had recently gotten a pup, and our daughters were smitten with him. His name was Jackson, which was funny because it was also Eric's nickname for Jackie.

We shuddered at the thought, and I said firmly, "No way. They're too demanding and chew everything. Dogs don't settle down until they're a couple of years old."

"You girls can get one when you move out," Karen said, signalling the end of the discussion.

*

The girls kept voicing their wish, but we held our ground, at least until Karen saw photos of baby retrievers on a rescue site.

"Maybe a puppy wouldn't be so bad," she said meekly, while her daughters hovered nearby. "Let me show you the pictures. This place is called 'Dog Camp,' and the lady said we could have our pick." I sat down at the computer while she continued. "Apparently, they don't have puppies at present, but they're expecting a shipment from Ohio this weekend."

"I still think a retriever's too big," I said, studying the cute doggie faces.

"That's too bad, Dad. We're getting one." Jackie smirked, knowing full well it was three against one.

"You're outvoted, Dad — so suck it up!" Meagan added with

a twinkle in her eye and stabbing a finger at me. She was mad with power.

"Okay, call and find out when we can visit," I said, trying to regain control of the situation.

Karen called immediately and booked us in.

"The puppies will arrive on Friday, but we have to wait until Sunday to allow them to settle in," she announced and hugged me. "Thank you, honey."

Things were moving faster than expected, and I was a bit dismayed. Damn internet; they would have puppy pictures on the website, and of course, you'd fall in love with them. But Karen was part of the problem too; she moved like greased lightning on these things.

"The owner's emailing some guidelines," she added. "One is that no one under sixteen is allowed to visit."

Jackie's eyebrows shot up, and she cried out in horror, "What? Why can't I come? Tell her we had a dog and I know how to behave with them."

"It's no good. I tried. She said they have about thirty dogs, and young people are too disruptive. If you're with us, she won't permit us to see them. It'll be alright. You can stay home."

Jackie stormed out of the room.

*

When the guidelines arrived, I stared at them in shock. "Are you serious? It's ..." I thumbed the papers she had printed. "... five pages long!" As I skimmed the writing, it was clear the lady had a compulsion for bold letters and capitals.

"The first item — **'BE ON TIME'** — is clarified in no less than half a page!" I read on in horror; the list ran on forever. "These aren't guidelines. They're ultimatums, and they're ridiculous! Look at this — **My house/My dogs/My Rules!**" I waved the papers. "What is this — a Nazi Dog Camp?"

Karen looked at me patiently. "I know it's extreme, but she's very passionate. They're rescue animals, so they've had a tough time. And she seems to care for them. Let's check it out; we may not find a dog we want, anyway."

I'd never heard of this lady before, but I didn't like her already. The pure audacity of the woman. However, I agreed to go because Karen had her heart set on it.

"Okay, but I won't put up with any nonsense."

"Oh, yeah," Karen said on her way out of the room, "she also sent an application form to complete before Friday. Don't worry. I'll fill it out."

I opened the attachment for the application form on the computer. Eight pages long — that aggravated me even more. I slumped in the chair. Every fibre of my body told me to forget it, but I knew it was pointless. Karen's mind was set.

*

On Sunday, we headed for the small village of Myrtle, which was an hour away. Meggy volunteered to stay behind with Jackie so she wouldn't be upset.

As we chatted in the van, Karen got annoyed with me. "Stop calling it the Nazi Dog Camp!" she demanded. "You're going to say it by accident in front of her."

"How about Mein Kampf?" I said and grinned.

"No! Now stop it."

"Okay, okay."

We rode along upbeat. It was a bright sunny day, which made the journey quite pleasurable. The sun's rays made the snow-covered fields sparkle like diamonds. At some length, we arrived at a farmhouse that had a fenced-in area behind it.

"There's a lot more than thirty dogs," I said, as we took in the hoard of beasts roaming around on the other side of the fence.

"That's good. We'll have more to pick from."

*

A short, portly, middle-aged, bleached blonde answered our knock on the front door. Her appearance wasn't at all what I expected. Hair hanging loosely to her shoulders, and not pulled into a tight tense bun, dressed casually in jeans: not the Gestapo uniform I envisioned. Her facial features were best described as soft and not the face of someone who sucked prunes for breakfast or suffered from a lifetime of constipation.

Managing a weak smile, she sized us up as we introduced ourselves. I felt better. The owner appeared normal; perhaps she just had an issue with fonts. With her encouragement, we waded into the melee, which swarmed around us like a herd of cattle. I asked about the puppies, thinking they were inside, but apparently, none had arrived in this shipment. It was likely just a ruse to get us there. Ten minutes into the crush of feet, snouts, tongues and tails, we spotted two possibilities, or rather they spotted us. A small black lab and a chubby golden retriever ran and played with the army of dogs but returned every few minutes to muzzle our hands. Both were very affectionate.

As we talked it over, a cute brown and white terrier in a red sweater jumping beside the owner caught my eye. He reminded me of Eddy on *Fraser*.

When I pointed, she said, "He's seven."

"No," Karen said with tight lips, brushing aside my interest. "You only want him because he looks like that one on TV."

She was right, of course, but I felt sorry for him so I played on her sympathies. "If we don't claim him, nobody will."

"Too old," she said mercilessly, returning her focus to the other two candidates.

The owner watched us from outside the fence and told us that the lab was nine months old, and the retriever two years.

"Why don't you take each for a walk and see how they do?"

That was a great idea. Maybe she did know her stuff. She

handed us a leash, and we trotted each one around the perimeter. Afterwards, we were still undecided. Karen favoured the lab, but I leaned towards the retriever who resembled a large golden bear. If the kids didn't get a puppy, at least they'd have their breed.

As I patted each, I looked at the woman. "They both seem nice and are friendly and calm."

"Yes, they are," she said, then nodding towards the retriever. "I keep him tired."

This comment puzzled me, but Karen whispered, "Let's take the lab. The other must have too much energy."

"My goodness, you're right."

We walked out of the pen, closed the gate carefully to make sure it couldn't be pushed open and approached the lady.

"We've decided on the lab," Karen said. The woman nodded.

She wasn't a purebred, but that was fine. Mongrels are healthier and have the best temperament.

Karen texted the girls. "They want a picture."

We tried, but black dogs do not photograph well; her face appeared as a dark blob. There was, however, a splash of white on her chest and feet, which made her a member of the tuxedo club. The dog had to stay to be microchipped and vaccinated, which the woman preferred to arrange herself. Months later, we learned that the woman had programmed her address into the chip so the dog would be returned to her if lost. We would have our vet change this to our information.

While I paid the deposit, she lectured us on greedy veterinarians who try to rip you off. Before we left, she handed Karen an adoption contract to sign and return before picking up the dog.

*

The jaunt home was even merrier than on the way there.

"I have to admit it was nice of her to tip us off about the other one's high energy."

"Yes," Karen smiled, "she asked me what we were looking for. Her purpose seems to be to get the right fit, not simply to unload them."

When we arrived home, the girls made it clear they weren't pleased with our choice. After all, she wasn't a golden retriever or even a puppy. Jackie made a face, and Meggy looked dishearteningly at the photo.

"Don't worry. They'll get used to her," Karen said, and she was unwavering. "It's our decision, after all."

*

I read the contract. A clause allowed repossession if evidence of abuse or neglect emerged. That didn't seem unreasonable, but others were. For example, another section gave the woman permission to visit our home and check the dog's condition. It also listed common canned foods that we had to agree not to feed her.

"Is she kidding?" I said.

"Well, if we don't sign, we don't get her."

"There is no way this is enforceable, so we can sign."

On Wednesday, we returned to collect our new pet.

"With the adoption fee plus vaccinations, microchip, collar and leash, etc., the grand total is one thousand and sixty-three dollars," said the owner.

Speechless with a smile frozen on my face, I handed over my credit card.

The woman processed it while Karen fussed over our new baby, undaunted by the exorbitant fee.

As soon as we were in the car, I roared in disbelief, "A thousand dollars? She's a rescue dog, for crying out loud."

Karen's reply was phlegmatic. "It would cost the same from the pound. Gone are the days when pets were free."

I whistled softly; she knew more about the current state of pet adoption than I did.

*

When we tramped through the door, Moochie's reaction was memorable. She looked up as if to say, 'Oh no, here we go again' and disappeared into the basement. Except for meals, we never saw her for two weeks.

"She's only nine months and this big?" Meggy asked skeptically. Her blue eyes had gone grey. Of the three women, only her eyes changed colour.

Initially, the girls shunned her but later yielded. After some discussion, we settled on Darla, after one of the *Little Rascals*, for a name.

"I don't like her," Jackie said flatly.

"Oh, Darla, cover your ears!" Karen cried.

Eric had been busy with his job in Hamilton, but his voice sounded excited when we phoned him with the news.

"She picked us," Karen told him. "She kept coming and snuggling up."

"Ah, that's nice."

We didn't know her history, but we could tell someone had abused her. She cowered whenever anyone approached and not just at the beginning, but for years. But Karen and I loved her from the start, and she was in a safe place now. When Eric came home, he made a fuss over Darla, which spurred his sisters to give her more attention.

"Ah, Dar-Dar," he said getting on the floor to caress and play with her. Then, he suddenly stopped, sniffed his hands and wrinkled his nose. "She stinks," he complained, "and there's an awful smell wherever she licked me." He got up and washed his hands.

Each animal has its own quirks. Milo farted a great deal, and they smelled awful. When he got going, he could easily clear the room. Fortunately, the vet suggested changing the brand of kibbles, and it made a world of difference. We stopped calling him 'The Gasbag.'

A few weeks later, while scooping kibbles for breakfast into Darla's bowl, I detected an odour that caught my attention. I took a deep breath from the heavy bag and almost fell over. That's why her breath smelled awful — it's the kibbles! Karen and I discussed the matter but decided not to change them because bad breath was far better than a gas issue.

She put the least demands on us of any pet I ever had. Content to lie in bed instead of running through the house, and never any pressure to take her for a walk, we could do that each day or not. And that's exactly how we preferred it; no high-energy pup for us. Although loving to everyone, she bonded most to Karen to the point of obsession. If Karen went out, she wouldn't eat until she returned.

*

Moochie did recover from the shock and resurface, but I can't say she ever grew to love Darla. She tolerated her; in fact, she bullied her. She'd push Darla out of the way and eat her food or move into the dog bed to show her who was boss. Moochie was the queen of the house and ruled her subjects mercilessly. I wondered if it was payback for Milo.

But even the queen had to jump out of the way when Darla came running, oblivious to whatever lay in her path. In the morning after I let them out of the laundry area, Moochie sat in front of the patio door, swishing her tail and waiting for breakfast. I feared for her as Darla charged pell-mell to the door, but then Moochie threw her front paws up in the air and leaped sideways, fleeing from the onslaught. It was either that or be trampled to death. Darla couldn't get outside fast enough, and once in again, she raced to her dish. If breakfast wasn't ready, she'd slam on the brakes and skid across the floor, claws digging into our hardwood floor. Mornings were when she was the most vigorous, and the cat had to beware.

In many ways, she was different from Milo: more than twice the size for one, despite being smaller than the average lab.

A neighbour was outside clearing his driveway the first day we walked by. He leaned his tall frame on the shovel and chuckled, "I see you finally got a real dog."

We laughed; I guess Milo was small. Another thing I noticed was that her head was less sensitive than Milo's. She couldn't wait for you to fully open a door and would bang it wide with her hard skull. It didn't seem to hurt her, but it sounded like a rock hitting wood.

*

The girls wanted to train her, which we permitted, but I was always skeptical about how much pets would actually obey. Years ago, we visited a friend named Jill, who lived alone with a little mutt who was a bit of Terrier and Collie. I commented on the candy bowl, which was on the coffee table and reachable by the pooch.

"Oh, Tammy's very well-behaved," Jill sniffed. "She never touches it."

Karen may have been impressed, but I found the statement to be annoying and pompous. In my experience, animals are sneaky and not as trainable as one thinks. In my youth, I discovered our dog was sneaking into my father's off-limits armchair whenever my parents went out. And teaching them to leave food alone is even tougher. It goes against nature. Cats? Forget it. They'll eat it right in front of you. Your only hope is to train the cat not to eat *you*.

So, I listened suspiciously. Though I had to admit that while we remained there, the dog didn't even look at the sweets. After a while, Jill offered us a tour of the house. Bored within ten minutes, I excused myself to go to the bathroom but stopped at the hall mirror to comb my hair. The living room was visible in the reflection, and I saw Tammy sitting staring at the bowl. Then she put her front paws on the table and licked the top candies. Next, she picked one up in her mouth and dropped it. Drooling, she studied it for a minute, licked it several times and then put it back in the dish.

The sound of the ladies approaching startled me.

Jill led us back to the sitting area. "Come, sit down and please, help yourself to the treats. I'll bring the drinks." She departed to the adjacent kitchen.

Karen sat beside me on the couch and reached for the candies. I touched her arm and vigorously shook my head. She shrugged as if to say — *what?* With it halfway to her mouth, I made a licking motion and pointed at Tammy. A look of revulsion crossed her face, and she quickly returned it to the bowl.

Our host reappeared, and Karen flashed a smile. "Delicious candies, Jill."

She grinned in response and handed us the drinks. "Thank you!"

Both of us watched stoically as Jill ate one of the candies.

*

The following Saturday, Karen returned from errands with Darla.

"She's soo cute," she crooned while unleashing her. "She sits in the backseat and looks at everything, happy just to be with her momma." Then a wide grin showed white teeth. "Oh, and I stopped at a red light beside a huge truck. Inside was this tough-looking truck driver, you know the type — crew cut and tattoos all over his arm. While I waited for the light, I heard a funny noise and looked over to see Mr. Tough Guy blowing kisses at Darla. When he saw me looking, he flinched, turned away and stared straight ahead, blushing." She cackled, "He wasn't so tough after all." Then she reached down and stroked Darla's head. "See, Honeybun, everybody loves you. *Don't* they?"

Darla had turned out to be our saviour and the best dog either of us ever had. It felt as if a ray of sunshine had broken through the clouds.

"See," Karen said, while our lab frolicked in the park, "I prayed for God to help us find the perfect dog, and He did."

Even in your darkest days, there's hope.

16
REACHING OUT

My ancestors wandered lost in the wilderness for
40 years because even in biblical times, men would
not stop to ask for directions." - Elayne Bossler

EVERY PARENT LOOKS forward to their child's firsts: first day of school; first time driving a car; first summer job, etc. Being the oldest, Eric achieved these milestones initially, but this week Jackie attained a unique one. The unappealing distinction of being the first and only child to tell us to F-off. Not exactly the achievement we had hoped for.

Don't get me wrong. Meggy had dropped the F-bomb before, most notably at the age of six. Upon leaving my parents' house, we had pulled into a KFC to pick up something for dinner.

"Looks like it's closed, Andrew. Gone out of business," said Karen as she stared at the empty store. "Now what do we do?"

There was silence while we considered the situation. Then I

shrugged. "There isn't another on the way home, so we'll make a quick dinner ourselves."

I heard a child's voice speaking slowly and softly behind me. "Daddy, if I don't have my Ken-fucky chicken, I'm going to be very upset."

We tried to stifle our laughter, but a sharp-eyed Jackie jumped on us. "What did she say?" she asked, glancing around at everyone. "What was it?"

"Never mind — but don't say it again, Meggy. It's a bad word, he-he."

These days she drops the bomb whenever she has a mishap, and I find it upsetting.

"Must you use that language, Meggy?"

"It's no big deal, Dad."

"Why don't you just say hell or damn instead?"

Karen and I never saw the need for vulgar words and found it upsetting when our daughters used them. And while Meggy occasionally said an expletive in frustration or anger at a circumstance, Jackie had directed it at us.

While Karen could shrug it off, it incensed me more than anything or anyone else. Not having experienced it with the other two, I wasn't prepared, and it knocked me off balance. Many a day, I walked in the front door, not knowing what to expect on the other side.

*

You'd think Jackie would have realized profanity didn't get her what she wanted and stop. But she didn't. The reaction was emotionally driven, and in this state, you couldn't reason with her. This turned out to be the beginning of an emotional ride with this child. Her brain swirling with new hormones, estrogen and progesterone, she'd be loving and fun one minute, then angry and rebellious the next. Apparently, the onset of puberty can cause more severe mood swings in some teenagers: those emotional highs and lows that feel out of control. Experts state that during the teenage years, the brain is being remodelled, and the frontal cortex, which exerts the calming, rational influence, doesn't fully develop until much later. Unfortunately, I wasn't aware of this at the time, but even if I had been, it probably wouldn't have helped me very much.

Meggy didn't behave belligerently; she was passive-aggressive instead. And she developed anxiety, often refusing to get out of the car when she and her mother reached her high school in Oakville. Because there was no bus, Karen had to drive her to and fro, which took her about three hours. The previous week, as they neared the school, Meggy complained she didn't feel well. Karen remained adamant; she had to attend. Spying a coffee shop, Meggy begged to use their washroom, so she pulled in. She waited and waited, but Meggy didn't reappear until half an hour later.

I shared Karen's frustration. Meggy was always stubborn. Many a time when she was younger, her siblings would try to help get her to agree to a movie or activity, and she would hold her ground beyond reason and refuse to compromise. When she was still old enough to qualify for the kids' meal in restaurants, she would insist to eat off the adult menu. Try as we might, I could only manage to get her to order the kids' meal for me, and I would order what she wanted and then switch. My thinking was that she couldn't eat the whole meal and I would finish it. But she always did.

*

We both sought outlets for our stress. I jogged four days a week, and Karen rode her bike on the park trails. One day, I heard that classical music reduces road rage, so I tried playing it on my commute. The relaxation response worked so well, I began to listen to the station at my desk. And once a week, I varied my drive home to pull over at a scenic view, such as open farmland or the winding Credit River, and savour the natural beauty for a brief time. These simple things helped changed my mind set. I slowed down and saw life as more about enjoying the present journey rather than rushing home each day.

And though I wasn't thrilled about it, Karen also found relief by sharing stories with other mothers.

"I don't believe in airing our dirty laundry in front of others," I complained when she mentioned some recent advice from her friend Sue.

Karen leaned back in the love seat and appeared indifferent. "We help each other. If I didn't have my girlfriends, I'd go crazy. I read once that if more people had good friends to talk to, we wouldn't need as many psychiatrists."

That was hard to argue with; she had a way of cutting to the bone on a subject.

*

Weekends still provided the best opportunity for unwinding. Karen and I enjoyed talking, having coffee and reading the newspaper in the early hours before the rest of the household woke up. And that's just what we were doing one morning when Karen peered over her section of the paper. "By the way, I talked to Eileen yesterday."

"How's she doing?"

"She and the family are fine. I told her about some recent battles with the girls and how Darla had brightened up our life."

"What did she say to that?" I asked, giving my full attention.

"She was wonderful, understanding and made me feel better. She offered to pray for us," Karen said and chuckled. "I said, please do, Eileen. Your prayers are very powerful. You're like the Pope. And she said, 'Yes, I'm the Popess!' She was funny."

That made me smile because Eileen's not even Catholic. And because she hadn't criticized us, I took comfort. We started praying more ourselves and attending church more frequently. The sermons had a calming effect and brought us hope that things would improve.

*

The following month, Karen surprised me with the news she talked with Dr. MacEwan.

"He didn't mind you seeing him about the girls?"

"Not at all. It is medical treatment, just mental rather than physical. He was very helpful and compassionate, and I felt less tense when I left," she effused. "After all, he had five children himself: four girls and a boy. He must have *really* wanted a boy to keep trying after all those girls, ha-ha." She gave me a nod of encouragement. "You should see him, too."

I hesitated. While I was very comfortable talking to our doctor, it never occurred to me to see him for domestic issues. But Karen seemed at peace, so I made an appointment. I needed someone to confide in and didn't wish to discuss our problems with anyone else.

Thursday at nine o'clock, I waited in the examination room. The door suddenly swung open, and in he strode. As he sat down, I noticed his hair was dishevelled, and I smiled. It looked like he had jumped out of bed and rushed in to work.

He looked at me curiously from under a mop of black hair. "What is it you're here for then?" he asked with his Scottish burr.

As he listened attentively, I described recent incidents with Jackie. When I finished, he opened up about his own experience and was very candid. His trouble arose mostly from his son.

"He took philosophy, but majored in Beer 101," he said with a disdainful expression, and then he stared off for a moment as the frustration resurfaced. "He flunked out of first year, and I told him to either get his act together or get out. At his age, I have no obligation to house or feed him, let alone pay for more education. I said to him, 'I'm your parent first, and if we happen to become friends — well, that's a bonus.'"

I admired his assertiveness, and the words about being a parent first rang true. Karen's problem was she wanted to be their pal.

"I agree, but the problem is Karen hates to discipline the girls. In fact, she'll often go behind my back and end the punishment early."

He leaned forward, rested his arms on his knees and looked me straight in the eye. "That's a problem," he said and pointed his finger. "She needs to be on board with you, or they'll manipulate the situation. And you can't elicit improvement if you're sending different messages."

He was absolutely right, and I thanked him as I followed him out of the room. On the drive to work, my outlook was more positive; he had vindicated my perspective on raising adolescents. And although I failed to convince Karen before, now I had Dr. MacEwan, whom she liked and respected, as an ally.

When I arrived home that evening, Karen asked me how my appointment had gone. I relayed the conversation and his advice to stand united and firm with discipline.

A pained look crossed her face; she clearly struggled with the concept. And when she spoke, there was a tremor in her voice. "I just want everyone to get along without all the fighting."

"I don't understand why you can't be tougher on them; you certainly have no trouble being tough with me."

The distressed look disappeared, and she smiled coyly. "That's different because you're a pain in the ass!"

But by the end of our discussion, she had committed to a more unified approach, and my heart felt lighter. Hopefully, the family dynamics would improve.

*

Boys can be as bad as girls, as Dr. MacEwan showed, and I pondered this at work the next day. From my corner office on the fourth floor, I had a terrific view of the courtyard below and nearby park. Often between conference calls, I'd relax by gazing out at the scene for five or ten minutes. Today, I watched the sun reflect off the stone patio, and a few office workers scurried along the pathway to other buildings. My week had started well, and I was upbeat, because I was meeting an old chum. Mike had transitioned from production into sales and invited me for lunch to discuss his company's consulting abilities in the hope that I might have some projects for them.

The alarm on my computer sounded, and I shook myself into action. I pushed my chair away from the desk and grabbed my jacket.

"I'm out for lunch. Be back in an hour and a half," I called to Brenda as I hurried by.

Even though it had been ages since we'd seen each other, I recognized Mike instantly in the restaurant. The person waving at me had the same ruddy face and bright eyes I remembered, topped off by that thick red hair. He grinned, shook my hand, and it seemed as if no time had passed between us, although he was older and heavier.

"What a shame it's been so long, Mike," I said, sitting down in the booth.

"Yeah, I know," he said, and his smile turned a bit sadder. He drew in a breath and added, "Everyone gets busy."

"Are you still off the cigarettes?"

"Yes, I am. It's been ... two years since I quit."

We ordered and, when the waitress left, caught up with each other. Mike had a slow manner of speaking, pausing frequently, a habit he had developed as a teenager. He told me long ago that as the oldest of five, he had parents who were very strict. They upset him so much that he refused to speak to his parents for over a year. Concerned, they took him to a psychiatrist, where they discovered this was his means of protesting against their severe restrictions. They adjusted their parenting style to be more flexible, which made him happier. However, he complained that his siblings had it much easier because he had broken the ground for them.

When he asked about my kids, I described their distinct personalities. Then, after some hesitation, I plunged in and shared some recent upsetting events with Jackie. He listened carefully and remained quiet for a moment before leaning forward. "Remember when we bought those cases of Premier Grand Cru?"

"How could I forget?"

During my single days, Mike and I bought expensive wines

together, and when his wife enjoyed a night out with the girls, we'd cook a gourmet meal to pair with it. In due course, we each bought a case of the most famous Bordeaux in a deal that was too good to pass up.

The waitress interrupted us with coffee. As she walked away, Mike huddled over his cup. "You told me years ago to drink them faster and not cellar them so long, that my son Christopher — we only had one child then — would bring his pals to the house after school and open them."

I beamed. That was just the sort of thing I would have told him. "Yes, I remember. I said the girls would find the wine bitter and mix grape juice in. Then you'd come home from work and discover only empty bottles of your glorious wine." I laughed deeply at the memory; in fact, I had said it to Mike on a number of occasions.

"Yes, that was it," he chuckled. Then he straightened up and his eyes crinkled in a rueful smile. "The funny thing is, you were right. Except it wasn't Christopher, it was our youngest, Ricky. He broke into my expensive wines one night, and boy, was I ever mad!"

"Seriously?"

"Yeah, it's true. He's away at college now."

"Well, it's nice of you to pay for his studies after that stunt," I said, appalled at the behaviour.

His face clouded over, and he stared at his cup. After glancing around, he said evenly, "Staying home wasn't an option. We couldn't take him anymore. We told him, 'either you go away to school or move out.'" He put his arm across the top of the booth and let his breath out. "We had a hell of a time with him between the booze and drugs."

I shook my head and sipped my coffee. "It's incredible how much grief our children give us, isn't it?"

He nodded slowly.

Back in the office, I reflected on our exchange and wondered what had possessed me to reach out. It must have been Karen's influence, but I'm glad I did. Instead of viewing me poorly, he empathized, which gave me a sense of relief. We can't be terrible parents if others have similar problems. In fact, Ricky had been much worse. And what Mike said made sense — get them out of the house if they're disruptive and uncontrollable. I filed that one away for later.

*

Summer was in full swing when Karen bounced through the front door on Saturday.

"Kurt and Sharon have invited us for a swim in their pool and a drink!"

I looked up from my laptop. "No, he's too weird. Tell them we're busy."

"Too late," she said, drawing herself up to her full height. "I already told her we would. Rod and Iris will be there, too, so it'll be a party. Come on, it'll be fun." She watched me as I hesitated, then shrugged. "If you won't, I'll go by myself."

I mulled this over. Rod and Iris *were* fun, and I didn't want her to go alone. "Okay, I will. When?"

"After two."

The clock struck two, and I had almost completed my report, but Karen wouldn't wait. "I'm heading over. Join us when you finish."

After fifteen minutes, I strolled into their back yard. Kurt was stooping over the water with a pool skimmer, picking leaves out. Sharon and Rod lounged in deck chairs with drinks, and Karen floated beside Iris in the pool. A striking woman with dark features, Iris enjoyed Karen's company. I slid into the shallow end beside them while Kurt left to fetch me a beer.

When he returned, Iris looked up at him. "Where's your other bathing suit?"

"I changed," he replied, handing me my drink.

Iris leaned against the side of the pool and flashed a wicked grin. "You should have seen the other suit. It said, 'Rub here and make a wish!' Ha-ha-ha.'"

I made a face. "Glad I missed it."

Karen chortled, "I said, 'Oh, I don't wish for anything. I have everything I need,' ha-ha!"

The ladies kept giggling as I dove under and swam the length and back underwater. When I resurfaced, Kurt lay subdued on a lounge chair in the shade. Although he was sixty, it didn't surprise me at all to hear he owned a bathing suit only a horny fifteen-year-old would wear. At any rate, at least he was wearing a normal swimsuit now.

Later at home, Karen laughed, "He took it off before you arrived. I think that's funny; he must have figured out that you can't stand him."

I smiled. The suggestion that I intimidated him was pleasing. "Yeah, I dodged a bullet this time! Let's just say there's a reason I never wanted our kids to go over there without us. To be honest, I used to wonder if even Milo was safe."

*

Like a burst of fresh air, Eric arrived the following Saturday after kayaking in the afternoon with the university Outdoor Club.

As we gathered around the table, Karen beat me to the question of how he enjoyed the adventure.

"It was bad. I hit my head on a lot of rocks," he said in his husky voice and frowned. "It was supposed to be a beginner's course, but the current was fast, and the water was shallow. So, when you flipped over, which everyone did, you couldn't upright yourself again."

"Didn't you have helmets on?"

"Yeah, we all had helmets, but I kept hitting rocks on the bottom. The current basically dragged me from rock to rock."

Karen studied him. "But you're alright, aren't you?"

"I'm alright. I had the helmet, but it was awful!"

The naivety of the organizers irritated me. "They shouldn't have taken you on that river, Sonny. Someone could have been injured."

"Yeah, they took a guy to the hospital because of cuts to his face."

"It sounds as if they didn't know what they were doing," I said, and I felt anger bubble through me. But I didn't complain anymore. At least Eric hadn't been hurt.

At midnight, as we turned our lights off, there was a tapping sound on our door.

Eric walked in, holding a hand to his head. "Dad, as soon as I lie down on the pillow, it hurts."

I switched the lamp back on, and we sat up in the bed.

Karen looked anxious. "Perhaps he has a concussion." She was beside him in a flash, running her hands over his skull. "He has no bumps, Andrew, which is when you should worry. Dr. MacEwan says if there's no bump on the outside, the damage can be internal. Maybe you should take him to Emergency."

I dressed quickly but tried to act nonchalant so as not to alarm him. "It's probably nothing, but let's not take any chances."

The idea of visiting the Emergency Department at this time of night was depressing; it was usually a four-hour wait. But to my surprise, the waiting area was nearly empty. Only one worried mother with her child sat there reading magazines. We had timed it perfectly. As we registered, Eric explained the issue, and we waited. After what seemed like an eternity, I checked my watch — over an hour had passed. I stood up, stretched and approached the cheery nurse behind the counter.

"Do you think it'll be much longer?"

She looked at me sympathetically. "Very soon. We had a serious emergency arrive just before you came in."

Bad luck, I thought, and then felt remorse. I should have been sorry for whoever was in there instead of complaining about the wait. Ten minutes later, she led us to a curtained-off bed. Momentarily, a tall Indian doctor pulled the curtain aside and entered. Balding with short grey hair, he carried a clipboard.

"Tell me what happened?" he said in a heavy accent.

As he began an examination of the skull and pupils, Eric explained he'd been kayaking, flipped over and hit his head on submerged rocks.

In a jocular tone, the doctor continued talking while evaluating him, "Why you do that? Don't do that again. It not good."

Eric chuckled.

After he finished, the doctor summarized the situation. "No concussion but mustn't do that silly head banging on rocks again."

"He's funny," Eric said after he left.

I crawled into bed at four in the morning, grateful my son had no serious injury but bone-tired, nonetheless. With three children, Karen and I used to chime, 'triple the kids, triple the fun', but now that they're older, it seemed more like triple the worry. Kids are exhausting and can scare the hell out of you. One minute it feels like you're roaring downhill on a roller coaster, praying it won't jump off the track. Then it levels off, slows down, and everything is fine. The terrifying part is — you know there's another dip coming; you just don't know when.

CANOEING THE CREDIT 17

"To succeed in life, you need three things: a wishbone,
a backbone and a funny bone." - Reba McEntire

ERIC AND I were travelling to the historic hamlet of Norval with a red canoe tied to the roof. As we chatted, the sun blazed through the windshield, and its heat wafted towards us. It was a gorgeous day. We were off to explore the Credit River, starting in Norval and finishing at Churchill Park in Brampton.

"Thank you for suggesting we canoe a local river, son."

Slouched in the seat with his long legs stretched out, Eric grinned. "Yeah, I figured it would be easier than a long drive up north. And there are a lot of places in the city where you can go."

"Look over there, Sonny — that's one of my favourite views." The scene resembled an old country painting with a stream snaking through grassland towards the woods. And on this particular day, we would paddle right into that vista. It was like a dream come true.

"One morning, I saw three deer moving through the tall grass to get a drink."

"Nice," he said, turning his head.

*

Within twenty minutes, we had reached our destination. Tucked away from the bustling city and painted by A.J. Casson of the Group of Seven, the quaint village of Norval is nestled on the banks of the Credit River. Some old, Victorian-style farmhouses with gingerbread trim caught my eye, but the paper mills that once dotted the shoreline had disappeared long ago. We drove into a public park and carried the canoe to a spot with easy access to the water.

The vessel slipped into the water gracefully and floated by the shoreline. Eric stepped in while I gripped the gunnel and steadied it. Then he sat in the bottom and dug his paddle into the mud to brace it so I could climb in the stern.

As I settled in, Eric thrust a small bright yellow bag towards me. "Here, Dad, place your cell in this dry sack."

"Okay," I replied, extending my hand to him, "but I wasn't planning to tip. It's pretty shallow this time of year, and there's been no rain."

Eric made no response but took it, rolled the bag up and sealed the phones inside using the attached Velcro strips. As we moved away from the bank, all was quiet, except for the soft plunking sound of our blades dipping into the water. I smiled broadly as we set out on our adventure, with no idea where or how long it would take. It was a warm morning with no breeze, but the slow current carried us steadily along.

With the best view from the front, Eric called out directions. "Go over there, Dad. It's deeper."

I steered over and then used the J-stroke to propel us straight-forward. Sitting cross-legged, and looking confident and hand-some, Eric moved his broad shoulders beneath his safari-style hat with each stroke. I was grateful for the opportunity to experience this with him.

"Isn't this marvellous, Sonny?" I cried with delight. "Although we're surrounded by civilization, it feels like the wilderness." Canoes are a link to our country's history and tradition, and I could imagine us as early pioneers on the waterway.

"Uh-huh, very nice," he muttered while gazing at the tall grass on the banks and the occasional tree trunk that lay against them. A large turtle with a bright yellow chin and throat basked lazily in the warm sunshine but dove into the water when we approached. It felt as if the daily tension were easing out of my body.

The current was light, so we needed to paddle but not hard. There was no hurry. We wanted to soak up all the enjoyment we could. The Credit isn't wide, nor is it deep, but it was perfect for us. Occasionally, we'd scrape bottom but never had to step out even once to lighten the load. We glided silently along, sneaking up on birds and spooking them when we got close.

As we rounded a bend, we came upon a man fishing with hip waders. He glanced over his shoulder, jumped and almost dropped his rod in the stream before moving over to let us pass.

I put my paddle down and chuckled. "Did you see his expression? It was like — what the hell?"

Eric's white teeth shone against the black stubble on his face. "That was funny. You could tell he didn't expect anybody to be coming down the river." His eyes surveyed the shoreline, covered with bushes and interspersed with small sandy spots. "I guess few people canoe it. I'll bet we're the first ones in years."

A pang of guilt surfaced in my mind. Karen loved nature, and she was missing out. The girls would enjoy it, too, but weren't strong enough paddlers to come alone with just me, and the vessel would be too heavy if Karen or Eric joined us.

"Your mother would love this. We have to do it again with her."

"Yeah, but there are too many shallow parts to bear the weight of three people. You guys should go alone."

"You're right, Sonny."

The pace of the water picked up. As we wound into the little town of Huttonville, we spied the submerged concrete sections of an old mill, and they had created a small set of falls and rapids. We needed to make a fast decision.

Eric pointed to the right and yelled above the roar of the falls, "Head to the other side."

The strong current fought against us, but with rapid, deep strokes, we reached the side channel. There, we had to swiftly navigate between large boulders as the channel circumvented the small falls. As the canoe slipped out of the side rapids, the water immediately became calm.

"That was a bit of excitement," I gushed, as the canoe glided along the peaceful flatwater.

He twisted his head slightly. "You may want to portage it if you bring Mother."

I lay my paddle across the gunnels. "I think we'll be alright because now I know what to expect. We'll just follow the same path you and I did."

*

Soon we approached some woods on the right bank. Between the trees were vans, campers and people. A sign said, "Eldorado Park," which told me we were back in the city and near the end of our voyage. Some teens were wading in the shallow parts, and we waved at them as we breached the distance between us. They appeared both amused and amazed at the spectacle of a canoe floating by. Sweet-smelling aromas of barbeques wafted out, making me hungry, and I looked at my watch. I couldn't believe it. With all the twists and turns, our twenty-minute car ride north had turned into more than a two-hour river journey back.

"Look — Lionhead Golf Course," I called out, sighting a wooden bridge across our path that enabled players to reach the greens on each side. A few golfers smiled and waved as we drifted by.

"We'll have to play here sometime. I didn't realize the course crossed over the Credit."

He took a gander at both sides. "We should. It looks pretty."

Passing under Steeles Avenue, we entered that picturesque setting I often stopped to gaze at. A parking lot here was our destination, and we scanned the shoreline for a safe place to disembark.

"There's a spot!" he shouted and manoeuvred the nose in. Grabbing the bow rope in his hand, he scrambled up the four-foot bank. With me pushing and him pulling, the canoe rode easily up and onto the grass.

I retrieved my phone from the dry sack. Karen was waiting for our call to ferry us to the starting point so we could collect the other van. While we waited for her, we sat on the grass and talked about the experience.

"That was wonderful. I loved it. Thanks for suggesting this!"

He beamed. "It was really good; I enjoyed it, too, Pops."

What a magnificent way to spend a Sunday afternoon, and soon we'd be home for a delicious dinner.

On the drive to Norval, Karen seemed as happy as we were. "What a great father and son activity."

"You have to do it with me, too," said I, sitting sprawled out in the passenger seat. "I feel so mellow: like I've been to a spa."

She glanced over and smiled. "Okay, if you want. You both seem very content."

I watched the countryside go by. "There's one tricky part at Huttonville with remnants of a mill, but I can manage that. Otherwise, it's pretty easy."

"I'm glad you enjoyed yourselves."

"One of the best days of my life." I sighed and closed my eyes in complete satisfaction.

*

The following weekend, Eric had arranged a camping trip with his girlfriend and another couple.

He dropped by on Friday to collect his gear, before picking up Gloria and heading to Algonquin Park.

As we waved goodbye, Karen snickered, "Backcountry camping, translation — no washrooms and no showers. No thanks!"

Eric was very keen on this type of camping and had purchased the necessary equipment: a water purifier; a single burner propane stove and a portable toilet called a 'Thunder Box' (for reasons you can imagine). Everything was lightweight and designed for carrying. They planned to hike a circular route around a lake for two days, pitching their tents wherever needed. It's not for the faint-hearted. And Gloria appeared to be more of an indoor girl: one whom I suspected had never become one with the dirt.

"I'm still astonished that she agreed to this," I said with a laugh.

"Shockeroo!" Karen exclaimed with a grin.

I studied her. "You know that's not really a word."

"Sure, it is." Karen smirked. "Like in — it was a shock. It was a shockeroo!"

She could be funny, and I chuckled along with her. Then she looked thoughtful. "They must be serious if she's willing to put up with this."

"It will be a real test of their relationship," I agreed, "especially when she has to use the 'Thunder Box!'"

Karen bent over, giggling.

*

After taking Gloria home late Sunday night, Eric dropped his gear off and had a quick bite before returning to Hamilton. We couldn't wait to hear the details.

"It was good," he said in his usual understated manner. But he patiently answered questions, and we had quite a few. "The last part was a bit difficult," he said, and his tone sounded serious, "because it rained, and we had to cross a bog by wadding up to our knees in mud. That wasn't much fun."

Karen's eyes widened. "How did Gloria like the mud bog?"

"Well," he said, reflecting on it, "that wasn't her favourite part, but she did it. The rest wasn't so bad."

"Wow, I'm impressed," I muttered.

After he left, Karen smiled at me. "It must be love. You won't get me on that kind of trip."

*

Two weeks later, I suggested doing the river to Karen.

"Really, you want to go again?"

"Yes, because I know you'll love the experience. An easy paddle, we'll drift along without a care in the world. Plus, we're getting rain tonight, which should eliminate the shallow spots and make it easier."

An avid outdoorswoman, Karen was always the first to suggest canoeing a lake, although, like Eric, she hadn't mastered the J-stroke and would rely on me to keep the vessel moving straight. Whitewater training many years ago had built up my confidence for rivers.

"Okay," she said, happily, "but we need to ask Eric to come home Sunday to pick us up."

*

Karen and I scrambled out of the van at Norval, eager to recreate my splendid voyage. I held onto the bank to steady the canoe while she climbed aboard. I noticed the water level was higher, just as I suspected it would be. As we assumed our places, I placed my Blackberry in Eric's dry sack. Since I knew what lay ahead, I was already more relaxed than on the previous trip. We pushed off from shore into the stream, and the flow moved us on our way.

"Oh, Andrew, I see what you mean," Karen effused, sitting with her long legs crossed and a pink bucket hat on top of her light brown hair. "This is a piece of heaven on earth." She twisted her head around to gape at the scenery, enthralled by its natural beauty. Excited whenever we spotted an occasional bird or turtle, sometimes we coasted, letting the current carry us.

We took our time, but eventually, we encountered the ruins of the old mill. Water seemed to rush faster between the boulders, and the troughs were deeper, which alarmed me. That far passage was riskier now, but the alternative was even worse — the pitch over the falls looked terrifying.

"Go to the right!" I yelled over the noise of the falls and dug deep to pivot us. We were in the thick of it, too late to portage. We had to make this work.

Karen's not a strong paddler, and although I worked furiously, the fast-moving water drew us closer to the ledge. All of a sudden, she stopped and turned completely around. "What do we do now?"

I stared in disbelief, and my heart sank. That was it; we were done. Her pause had swept us to the brink. The expression *kiss your ass goodbye* popped into my head, but instead, I shouted, "Hang on."

She turned back and faced forward as we went over the edge. I watched her and the front of the canoe disappear before my eyes into a three-foot hole of swirling water. I feared the vessel would break in half, but it didn't. Incredibly my half followed the front, and after some heart-pounding terror, while the river roared and swirled us around, it righted itself and shot out into a placid pool as if it'd been spit out by the rapids.

"Are you trying to kill me?" Karen wailed. She looked like she'd seen a ghost.

I let my breath out. "Thank goodness we made it safely," I said, as she stared at me in horror. "Don't worry, that's the worst part; the rest is easy." But I bent over to calm my racing heart.

"I hope so because I thought I was going to die back there," she said, disheartened.

*

After a moment, I grinned. "Whew — that was like a wild ride at Wonderland."

She grimaced and picked up her paddle. She was a good sport, and I was proud that we had managed the toughest piece. Kicking off my water socks, I tossed them in front of me and wiggled my toes. I relaxed my posture and resumed an easy paddling.

Ten minutes later, we rounded a turn, and I spied yet another bend with the large branch of a weeping willow hanging out across the middle.

I studied it as we came closer. "Go to the left," I called out.

The current picked up and became ominously fast. Although I tried to steer us to the left side, it propelled us the other way. As we sped forward, I could see the bough was too low to pass under, and the outcome didn't look good.

"Get ready to push off from the branch," I instructed.

I had the notion Karen might be able to deflect us away. To my dismay, she grabbed hold of the branch, and as she did, the stream swept the canoe out from under us. I hit the water in shock. It was deep and cold, but the life jacket kept me afloat. I seized the end of the canoe to prevent it from washing away. As I held on, the strong flow dragged me along until my feet found the bottom, dug in, and I could brace myself. I caught a glimpse of half a broken paddle floating away.

"Grab the canoe!" I shouted to Karen, who was making her way to shore.

She did an about-face, took hold and stopped it from dragging me. Together we pulled it over to the side where the water was shallower and out of the rush. But it was full of water and heavy, so I dug my toes into the soft mud and, with all my strength, lifted the stern. With Karen's help, I tipped some water out. We repeated this step several times until the canoe was drained.

She leaned back against the bank and fixed her eyes on me. "Seriously, are you trying to murder me?"

My heart was still pounding, but I wiped my face, squinted at her and sputtered, "The rain made us go faster." We breathed heavily, trying to catch our breath, and I pondered what had happened. "To be honest, I don't remember that branch. Maybe because the level was lower, there was more clearance." Then I asked her the question that had been puzzling me. "Why did you grab it? I said, 'Push off', not 'grab it.'"

Her face soured, and she hollered, "Well, I couldn't push off unless I grabbed it first!"

"Okay."

I dropped the matter. What was done was done, and we probably would have ended up in the drink anyway.

I took stock of the situation. "Luckily, the dry sack's still in the bow."

"Aren't you glad I insisted you tie it there?" she asked smugly.

"Yes, I am." At first, I had simply put it loosely on the bottom, so it would've been long gone by now. But Karen's persistence made me listen to her. The front and back straps of my expensive Tilley hat had kept it around my neck, which was a relief, although it made me feel like a drenched rat. "I lost my water socks," I mumbled and pictured them floating downstream.

"A duck's probably wearing them." She laughed. Then she looked around. "Where's the other paddle?"

"It broke in half and floated downstream, but don't worry. We'll be alright with one." I held the canoe so she could climb in. "We're nearly finished; there's not much farther to go."

*

She relaxed while I did the work. Momentarily, we approached the golf course.

She watched the shore closely. "Andrew, there're golfers. You better signal for them to wait."

I spotted them. One guy was preparing to hit over the water while his buddy stood by. I waved my paddle at the second guy and caught his attention. But instead of telling his golf partner to halt, he just stood and stared. The ball was hit — a line drive hard into my chest. Inches higher and it would have struck my throat, nose or sunglasses.

She swung around as I yelled, "He hit me!"

"Are you alright? Why didn't he wait?"

As we floated away, I shouted at the moron who still stood rooted to the ground, "Thanks a lot ... **you ASS!**"

Karen's face turned angry. "You should tell the golf club what happened. You could sue them!"

"No, it was an accident, and to be fair, they don't expect anyone on the river. But that other guy makes me mad. He saw me, and it's not as if you can put the brakes on this thing until they finish their shot." I steered over to the middle of the river. "That was a bad shot, too. It would've never made it over."

"Thankfully, you weren't hurt."

"I felt the impact through my life jacket. It would have done some damage if it had struck me any higher."

Shortly after, I saw the endpoint downstream. "Okay, watch out. I'm going to land at the same place I did with Eric. Since you don't have a paddle, you'll need to jump out and hold it in place."

She executed this perfectly. I climbed the bank and, after hauling it up, flopped on the ground, exhausted. The possibility that our trip would not be the same tranquil experience as before had never occurred to me.

Karen sat with her arms around her knees. After a minute, she said, "You better call Eric."

Fifteen minutes later, we could see his van making its way down the dusty road.

He jumped out with a big smile and looked down at us from his tall height. "Well, how'd it go?"

"It was good," Karen answered, "but we hit a branch and got knocked over. So, we lost a paddle, and Father's water socks."

"I knew you'd capsize!" He laughed.

"That is so annoying," I said with irritation, wondering what he meant by that.

We tied the canoe on the roof, and as he drove, we recounted the harrowing adventure. He laughed at each episode, and so did we.

Not quite the dream experience I had envisioned, but at least we survived, although I discovered I had broken a toe digging into the riverbed.

*

When I got home from work on Monday, Karen greeted me from the living room with an impish smile. "I told Vicky our adventure story."

Vicky was one of her best friends, kind and very petite. So short in fact that when she sat on our couch, her feet dangled above the floor.

I smiled in embarrassment. "What did she think of it?"

"She laughed so hard she almost fell on the floor! The only thing missing, she said, was when you got out of the canoe, a dog should have jumped up and bit you in the ass."

I dropped onto the sofa. "Somehow, it's funnier when you're not living it."

*

When I was single, I never thought married life would be so exciting or dramatic. After all, I grew up watching *Leave It to Beaver*. The only drama there was provided by Wally's friend, Eddie Haskell. When I looked back at all the heart-pumping, near catastrophes Karen and I have had, I realized that our personalities and love for physical activity had led us into some of these. Most of our friends were less adventurous and tended not to take risks. Although scary at the time, I like to think that we lived life fuller and, thus far, have survived all of the mishaps.

In this case, we had achieved what few people have done — we canoed a river running through our city. Not many have done this, and in the future, there would be two fewer. Karen told me quite clearly that this was one adventure she had no interest in repeating.

THE MOONING

*"Some days it feels a bit more like hostage negotiating
with a band of drunken bi-polar pirates than
actual parenting." - @mommaunfiltered*

THE END OF summer had snuck up on us quickly. In many ways, I've always found September to be a bittersweet month. The vacation time is over, and a sadness hangs in the air because school and all the activities that go with it resume. Much of Karen's time was spent ferrying our daughters to and from school. It was a far cry from the world I grew up in where we walked to school with friends. However, it had become the norm in order to keep your kids safe. Jackie started grade eleven, Eric continued at the co-op job, and Meggy graduated but was still looking for work.

Getting the kids ready for school was another stress in the McKinney household. When Meggy was in school, she made everyone late. It didn't matter how much you yelled or tried to hurry her; she was never ready on time. Eric was pretty good, but in high school even he had to bolt out and race over the neighbours' lawns to the bus stop. Sometimes Karen drove him when he missed it. But the driver held the bus most often for Jackie, so much, in fact, that we gave him a card and gift certificate at the end of each term as a thank you.

When the girls did miss the bus, Karen would chase it, driving fast and leapfrogging ahead to the next stop. If that didn't succeed, then she drove her to class in her pyjamas with her winter coat over top. Child experts will tell you it's wrong to rescue them, but when you're under pressure as she was to get two girls to school, you do it. I did this several times myself before work in order to help Karen out. No question about it, the effort spent to wake adolescents up and get them moving is a source of frustration for many parents.

On the second weekend after the start of classes, Jackie moaned about her lunches. "A wrap with only cheese in it is disgusting." She put a finger in her mouth and made a gagging noise.

"What's wrong with that?" Karen asked in surprise.

"Yeah, I remember them," Eric chuckled. "They were pretty bad, Mum."

"I threw it out and bought a cookie," Jackie said with a smirk.

"I've run out of ideas. How about I let you make your own lunch?"

This proposal was met with silence. Karen continued to make cheese wraps, and although she suspected they weren't eaten, no more complaints arose.

*

And through it all, my career went on. The head office advised me I needed to qualify as a Global Auditor if I wished to continue inspecting our local third parties. Since they were critical to the local supply of medicines, I attended a four-day training program in New Jersey. I easily passed the exam; however, the ultimate test was to perform an inspection under the evaluation of a global manager.

"They scheduled me to do two audits in Ecuador: on a distributor and a third-party warehouse. So, I'll be gone for a week," I said when I broke the news to Karen.

"That's no problem," she said quickly and rubbed her hands together. "Think of the reward miles!"

"Terrific," I teased, "most women are upset when their husband leaves, but you're thinking of another holiday on frequent flyer miles."

"I'm kidding. I know it's your job and these trips aren't fun. Take some extra time and explore the area."

"In Ecuador? By myself?"

"Sure, I would, if it were me. When do you leave?"

"The Sunday before Thanksgiving. Thanks for the suggestion, but I'll come straight home. It'll be tiring enough doing two audits."

However, I did feel a twinge of guilt. I couldn't deny that escaping the tension in our nuthouse, flying business class, staying in a grand hotel and eating superb meals didn't have its appeal. This would be just what I needed to put me in a better frame of mind for Thanksgiving.

*

The flight to Quito was tedious — with a five-hour layover in Miami, it totalled twelve hours. When I finally landed at ten p.m., the airport was in chaos. There was no apparent separation between arriving passengers and locals waiting to welcome friends or family. I disembarked from the aircraft steps into a sea of people swarming around me, which didn't feel safe. But I straightened up, hoisted my laptop bag onto my shoulder and waded through the crowd, feeling like an adventurer arriving in a third-world country in the 1940s.

After collecting my luggage, I joined a line for entry checks, although it appeared I could have bypassed it. How they discerned a new arrival from the mass of humanity milling in and out was beyond me. They must worry more about smuggling out of the country than in. The bored-looking official with a small moustache seemed more interested in the length of the ever-growing line than my details, barely glancing at the passport before stamping it and waving me through. I scanned the room for the driver my company had arranged to meet me. After a minute, I spotted him at the side; a short, dark-haired young man, smartly dressed and holding up a sign with my name. I nodded and followed him through the exit to a car parked on the small road by the terminal.

He placed my suitcase in the trunk and motioned to get in. "Wait here a few minutes. I'll be right back," he said and disappeared inside again.

I sat unhappily with the windows down and waited. The air was warm; while we had entered fall, the Ecuadorians had begun spring. I glanced nervously along the street. Graffiti covered a wall along the side of the road, which was lined with older model vehicles. Paul, my country manager, had warned me that Latin American countries weren't safe and said he often travelled there with a bodyguard. I wished I had one now. Twenty minutes passed. Perhaps he left me to be murdered for my belongings, I wondered. I decided to send Karen a text to let her know I had arrived. And before I could add a description of the sketchy vehicle I was in, to aid them in locating my body, the driver reappeared. My fears soon dissolved, for he was friendly and articulate, and as we talked, I learned that he did considerable work for our company.

*

Pierre Faucher, the person sent to evaluate me, had suggested meeting for breakfast. I saw him enter as the waitress was pouring my coffee and taking my order. We had met during the training session. He was younger than me, short, fat and, like many Swiss employees, tense. He gave me a quick nod, scanned the menu and made his selection. Once the server left, he appeared to be more at ease and pleased to see me. Balding, he wore his hair short and a suit with no tie, while I was attired more comfortably in a simple dress shirt and slacks.

"Patricia De Breto, the site Quality Head, will collect us each morning and take us to the location," he said dourly.

The talk turned to my agenda and the two different facilities. There had been plenty of information about them in our global database that I had read beforehand, and I shared it with him. By the time we finished eating, I was eager to begin.

The air was warm and fresh as we stood on the sidewalk outside the hotel. I couldn't remember which of the ten women I met in Florida Patricia had been. But all of a sudden, a subcompact pulled up, and I recognized her. She had been very quiet during the meetings but flashed a broad smile today and was decked out in smart business attire. Her English was extremely limited, but we managed to chat a little during the drive. When we reached the corporate building, she led us to the general manager for a brief introduction before commencing our activities.

The 'brief' intro ran over two hours, and Pierre was frazzled as we descended the staircase to the floor below.

He tapped his watch in alarm and screwed up his face in annoyance. "We have to make up for the two hours!" he hissed.

I waved him off. Was he kidding? There was nothing to worry about; we'd just arrived, and I had no doubt we'd finish everything. Patricia had advised us that only even-numbered licence plates could drive in the city on certain weekdays and odd numbers on the other days. So, we'd have to alternate between this site and the warehouse location. That was doable, but as I digested the information about this form of traffic control, I concluded it would never succeed in a large city like Toronto with so many more cars and industries.

*

During the first day, Patricia kept asking if I was alright. Short, plump, with blonde hair, she sounded apprehensive.

"No problems," I answered each time. "I'm fine."

A regular jogger and fit, I had no medical issues. But I understood her concern better after she described a previous visitor who required hospitalization. At the contractor's facility, I climbed the steps two at a time and felt marvellous.

On Tuesday, Pierre mentioned he had a headache, and then confided more over dinner. "It started when I woke up and stayed with me all day."

I had no idea he was ill, probably because his expression was dreary by nature. I thought little of it at the time. But that night, I woke up with my head pounding and had trouble catching my breath. It was scary, and it occurred to me that this might not be my week. Besides the long hours I was spending at the two facilities, I had to write up formal presentations of my findings for each site, and now I was hovering on the brink of cardiac arrest in a foreign land. When I reached the warehouse that morning, I didn't run up the stairs; I halted halfway to catch my breath. In due course, we stopped for a coffee break, and I casually disclosed my splitting headache to Pierre but not the breathing issue.

"That's exactly what happened to me yesterday," he said, nodding vigorously and sipping his coffee, "but the next day, I was fine. Because I'd been in Peru previously, I believed I'd adjusted to the altitude, but Ecuador is even higher." His expression became earnest. "Quito is the second highest capital city in the world."

I choked on my coffee and entered a coughing fit under his watchful eyes. I'd been so busy with my preparation, I hadn't bothered to learn anything about the city itself. And because it took four days to hit me, I didn't suspect altitude as the cause. Now I experienced a wave of relief at the realization it was because of our height above sea level.

We went back to work, toiled hard at reviewing documents and systems and grabbed a late dinner in the hotel dining room. As soon as I got to my room, I called Karen.

After hearing the symptoms, she urged me to see a doctor, but

I reassured her, "The migraine's gone, and since Pierre had one too, I'm not worried. My breathing's still a bit laboured but not as much as before."

She remained concerned, however, so I agreed to seek medical attention if I wasn't better tomorrow. Then I went to bed and had a good sleep. In the morning, my energy was rekindled by the knowledge that the illness had passed.

Thursday, as we drove through various streets, I realized how much I enjoyed watching people in other countries start their workday. A pickup truck ahead of us caught my attention, its open back full of dark-skinned, black-haired men and women. Clearly, the workers had never heard of seatbelts. Like a scene in a postcard, the Ecuadorian women were dressed in colourful shawls and the men in blue ponchos. Both sexes wore black fedoras on top of their jet-black hair, a hat style long out of fashion in North America.

Patricia sat stiffly, gripping the wheel and elaborated, "A lot of them work outside the city, picking coffee beans for export."

The glimpses of countryside that I had during these journeys revealed barren land, and I wondered if anything but coffee would grow there. At lunch, we visited the company's cafeteria. I followed Patricia in line, and she described the choices.

When I took soup, she pointed to a large bowl beside it. "Popcorn."

Seeing my confused expression, she explained, "Eets customary to eet soup here with popcorn."

"Okay, I'll try it." I dished a few spoonsful into my bowl. After all, our custom at home is to add crackers. The sogginess was not unlike the result with crackers, but the hard kernel bits remained a challenge. I put them on my plate and finished the soup to be polite.

*

That night, I sweated over my slide presentations until one o'clock in the morning. There's never an easy way to deliver bad news. You need the right balance of praise in some areas while alerting the client to the significant deficiencies in others. Pierre and I had a brief discussion before, and he called the Swiss office to alert them that there were significant flaws in the quality systems of each site. While alarming, the general managers accepted the results. As disappointed as they must have been, it was impossible to argue their validity. On the way out, we stopped for hamburgers and fries since it was too late for a nice dinner. Pierre told me I had succeeded and would receive certification.

In between mouthfuls, he continued. "I'm impressed by your knowledge and technique. You never worried about finishing all the work needed. I'm hoping you might assist training some of our new auditors."

This positive feedback was a terrific lift after the gruelling week that I had.

*

My plane landed on Friday of the Thanksgiving weekend. When the taxi dropped me off, I found Karen, Eric and the girls had loaded up the van so we could travel straight to Steven's cottage. While she drove, I ate sandwiches she had made, and we updated one another on events of the past week. We had missed each other, and although tired from the long flight, it was good to be back with my family. As I thought about it, business travel likely helped our marriage during those years because occasional absence does make the heart grow fonder.

Turning onto the small country road north of Parry Sound that led to Steven's, we marvelled at the blazing scarlet sumac bushes on each side. And the multicoloured leaves on the tall, sturdy oak, maple and birch trees gave the impression that someone had taken a palette with yellow, orange and red paints and dabbed them with all the possible combinations. Russet, amber, yellow, orange, brown, dark red and all the shades in between were vibrantly visible as we motored along. Steven greeted us when we pulled into his gravel driveway and helped unload. The girls embraced him happily; he was like an uncle to them, as he grinned broadly beneath his moustache. His cottage had a dark brown wood exterior with black asphalt tiles. The roof and ground were covered with fallen autumn leaves and the eavestrough was stuffed and overflowing. Inside, the walls and ceilings were all tongue-in-groove pine which evoked a Scandinavian ambiance to his woodland home. The girls stayed inside on their phones while the rest of us took Darla for a walk. The pungent, earthy aromas of decaying leaves coated each breath of air, and we caught sight of the lake frequently through trees now partially bare of their foliage.

I felt displaced as I ambled along the gravel road. That morning, I stood in the barren, brown and arid land of Ecuador, but only hours later, here I was on a country road with the beautiful Canadian landscape before me. The contrast was mindboggling. By the time we departed for home on Monday, my mind was unencumbered. Nature, it seems, has the ability to refresh our spirits.

*

Home again, the weeks and months clicked by. One Saturday night in January, Jackie left with Katie for a sleepover at Chloe's, a new friend who'd been to our house a few times. It seemed strange, but parents no longer came to the door to pick up their kids. They'd simply text them to come out from the driveway. So, we had never met Chloe's parents, and perhaps that's why she thought we wouldn't check her plans. But we did. Karen got her mother's number from Diane.

"Jackie isn't staying at her house," she declared after reading a response from the mom. "They've gone to a hockey game where a boy named James is playing. And there's a party after — at the coach's place."

I pricked up my ears. "James .... why that's the glib young man I met at Katie's when we busted their other scheme," I exclaimed.

Her cell dinged again. "Okay, Chloe told her mother that Jackie and Katie's parents gave them permission to go to the party, that there'd be drinking and they'd sleep over. The coach said it was all proper, though. Girls will sleep in a trailer in the driveway and boys in the house." She scowled. "Is she kidding? Drunk girls in an unchaperoned trailer and inebriated boys within twenty feet. There's no way she's staying there. What is this, a reward for his players? Okay, guys — here's some intoxicated teens to have fun with."

My minded clouded over. "That's disturbing. If you ask me, the coach should be investigated."

Karen called Diane, who knew nothing of the actual plan and filled her in.

"I'm going to fetch them from the party and then take Katie home," she said, getting up from the sofa.

"I'll come with you. I want to see the faces of these partners in crime."

The ride was quiet, but after Katie was dropped off, Jackie ranted, "That was *sooo* humiliating! Why don't you work like other mothers? You're lazy, aren't you?"

"Lazy?" Karen yelled, "That goes to show how little you know about everything I do for you. Running you around is a full-time job."

Jackie glared at us, ran upstairs and slammed her door. Out-flanked again. Score — kids zero, parents two.

*

Fighting continued in the household, and even though Karen tolerated disrespect better than me, it wore her down. On Wednesday afternoon, I opened the front door just as Jackie landed in front, having leaped off the landing.

"Jackie, don't run so fast. You'll trip and hurt yourself."

But she had already sped around the kitchen wall, ignorant

of my concern because of the headphones she was wearing. In a moment, she bounced back into the room, with the headphones around her neck.

"Father, Mother embarrassed me today," she said solemnly, as I hung up my coat. When Jackie relayed a story, her voice was always calm and pleasant, quite contrary to her tone during the actual event. So, I greeted her story with suspicion, sighed and said nothing.

"She *mooned* me."

"Mooned you?"

"Yes, and Katie, too!"

"What do you mean?" I asked, hanging my keys up in the kitchen, where Meaghan and Karen sat eating crackers and hummus.

Jackie had followed me. "She pulled down her pants, jiggled her rear, and yelled — '**Kiss my ass**!' It was so embarrassing!" Then our daughter doubled over with laughter. Her blonde hair hung down to her knees, and she clutched her stomach while her face twisted in pain from the unrestrained hysterics. Stunned, I looked to Karen for a denial or explanation.

To my surprise, she squealed, "They were bugging me! I forget what it was about, but they really annoyed me."

I blinked. "You pulled down your pants in front of Katie?" I looked around me, not understanding what had happened and why Karen wasn't embarrassed.

"Don't worry, I only showed them my crack," she said with a sheepish grin.

"Nooo. She showed her whole butt, jiggled it and yelled, 'Ha-ha, kiss my ass!'" Jackie fell into another giggling spree.

Meaghan's body shook with convulsions, too, and she gestured at her mother. "What ...were you... thinking?" she stammered, trying to catch her breath.

"I think Katie's still traumatized from it," Jackie added. "Your butt is burned into her mind!" She threw her blonde head back and cackled even more.

"Why would you show them your rear?" I asked Karen in a daze.

"They pissed me off!" she said, and she answered just like it was normal behaviour.

"She uncovered her *ass*!" Jackie continued, not wishing to let the joyful moment go. "I think it's burned into Katie's brain."

"Okay, well, I'm glad everybody had fun," I said with an exasperated sigh. Then I sat down and helped myself to the hummus.

After our daughters ran upstairs, I whispered, "Were you drunk? How could you do that?"

Offended, she gave me a dirty look. "No! Of course not. I was mad at her. I don't remember what she did, but it irritated me."

"You're lucky they didn't film it on their phones," I warned.

A troubled look crossed her face, which indicated she had registered my point.

"Just so you know, dear, they didn't see my whole bum," she added, as though this was a defence.

But a young voice shouted out from upstairs, "Oh, yes, she did. We saw the whole butt, ha-ha-ha."

How could she hear us whisper from a different floor but not when we talked to her in the same room? That is one of life's great mysteries.

I shook my head. "For your information, it will be formal dress for dinner tonight, dear. Pants are required!"

At least she was listening to Dr. MacEwan and attempting to stand up for herself more, although mooning the girls wasn't exactly what I had in mind. We both carried enough pressures in life without our kids adding new ones, but they seemed to have a propensity for it. It felt like our house was in a perpetual state of chaos. Like the law of entropy in thermodynamics — left unchecked, everything approaches a state of randomness or chaos. That was it. If entropy is defined as a measure of the disorder, then my life was proof of it.

*

Humour was a coping mechanism we used to dissolve some of the anger, friction and hurt feelings that arose. And I was reminded of a story from a senior person in Switzerland. Tomas, an older, portly Irishman with white hair and a strangely colourful tie worn on an ordinary shirt with no jacket, sat surrounded at a cocktail event by underlings striving to impress him. After a long career in the industry, he retired only to be recruited by our corporation. I joined the group in time to hear him talk about his daughter, who was employed at another pharmaceutical company.

"Yes, she works in the laboratory. Everybody there asks her how she manages to get along with her boss — apparently, he's a real SOB — and she told them, 'If you think he's bad, you should meet my *father!*'" He slammed his hand on the table, and the glasses shook and clinked while his belly heaved with laughter. The entire group, me included, erupted. It was funny, although I hoped the girls wouldn't say that about me one day.

AUTO SHOP

"Things I've learned in school: 1) How to whisper;
2) How to text without looking; and 3) How to
look like I'm paying attention." - lolsotrue.com

"**W**HY DON'T WE arrange for a tutor?" Karen suggested after dinner.

Jackie struggled with math this term. Her mark to date was in the fifties, and she confided to Karen that she was scared of failing.

Our blonde daughter brightened up at the idea, but I shook the suggestion off. "We don't need a tutor. I can teach her."

"That would be great if you could," Karen said, warming to the idea. "Your father is excellent at math. He helped me with statistics in university and Meggy with grade nine math, and we both got terrific marks."

"And ninth grade is a tough year for math; there must be thirty formulas to learn," I added proudly.

Then I turned to my tall daughter. "Bring me your homework, and I'll help you.

She perked up and smiled. "Thanks, Daddy."

Only ten minutes passed before she stormed out. "Father's so mean! I'm not working with him anymore."

"What happened?" Karen sputtered, looking up from the book she had just started reading.

"That kid's a brat, and she's lazy," I fumed. "She wants me to give her the answers, instead of thinking for herself!"

A voice yelled from upstairs, "I don't understand it — and Dad's nasty!"

I remained silent for a moment. That kid hears so well she could be part of the early missile detection system if she put her mind and ears to it.

"I'm calling the tutoring company," Karen said, flatly. "You two butt heads too much."

The blood was pounding in my veins, and I felt insulted. Over the years, I'd been complimented on my ability to train staff. One boss went so far as to say I'd make an outstanding teacher. But at home, I couldn't instruct my own daughter without losing my temper.

When she was younger, Jackie had excellent marks and was very proud of them, but now she didn't seem to care. Some teenage girls 'dumb themselves down' in order to appeal to boys; I'd seen it happen with a friend of Meggy's. But I doubted this was the case with her; she had loads of confidence. Be that as it may, after this singular attempt, I abandoned the idea of working with Jackie for the sake of peace in the household.

*

Karen put the phone down. "He'll start next week. You'll see — this will be better."

Since we had paid for Meaghan's private schooling, I suppose we owed Jackie some support. Besides, the cost was worth it to avoid fighting, and a professional might get her motivated about learning again.

"Close the pocket door so you aren't undisturbed," Karen instructed when the tutor arrived, and they entered the family room — the same place where I had tried and failed.

Although pleasant enough, his youthfulness had surprised me, and Karen, noting my startled look, advised me that he was in first-year university. So, only two years older than Jackie.

While they laboured, we finished dinner with Meggy in the adjoining kitchen. She kept glancing at the glass pocket door curious about their progress.

A month later, the tutor reported she was making excellent strides. But as soon as he exited, Jackie marched angrily into the kitchen.

"Oh ... my ... God, that was so embarrassing!"

Our jaws dropped as she proceeded to tell us off. "We tried to work while listening to you two tell stories about dogs pooping, and you were laughing! I was so embarrassed."

Karen looked around uncomfortably. "You could hear us through the pocket door?"

She nodded vigorously. "Yes! And he could hear you too, telling your gross stories. How humiliating!" Off she ran in disgust.

"Sorry!" I called after her.

*

Parents aren't bothered by pooping stories. They consider them funny. But I felt ashamed that he had overheard us. However, despite a brief awkward moment at his next visit, the tutor and Jackie were able to continue unperturbed. At the end of the year, we eagerly awaited her report card to see the improvement.

When Jackie brought it home, Karen read it out loud. "Fifty-nine?"

"Yes," she said and looked away.

"What was your mark before the tutor?" I asked, as the disappointment sunk in.

"Fifty-nine," she responded, shuffling her feet.

"Exactly the same mark as now?" I asked in horror. "All that money and time wasted. Now that's annoying."

She ran upstairs.

"Oh, well," Karen said, trying to make peace. "At least she passed."

"Well, she couldn't have put in much effort." I lowered my voice. "Perhaps she thought you learn by osmosis, from sitting beside someone who's an ace in math." I cast my eyes up to the ceiling. This was unbelievable. However, she must have made an impression on the tutor because a few years later, he tried to friend her on Facebook.

"Ewww," she cried at the time. "I'm not being friends with that old man!"

*

Jackie wasn't the only one who needed tutoring. Although the family benefited from Karen staying home with the kids, it had made her somewhat technology-challenged. She missed out on computers in the workplace and, now that the girls were older, often needed their help with a text or email. At first, they gladly assisted, albeit with considerable chuckling and mocking, but as time went on, they became more and more frustrated.

"OMG... you do... this!" Jackie yelled as she hovered over her mother.

"Well, I don't know," Karen howled. "I didn't grow up with them like you did. You girls practically came out of the womb holding a cell phone."

Daughters are quick to criticize their mothers, I've noticed. The last time we visited Karen's hometown of Fort Erie, we had dinner at our good friend Maria's house. She invited Darlene, another old friend, and her daughter Amanda to join us.

I'd only met them a few times, most recently at Maria's older daughter's wedding. Amanda was slender and pretty, with dark hair cut in an elegant long bob and the same age as Maria's youngest, Stacey.

Before she disappeared with the others, I said, "Amanda, I saw you dancing at Annie's wedding. You were doing the Swim." And I chuckled at the recollection of her holding her nose with one hand while lifting the other in the air and sashaying down to the floor and back. "You're a great dancer." A smile flickered across her face, and I continued, "I've only seen that dance in the beach party films of the '60s. I'm surprised you knew it."

She wrinkled her nose, laughed and I turned to her mother. "Were you aware she could do the Swim?"

Darlene pursed her lips. "Nooo, I wasn't." Then she chortled, "The rum and coke might have had something to do with it. To be honest, I was a little worried about how much she drank."

The memory of those underage girls huddled together, covertly sipping drinks the bartender generously supplied, floated through my mind.

"You've grown up, Amanda. You're very pretty," Karen said, jumping in during the pause, "and the spitting image of your mother at this age."

Amanda smirked. "Oh yeah, I've heard she was attractive ... when she was young."

I winced at the words — *when she was young* — ouch! Girls can be cruel.

*

Even though our daughters were often harsh to her, Karen could still not resist shortening their punishments. Wednesday, I entered the front door and found Jackie sitting in an armchair engrossed with her cell phone. She had lost it for three days for swearing at her mother.

I studied her with annoyance. "What are you doing with that, Jackie? You lost it."

Her eyes never moved from the phone. "Talk to Mother."

Smouldering with irritation, I went downstairs to where Karen was doing laundry and accused her of caving in again.

"But Andrew, you have to realize how upset she is." Her face twisted in anguish. "The dance girls are cliquey and obnoxious to anyone outside their group. Jackie joined a year after most kids, so she wasn't included — not that she'd want to belong to that snobbish gang, anyway — but we've talked about this. If we take her cell away, she becomes a social pariah." She tossed her hair back. Karen had gotten a cut today and her light brown hair looked fetching.

"Okay, but she doesn't have to lose it. She can choose to behave," I said firmly, not wanting her to play the girl card again, even though I'm the first to admit I don't completely understand the women in my family. Honestly, why can't they just be more logical?

Karen sighed. "Yes, but teenage girls are very emotional. Besides, she apologized to me, so I forgave her."

"That's fine, but it still isn't right. Remember what Dr. MacEwan said? Stick with the punishment or the behaviour won't improve."

Her face softened, and she looked down at the floor. "Today she told me she wants out of Hillside and to return to the other school." The news was staggering, but when I started to say something, she waved me off. "I said that was out of the question. It took a lot of effort to get her in there, so we're not taking her out."

"I agree. It's ridiculous." I frowned. "She has to learn to stick it out."

"We came up with a compromise," Karen said, looking at me hopefully. "If she didn't want to do the dance program anymore, I said I'd request a note from the hospital that fitted her back brace to state she had to stop due to pain from the scoliosis."

I tilted my head and considered this. The fact that she created solutions to our daughter's complaints was distressing. Upon seeing my skeptical expression, Karen quickly added, "No, it's true. She found it painful. However, another big reason is those dance girls."

I shrugged. "Alright, try that and see what happens."

She succeeded. They permitted Jackie to drop out of the dance program but still attend their school. Jackie was elated, and another mini crisis had been averted.

*

Experts say that teens are simply asserting independence when they're angry and rebellious, but that doesn't help when parents or siblings have to deal with it constantly. Eric had noticed the tension during his last visit.

"Why is there so much anger in the house?" he asked in bewilderment.

It made us stop and think. I guess we all had become so conditioned to the fighting that we didn't notice it anymore. I blamed the girls, but after he left, Karen told me that my face was always angry.

"You're a grouchy man, always looking grumpy."

That hit me like a bolt of lightning and hurt my feelings. Sure, I wear a serious expression at the office and possibly at home. And when I tell jokes, I prefer to keep a straight face and surprise people with the punch line. But I wouldn't describe that as 'grouchy.'

During our last visit, Maria said, "You have a dry sense of humour, Andrew. I can never tell when you're joking!"

That pleased me because it was exactly what I was going for. But after what Karen said, I worried my employees might view me as grouchy, too. Maybe all the stress from my family and job had caught up to me and soured my features. The next morning, when I entered the kitchen area at work, Sarah and Suzanne were making coffee.

"Let me ask you something if you don't mind?" I said, and I noticed Carol had joined us. "Do I look mean?"

They looked at me curiously and glanced at each other. Then, Suzanne spoke up, "No, you don't." The others nodded their heads in agreement.

"Okay, thank you. The reason I asked is that Karen and the girls tell me I look crabby all the time."

A smile formed on their lips, but Carol and Sarah echoed Suzanne. "No, not at all."

I hurried off for a conference call and shook my head as I dialled the number. They must have thought I was nuts to ask that question, but then they have teenagers so they should understand. In my career, I've often felt like a hero, but at home, the family often sees the worst in me. I couldn't wait to trumpet the news to Karen.

"So, there you go, dear. You're wrong," I concluded smugly. "I'm not mean looking at all."

"Well, maybe you're happier in the office because you're the boss, and they have to listen to you," Karen rebutted. Then she smirked. "I can't believe you asked your staff if you look mean!" She broke out in a full laugh, while I watched in bewilderment.

*

Afterwards that night, I called Eric. "When are you coming home, Sonny? I need some male hormones in the house."

The voice on the other end chuckled. "Are the girls getting to you?"

"Not just them. Your mother, too. I could use some male companionship — even Darla's a girl! Although she doesn't bother me as much. In fact, there's many a day when she's the best-behaved girl in the house."

He's a good son. He brought Gloria for dinner that Sunday, which helped break the crabby pattern that I had fallen into.

But after they left, Meggy complained, "Eric is such an ass."

"What did he do this time, Meggy?" I sighed.

"He farted, and it stank," she said, and displeasure was written all over her face.

I shrugged my shoulders and muttered, "So, just walk away."

"I couldn't because he grabbed me."

"What do you mean, he grabbed you?" I asked, snickering. I knew what he had done; my brother did it to me. Once he even sat on me so I couldn't get away.

Although she tried to act mad, her face broke into a smile as she gestured with her arms. "He grabbed me like this and lifted me up, saying, 'You're vegan weak. You can't get away!' and he let out an evil laugh."

Now I really howled. After a moment, I wiped the tears away. Trust Eric to add that twist of vegan weak, ha-ha.

"Where was Gloria when all this happened?"

"She was standing right there!" Meggy answered and then added with some annoyance, "For your information, vegans are as healthy as meat eaters."

"Yes dear, you're right, but it *is* funny."

Then I quickly changed the conversation to avoid another vegan rant. "I'm surprised he did that in front of Gloria, ha-ha. Well, today she got a taste of what she missed by not having a brother!"

With only a younger sister, Gloria couldn't have learned how weird brothers are. Although I received the same treatment from Peter, I presumed older brothers treated sisters better, but I was wrong. When we repeated the story to friends, we learned that most of the men had behaved similarly with their younger sisters.

Ed denied it, but Greta, whom he started dating in high school insisted, "Yes, you did!" she squealed in delight at the chance to tattle on him. "I know because I saw it. You farted and held Betty down on the couch."

Ed stiffened noticeably at being upbraided in front of us. Ever since I had met him, Ed was the epitome of culture and good manners. But the gleam in his eye told me Greta had struck a chord. He left the room on a pretense of fetching something from the kitchen. Both Eric and Ed had corrected my assumption of sibling behaviour.

*

The fall air had turned colder. We were approaching winter and would soon see snow. On Sunday afternoon, I put on some old clothes and, going downstairs, spied my daughters.

"Jackie, come and give me a hand putting the winter tires on," I called out to her.

"What?" The cute face under the blonde hair registered shock.

"You took auto shop last term, so this will be good practice for you."

Frankly, when I heard she had registered for this class, I was impressed. She'd never shown any interest in cars before. Reluctantly putting her jacket on, she trundled outside after me with her ponytail sticking out from the back of a cap. I couldn't hide my pleasure. Without Eric around, I had no one to share manly chores with.

"It's great you took that course," I said, opening the garage door to reveal the set of winter tires. "Girls need to learn these things in case their car breaks down."

"Whatever," she muttered indifferently and then added, "I thought it'd be an easy credit, but there was more involved than I expected."

"Really?" I felt my pride deflate. "Don't worry. This won't take too long." I pointed to the tires. "Bring one over and we'll get started."

"They're too heavy for me," she wailed.

I stared at her. "Just roll it. How'd you move them in class?"

"Oh, I got one of the boys to do it."

Then I understood. A beautiful blonde in shop class, *Oh, could one of you big, strong men help me?* Those hormonal adolescents must have fought over the chance to assist. While she watched me, I quizzed her on the steps. It was obvious she had no idea.

When finished, I popped the hood. "Alright, why don't you check the oil? That's easy enough."

"I don't know how to do that," she replied indignantly.

I sighed. "It's hard to believe you passed the course."

"Yeah," she chuckled, "and I got a B." As I rolled the summer tires into the garage, she warmed to the subject. "It was kind of funny, Dad, because we had an assignment to do, and this boy let me copy his. But I thought, copying the whole thing was too much work, so I whited out his name and wrote mine over top."

"Did you?" I said, leaning against the wall. She had my attention now.

"Un-huh, but I got caught. The teacher said he simply held it up to the light and saw the other student's name underneath. I'm so embarrassed I did that, because it wasn't very smart, ha-ha-ha."

My jaw tightened, and I tried not to frown. Her gaiety in describing this horrendous event confused me. "That's crazy. Did you get a zero on it?"

"No, he let me do it over."

"You were lucky," I said seriously.

"Yeah, and he gave me a B!" Her eyes twinkled with delight. "I baked him some cupcakes, and he told me I reminded him of his daughter."

"Did you ask if she was in jail?"

"Good one, Dad, he-he. Yeah, I should have asked him that."

I didn't lecture her, beyond saying she was fortunate not to receive a failing grade. She'll get caught one day, learn an important lesson and change her ways. Surprisingly, she'd prove to be more cunning than I anticipated.

NAKED GIRL

*"When your children are teenagers, it's important
to have a dog so that someone in the house
is happy to see you." - Nora Ephron*

WALKING DARLA WAS uplifting, and we watched her run through the park like an excited kid. She found a dead stick in the snow, gnawed on it and then carried it around like a trophy, not caring how goofy she looked. Holding the stick on the ground with her paws, rump in the air and tail wagging, she teased us with it, growling as if to say — *try and get it*. Of course, as soon as we made a move towards her, she bolted off like a little brat and pranced around with the wood protruding from her jaw. She made us laugh. A thirty-minute walk in the park felt like a therapy session, and we returned home refreshed and cheerful.

Still, she was a different dog than Milo, and we had to adjust. Black, whereas he had been brown and white with black splashes and taller. Darla's tail could be an unintentional weapon no matter whether happy or nervous. On Sunday evening, Karen and I sat on opposite ends of the sofa watching TV in the family room. Moochie lay in between us, purring contentedly. Her eyes looked softly at me as if to say — *I love you.* Or maybe it was — *I'm going to kill you.* With cats, it's hard to tell. Darla entered, approached the couch and stared at us expectantly. Karen patted the spot beside her and coaxed her up. "Come on, honeybun. Don't be shy." Darla jumped into the small area that remained between Karen and the cat and lay down.

"There you go. See, you can join us," Karen said softly, stroking her black head.

Moochie lifted her head and assessed this turn of events. The dog's eyes rolled nervously and her tail started whipping from side to side, right into Moochie's face. But the cat didn't move. She just lay there grimacing while being smacked back and forth.

I tried to intervene. "Stop it, Darla. Watch your tail!" I said, placing my hand on her side to calm her, but her tail beat even faster.

The cat could take no more. She heaved herself off the couch and onto the ground, giving us a pissed-off look before shuffling off. Was the dog aware her tail had been hitting the cat in the face? She didn't seem to be, but sometimes I wondered.

And that tail could wreak havoc. Many a time, she sauntered into the kitchen and cleared all the pictures off the low corner shelves of the cabinets. Even worse was this Saturday morning. I lay against the end of the couch talking to Karen when Darla strolled by. Her swinging tail was level with the coffee table and did its work. Before I could move, my glasses, tea and the remote control all went flying. I jumped to rescue my glasses before she stepped on them and then ran for a rag to soak the tea up from the carpet. Our lab observed me curiously, wondering what all the fuss was about.

*

Moochie wasn't perfect either, and her idiosyncrasies continued to catch us off guard. The previous week, Karen brought the groceries in and put them on the floor by the stairs to take down to the spare fridge after she finished unloading the car.

When she came in from a second trip, I heard her yelling, "What the heck are you doing? Get away from there!"

Her anger startled me, and I rushed over in time to see her carry a bag of milk to the sink. She glared at me. "The stupid cat chewed through the bag!"

As I wiped the floor with a rag, Karen dumped the contents of the torn pouch. For the past few years, we'd had to store the kibble bags on a shelf that Moochie couldn't reach. But the milk was a new low.

"From now on, I'll have to put the milk on the kitchen counter while I unload." She fumed. Nowhere to be seen, the cat had wisely disappeared. "She's smart to beat it, or I'd give her rear end a smack."

I rubbed my chin. "How could she know that milk was in the bag? She must be smarter than I gave her credit for."

"Oh, she's clever alright — when it comes to food."

*

Eric brought Gloria to the house again the following weekend, to see us before our Bahamas trip. Unfortunately, he couldn't go with us because of his limited vacation. At first, Karen wasn't sure if we should go. It'd be our first March break without him. However, he'd gone to Punta Cana last year with his university chums, so the girls dismissed our concern.

"No problem," Meggy quipped. "We'll Photoshop him in."

We decided to go ahead because it was important to enjoy ourselves and escape the pressures of school and work. Karen took the girls shopping for new bikinis, a concept that was strange to me. I've been quite happy with the same bathing suit for the past ten years.

When our son arrived, he wore his new engineering jacket with the graduation year on it, and Gloria had a full-length beige winter coat. They were a nice-looking couple. As they handed me their coats, Darla strolled in to say hello. Gloria backed up; she didn't fancy animals. But quick as a flash, Darla's head moved forward and licked her leg below the skirt. I watched her recoil in horror.

"Don't worry, Gloria. She won't hurt you," I said. "She's showing affection."

Eric looked at me and grinned. "Yes, Dad, but the problem is — Darla smells like **ass**!"

Well, that did it — '*like ass*', he said. A look of revulsion crossed everybody's face, especially Gloria's.

"Ewww," Jackie cried.

That was it. He had succeeded in planting a graphic image in our heads that was hard to shake. Sure, her mouth had an unpleasant odour. Maybe she did smell like that, but I knew better as to the reason.

"No, Eric," I said, shaking my head and trying to calm everyone down. "Her breath is bad, but I took a sniff of the kibbles, and that's exactly how they smell. Her breath is like that because of her food. Don't tell people she smells like ass. It's disgusting."

But he just stood there snickering, white teeth bright against his black stubble, pleased at his wit. The dog looked around nervously, searching our faces to understand what was wrong. Poor Darla, how he misjudged you.

After that, I knew Eric's girlfriend would never love our black lab, which is a shame because she was so good-natured. If we stopped to talk to a neighbour, she sat patiently and waited. When I worked in the study on the weekends, she'd push the door open, saunter in and muzzle her head into my hands.

I just had to look into her brown eyes to understand what she wanted. "Are you hungry, Darla? Do you want a treat?"

Her body wiggled, and she did a little dance by stepping her front foot forward and back. Then, just in case I was too dense to grasp the idea, she licked her lips a few times.

*

March break came upon us before we knew it, and the bright Nassau sunshine made me blink as we disembarked down the passenger stairs from the plane. What a terrific escape from the winter blahs, I thought to myself. Mind you, I could never have lived in a place that didn't have four seasons. I loved each one, from the frigid air of winter to the sweet smell of cut grass on a hot summer's day. Even the in between seasons were a pleasant change; the earthy aromas of spring as they reveal themselves from under the melting blanket of snow and the colours and smell of autumn leaves in the cool fall air. In a sense, we were getting a jump on spring with this trip.

Our daughters had been on their best behaviour before leaving, and as we rode the free shuttle bus from the airport, they gazed excitedly out the windows.

"You were here before scuba diving, weren't you?" Karen asked as the bus bumped along the road.

"Yes, I got certified on that trip. That was over thirty years ago, but I have wonderful memories. Over twenty university students came down, mostly girls, and we took over the place for a week. We had a party outside, danced by the pool, and then everyone jumped in and continued rocking in the water."

"Sounds as if you had a great time. It's funny, I also came to the Bahamas to get certified but on a different island. Isn't it odd how we both did the same activity but years apart?"

"Yes, it's nice to marry a younger wife." I smirked.

"Un-huh, and it shows we share common interests."

We had reservations for two ocean-front suites at the Breezes, an all-inclusive resort and definite upgrade from my single days.

*

"I'll wait in line, and you grab us a drink." Karen motioned to the hotel staff, dressed all in white while walking around with trays of rum punch. A classy touch, and we had refills because checking in took forever.

When we finally registered, Karen squealed, "Alright, let's drop our bags in the room and hit the beach!"

We pulled some lounge chairs together on the sand, and I lifted the backpack and pulled out the sunscreen.

"No, I don't want any," Jackie said, waving me off before I could say a word.

"Yeah, Dad, we always come home as white as when we left. I want a tan," Meggy said, sitting next to her sister in a skimpy red bikini and gazing at the ocean.

The girls had a point. I had worked for a sunscreen manufacturer for seven years and learned about the sun's damaging effects from their research scientists. Hence, we slathered it on. Although I try to present the facts, the girls were old enough to make their own decision.

"Let them do as they wish, dear. If they burn, that's their problem," Karen said. Then she looked at the bottle and frowned. "Wait a minute. It's expired."

"Don't worry about it," I responded. "Sunscreen chemicals are extremely stable. They never used to have an expiration date, but the government makes them put one on because over time, the viscosity can be affected, or they can get micro contamination from multiple use."

"What does viscosity mean?"

"Thickness — that's the scientific word. We even had an instrument — a viscometer — in the lab with a metal spindle that we lowered into the cream. It twirled and measured the viscosity."

"Oh, I like that word. Viscosity!" Karen said as she reclined in her chair.

I glanced at my watch. Three-thirty. "I guess the sun isn't so strong now. I won't put any on either."

After all, I had my wide-brimmed hat — always a necessity lest my bald spot burn — shorts and a short-sleeved shirt. Karen was in a black beach cover-up and a large beige hat, but our daughters only wore bikinis and no hats. At least, they had sunglasses on. We spent a few hours inhaling the salt sea air and enjoying the warm breeze. Twenty-eight degrees Celsius: a big change from minus fifteen at home.

*

The next morning, I noticed that my skin was slightly pink, surprising given the time of day we'd been by the water. Still, it was too little to worry about. As Karen showered, I went into the hallway and tapped on the kids' door to check if they were awake. No answer, so I unlocked it with the spare key.

"Rise and shine girls," I yelled to the lumps in the twin beds.

No response, so I shook their feet. "Come on. We have to go downstairs for breakfast; there's a full buffet."

Jackie rolled onto her other side. "That's okay. I'm not going."

"Me neither. I'm not hungry," Meggy said without opening her eyes.

I tried to cajole them for a few more minutes, then gave up and left with Karen for breakfast, disheartened.

"That's okay. They're tired," Karen said, tucking into a plate of scrambled eggs and fruit. "It's their holiday, too, so if they'd rather sleep, so be it."

"I guess," I mumbled and took a sip of coffee. No point in letting them spoil my mood.

It turned out; they weren't just sleepy — they were burned.

"I'm fried," Jackie wailed when we tried to rouse them after breakfast.

"I didn't think the sun would be so strong," Meggy whimpered from her bed.

"Okay." I sighed. "Now you understand why I always put

sunscreen on. The sun's rays are stronger down here, and the sand reflects the ultraviolet light to give you double the dose." I looked at Jackie's red face. "Besides, you burn fast if you're blonde and blue-eyed."

I sympathized with Jackie. Like me, her skin burned easily. As Woody Allen said, "I don't tan — I stroke!" Meggy, on the other hand, took after Karen, whose skin had more melanin, and tanned a nicer colour than either me or Jackie.

"You were right, Dad," Jackie whimpered, "but I don't feel well. I want to stay in bed,"

And that was what they did for the entire day.

*

The next day, Karen suggested we go shopping.

"Why? Are we being punished?" I said sullenly. Shopping on holiday was my definition of purgatory.

Karen stared at me. "Ha-ha. Well, the girls need an activity that is out of the sun, and I want to get some souvenirs."

I had to agree. There really wasn't a choice. They marched me through a number of shops in Nassau, all offering the same junky trinkets and shirts for sale. It was endless and very tedious and reminded me of when I was five years old and had to go shopping with my mother. Waiting endlessly in stores with no toys. Good grief, is there anything more boring? Then I wondered — did I ever like shopping? My thoughts were interrupted by the sight of another disinterested tourist, probably a husband, stepping out onto the porch where I waited.

After a while, Karen and the girls came out of the store with a bag of T-shirts, which they showed me.

Karen looked at me with a smile. "You're funny. The girls said, 'Who's Dad talking to?' and I said, 'Oh, that's his new best friend!'"

I grinned sheepishly. "Yeah, he's a nice guy — from New Jersey. We were comparing things to see on the island."

"You learned that from me, dear," she said smugly.

"You're right. I did."

I used to figure, why bother talking to strangers? I'd never see them again. But I learned by watching Karen that you often get valuable information from others, and besides, it's enjoyable. Yes, she was right; she did influence me.

*

We spent the next few days exploring the island and swimming at the beach, but it seemed quieter without Eric. At least, it did until Wednesday when there was an invasion. The beach and pools swarmed with hordes of rambunctious young people making merry. Karen asked the front desk what happened, given that it had been blissfully calm beforehand.

Two hundred college students had flown in for a three-day spring break holiday. More specifically, a sorority of attractive young women in skimpy bikinis with a few boyfriends in tow.

"Keep your eyes in your head, dear!" Karen instructed. "They're young enough to be your daughters."

Uggh! Karen can be a complete buzzkill at times. But besides being easy on the eyes, they were fun to watch. And the owner of the cruise ship in the harbour was ecstatic. Dressed in sailor whites with a captain's hat, he had walked up and down the hot beach all week in an effort to sell tickets to his excursion.

Karen shook him off. "He said it only sails in this bay, and all drinks are included. It's a booze cruise, and we're not interested."

But now the captain and his crew had customers. When the boarding horn sounded, the gang that had been drinking and tanning on the sand in front of us skipped over to the dock, drinks in hand. The boat pulled out and veered to the right, blasting its music to show the people on shore how much fun they were missing. When they lit into "Sweet Home Alabama," a loud cheer rose from all on board. Fifteen minutes later, they were back, motoring in the other direction. Each time they passed by the resort, they played "Sweet Home Alabama," hoping to entice more clients for the next day's cruise. After twenty minutes, they returned to dock and released the party animals.

"I never feel the urge to drink sitting on a beach under the scorching sun. The alcohol would make me feel terrible," I whispered.

"I agree," she said, chuckling softly as we watched the gang stretched out again on their blankets with plastic cups in their hands.

*

Walking from the shoreline to the resort for lunch, we had to be careful not to step on one of the young people. They were all over the pool area, sitting on chairs or lying on towels.

"Those kids will be tired tonight," Karen said. If our daughters wished to be part of this young group, they didn't show it. They seemed to be having a grand time with us.

During the night, there was a noise at one o'clock in the morning. Karen whispered, "Andrew, there's someone in the hall."

"Mmmh," I mumbled, half asleep. If I got up, I wouldn't be able to sleep anymore. But if I lay there, maybe I could doze off again.

Again, there was this noise, a small tapping sound. "Anna, let me in ... tap tap ... Anna, let me in...."

It continued over and over until Karen finally said, "I'll see who it is."

"Be careful," I mumbled, as she got up. "Don't go into the hall." I lay there listening to muffled voices.

Then Karen came back. "I'm lending her something," she said as she passed by the bed. "The poor girl is naked."

Now I was definitely awake.

I listened for another minute before she returned, and we both drifted off to sleep again. I relaxed because I knew I'd get a full account over breakfast. As the girls gathered food from the buffet, a smiling Bahamian waitress brought coffee. When she left, and our daughters returned, Karen told us the story.

*

Half asleep, she had cracked open the door only to find a young woman, undoubtedly one of the Alabama group, knocking lightly on the room beside us. She was attempting to rouse her roommate without awakening the whole floor. A security guard stood at the far end of the hallway observing her. When Karen asked what the matter was, she explained that she had been locked out.

Karen nodded and said, "Go to reception, honey, and they'll give you a key."

"I can't because I'm naked."

She opened her eyes wider and saw the girl standing with arms crossed to cover her breasts and wearing only a small pair of panties. "Wait a minute, and I'll get you something to wear," Karen said.

The knocking stopped while she waited. Karen returned and handed her a T-shirt. "Here, honey, take this. Don't worry about it. We bought it as a souvenir. You can have it."

The young lady thanked her, and Karen came back to bed.

"You did a nice thing for her, dear. That was very gracious of you."

"I felt sorry for her. Something must have happened to put her in that situation."

Jackie asked several questions, explaining she had slept through the entire incident.

"You mean you missed Naked Girl?" I teased. "Your mother was kind and helped her out."

Karen looked up from her eggs. "Oh, it's the least I could do. Poor girl. Imagine how she felt. I only hope somebody would help our kids if they were ever in a similar spot."

"Hopefully, they never will be," I added, touching the wooden table. I smiled absently and Karen nudged me. "I'm sorry," I said, sitting up straighter. "I was just imagining what might have caused her to return to her room with no clothes on."

"Oh, stop it!" she giggled.

That afternoon, we discovered the T-shirt tied around our doorknob.

*

The next day, we travelled to Paradise Island so the kids could do a dolphin encounter. They had been too young when we went to Florida, where Eric swam with them. I was just as happy. With our dollar worth only sixty-two American cents, it was too expensive. I could have bought a dolphin for what it would have cost us all to swim with them. This attraction was more affordable, but it still was a great show. Ten dolphins lined up in the lagoon, each opposite a person floating in a life jacket. When the trainer's whistle blew, the dolphins approached their partner, shook hands with their fins, danced with them, kissed their cheek and then started a splashing contest with their partner. Everyone had fun. Then our daughters posed for a picture with their dolphins. Meggy, raven-haired in a red bikini, and Jackie, blonde in a pink one. The two dolphins smiled as broadly as the girls.

When they finished, they were directed to swim away so another group could take their place. As they did, a dolphin farther down the line broke rank and followed them. It insisted on repeating the same routine again with Meggy, much to her embarrassment and the trainer's annoyance. Something about Meggy had drawn the rogue dolphin to her. She always had a special way with animals, and we called her the Dolphin Whisperer for the rest of the trip.

*

When we reached the resort, Jackie and I headed to our rooms to change, while Karen and Meggy grabbed a table for dinner. Two young women, with dripping hair and wearing towels over their bathing suits, were already in the elevator when we reached it.

"How's the water?" I asked. They had obviously come from the pool.

The short brunette perked up and smiled. "Oh, it's good. A bit cold but good." She pulled the towel closer around her. The husky voice sounded familiar. I glanced at the panel. We were on the 14th floor, and no other button was pushed, so they were headed there, too. When we reached the destination, we let them exit first.

As we followed them down the hallway, I motioned to Jackie to walk slower. Sure enough, they entered the suite next to ours.

I laughed softly. "That's her, the Naked Girl. The one who woke us up banging on her door. I recognized the voice."

Jackie chuckled but didn't seem that interested. However, Karen was.

"What did she look like? I was too tired to notice," she asked at dinner.

"Uh, pretty..." I thought for a minute, "close to Meggy's height, dark hair and friendly."

"Did she realize you were their neighbour?"

"No, they walked ahead and reached their room first." I smiled smugly. "I recognized her voice, though. It's distinctive — husky, almost hoarse. I can still hear her calling, '*Anna ... Anna, let me in.*'"

"Oh well, I'm glad she's okay."

The next day, we took an excursion on the other side of the island to swim with the sharks. This was Karen's idea, and while I wasn't keen on it, I wasn't prepared to let her do it alone. The girls came along for the ride but steadfastly remained in the boat. With twenty other tourists, we climbed into the ocean and peered downwards through our masks. A metal cage holding chum (fresh chunks of fish meat) was suspended about a hundred feet below, and twenty small reef sharks were swimming around the bait. I floated nervously on the surface, thinking of the movie Jaws and worrying that the crowd of tourists, swimming, splashing and kicking the water, might attract the beasts away from their designated meal below. Finally, our time was up, and I breathed a sigh of relief. As the crowd moved towards the boat, I hurried Karen aboard, fearful that the commotion involved in reboarding might draw the sharks.

Karen dried off, and it was obvious she had enjoyed herself. "That was fun, but I hope it doesn't hurt them."

"No, they seemed happy," I assured her. "I even saw some grinning. Well, I think they were grinning because I saw their teeth."

"Oh, stop it," she laughed.

*

As we sat on the flight back to Toronto, the girls a few rows ahead of us, Karen looked at me.

"I can't believe we did that, Andrew, swam with the sharks, I mean. We must have been crazy."

"Speak for yourself. I didn't want to do it."

"Then why did you?"

I rolled my head around and took a large breath. "I couldn't let you do it alone in case something happened to you."

"Oh, that's nice. My honey was protecting me," she said and stared at me with love in her eyes. After a minute, she frowned. "I don't know why I did that. I must be having a midlife crisis or something."

I smiled. "Yeah, something called teenagers."

She leaned her head towards me and took my arm. "We needed this, Andrew, for our sanity, but also for bonding time with the girls."

It's true. On holiday with no school or pals, the kids were forced to spend all their time with us and we had fun together, which we didn't do often enough at home.

Because of this, I smiled and was foolish enough to be optimistic. Perhaps we'd turned a corner on the behaviour issues. Little did I know what was still to come.

21
THE BIRTHDAY SURPRISE

"Today me live in the moment, unless it's unpleasant in which case me will eat a cookie." - Cookie Monster

ANNA GREETED US cheerfully when we opened the door, but her welcome paled in comparison to Darla's, who, beside herself with joy, danced around, licking and sniffing each of us. Afterwards, she ran to her bowl and gulped down the food. In her usual fashion, she had been on a hunger strike during our absence, likely from fear we wouldn't return.

And we did Photoshop Eric into a picture: a beautiful one of us in our swimming suits under a tree by the ocean. Gloria found a photo of him in summer attire to match our outfits and did an excellent job popping him in beside us. It became the Christmas picture we would send to friends and family that year.

A honeymoon period followed, with no fighting or angry words, only the memory of our wonderful holiday together. Everybody was pretty chill. And being down south had also bestowed the sense that winter was behind us, which made everyone cheer up. And sure enough, the days flowed quickly into spring.

*

A voice called from upstairs, "Andrew, shouldn't you be leaving? I thought you were meeting Eric at one o'clock."

Leaving my roast beef sandwich on the table, I went into the hallway and shouted back, "Yes, dear, I'm having a quick bite first. And please don't yell from upstairs. Come down and talk to me."

When I returned to the kitchen, there she was, the demon cat with my lunch on the floor. Miss Piggy had struck again.

"Moochie! Get out of here!" She didn't budge, so I pushed her with my foot. That still didn't move her. She just grabbed chunks of meat faster, trying to wolf down as much as possible. "Stop it!" I yelled and smacked her bottom. "Bad cat!"

She shuffled stiffly a few feet away, where she chewed the remnants in her mouth. I scooped up what little was left and threw it in the garbage. The bane of my life must have climbed up on my chair to pull it off, and I had fed her before I sat down to eat!

Now I had to make a replacement meal quickly. I opened a tin of pork and beans and ate them miserably while Darla watched me. The splash of white on her chest and throat was all that stood out in the black shape by the entranceway. Even her eyes were dark brown. Moochie had wisely vacated the vicinity.

"Good dog, Darla. You wouldn't do that, would you, girl?" Darla perked up, thinking I might be offering my meal.

Then something came to mind. I remembered coming back from the washroom one day and discovering an empty saucer on the coffee table. Didn't I have a cookie on that plate? Not a crumb remained, and I didn't recall eating it. Darla watched me curiously as I scrutinized her face. She looked guilty, but then she always did, a common characteristic in rescue dogs no doubt. She was a wonderful dog, and while I had my suspicions, I could never prove she'd eaten that cookie. I was stumped. However, it has been my experience over the years that pets have their own personalities and peculiarities. Moochie was an unabashed pig about food, while Darla was a sneaky thief.

*

The university term finished, and Eric needed my help moving again. His roommates were graduating, but because he took the co-op program with an additional year of studies, he wasn't finished and needed to find another shared accommodation. I drove out to Hamilton, and we loaded the van with his things, then made our way to the new place which he would share with three other students. The afternoon sun was shining, and the streets were busy with carefree students and parents moving in or out of accommodations. Garbage bags and cast-off furniture sat idly at the curb on both sides of the street, waiting for pickup. As we pulled into his new driveway, I observed it was yet another rundown house rented to students with low expectations.

But I hopped out eagerly. It was exhilarating to help him begin a new chapter in life. As I carried in a container of kitchen supplies, I glimpsed two tall young men moving between rooms, unpacking and arranging things. I noted that his new kitchen was smaller than the previous one, and bins covered the counter and floor. A short, perky brunette introduced herself as Emily, or Em for short, smiled and directed me to take my box back to the van.

"We already have enough plates and cooking utensils," she said without even bothering to examine its contents. I gaped in surprise; Em had clearly taken charge.

Next, we carried the box spring and mattress out of the van and up a steep flight of stairs. "I wouldn't want to climb these after a night in the pub, Sonny," I said as my feet felt the soft carpeted edges of the steps. "You'll go flying down them."

Eric grinned while handling his end easily. "Yes, Father, hilarious, ha-ha-ha."

I didn't get a chance to meet the other boys; they had left by the time we came downstairs. When we finished unloading, Eric thanked me and quickly hustled me out. I seemed to have been the only parent present. The others must have moved in by themselves.

Returning home, Karen asked my opinion of his new place. "It's smaller and not as nice as the other house, but it'll probably suit him fine," I answered diplomatically, not admitting the truth that it was a dump.

I had noticed a tap in the upstairs bathroom sink dripped continuously, and there was a significant hole in the exterior wall that would let flies and other bugs enter. I offered to come back and fix these items. Landlords of student rentals are notoriously unresponsive, so unless it's major, you're better off repairing it yourself.

But Eric shook his head. "We'll all be out of here in a year, and we really don't care."

Despite my feeling otherwise, I had to accept his decision. Later that fall, the sewer would back up and flood the basement, making it miserable for the guy who lived down there. Fortunately, Eric was unaffected, having taken the higher ground. The landlord repaired it but not as fast as they wished and only provided a temporary fix. He said he didn't want to spend a lot of money because he planned to sell the building when their lease was up. However, when Eric left the following spring, it was still posted for rent.

*

In May, we geared up to celebrate Jackie's sixteenth birthday with a special dinner at home. Gifts were purchased, her choice of meal selected, and Karen made a special run to pick up the cake. Late Saturday afternoon, Eric arrived with Gloria and fussed over his little sister's sweet sixteen.

Looking out the patio door, I noticed a dark brooding bank of clouds in the sky.

"I think we might be in for a thunderstorm," I commented as we sat down at the table.

Karen had set out the best china, and we chatted around a dinner of oven-roasted rack of lamb and vegetables that I had prepared. When we finished, Meggy offered to make decaf coffee and tea, and Karen stood up to make an announcement.

"We have an ice cream cake for dessert!" she declared, and this was met with murmurs of eager anticipation. She grinned girlishly as she placed the candles into the cake.

"Okay, I'll light it, and we can all sing 'Happy Birthday.'"

Jackie got up and strolled over to the counter to check out the inscription. She froze on the spot. "This is Reese's Pieces," she declared. "I hate this cake!"

Karen looked confused. "What do you mean? Reese's Pieces is your favourite."

The rest of us stared in disbelief.

"No, it's not!" Jackie insisted and her eyes shot laser beams at her mother. "It's Eric's favourite! You don't even know what I like."

The cake sat there with half the candles lit while Karen protested, the lighter still tightly clasped in her hand "I'm sorry. I can't remember what everyone likes and dislikes. But it's a nice cake!"

"Oh, my God, I told you last year. This is the *second* time you've done this to me," Jackie roared. Then she spun around on her heels, and stomped out of the room yelling, "Arggh!"

Everyone glanced at each other, not sure what to do. Our daughter had freaked out in the presence of Eric's girlfriend, and we were mortified.

Karen brought slices of the cake to the table and tried to fill the awkward silence. "You have a sister, Gloria, so I'm sure you're used to these things."

We ate quietly, and when we finished, Gloria spoke up. "I think Jackie should open the gifts now. I have something that might make her feel better."

Karen brought Jackie back to the table, and as she stood sullenly, Gloria placed a wrapped box in front of her.

She squealed on opening it, "Oh, I love it!" And she gave Gloria a heartfelt hug. "Thank you!"

We squeezed beside her and peeked into the box. It was a giant cookie with the words, '*Happy 16th Birthday*' written in white icing.

Handing Jackie a plate, Karen gave Gloria a big smile. "You really saved the day."

I echoed the sentiment. "You're our hero."

"I'm glad it helped," Gloria laughed.

The storm clouds rolled away, and the sun came out. The evening had been salvaged.

*

A few days later, Jackie rummaged through the fridge. "Where's my cookie?"

"It's there. Search for it," I answered. She always did this, calling for help before making an effort. After more shouts from her, I threw my serviette down and pushed my chair back. "Alright, alright! I'll get it for you. Honestly, you couldn't find something if it bit you in the ass."

Standing arms crossed, she watched me. "See, it's not there."

"Just a minute. Let me move this." I rustled some containers and bottles around. "Okay, I don't see it."

"I *told* you," she cried, and her face clouded over.

"Let me ask your mother, but take a look downstairs in case she put it in that fridge."

Karen was upstairs sitting on our bed folding laundry when I found her.

"Where'd you put her cookie?" I asked. "We've searched everywhere."

She lifted her head briefly and put it down again. "I ate it," she said matter-of-factly.

I stared open-mouthed and heard Jackie go ballistic downstairs.

"You ate my birthday cookie. I hate you!"

Somehow the radar ears had heard. While listening to the ranting below, I leaned against the dresser, feeling like the roof had fallen in. "Why did you eat it?" I said weakly.

"Oh, I just had a little piece one day, then another, and then another. It was delicious," she said with satisfaction.

"But that was her gift."

"I thought she forgot about it. Besides," Karen frowned, "I was mad at her."

I gazed at the ceiling. "Great, but that's really not going to help us now."

Sometimes, I think I have four children. And I realized that people at work are much easier to deal with: they listen to me; nobody has a meltdown, and no one eats someone else's food or steals their beer. Simple rules for a happy life.

The dust had settled by Thursday when Eric phoned.

"What??? You ate it, Mom? You shouldn't have done that," the tin voice squealed from the speaker.

"She pissed me off, okay? She was such a brat at the party, and besides, it was very tasty."

More plaintive squawks were emitted from the phone.

Karen became cross. "Look, I apologized, and I don't want to be scolded about it."

And that was the end of it for the time being.

Eric and Gloria returned for dinner the following weekend and brought a second big cookie. Jackie giggled as she read the inscription. "Property of Jackie. No one else is allowed to eat it! Hear that, Mom!"

The room erupted with laughter, and we all embraced her. Afterwards, we told Eric that Gloria was a keeper. How many girlfriends would return with a second cookie? Most of them would have run for the hills; I know I wanted to. The best part was that Karen managed to keep her mitts and mouth off, and Jackie munched happily on her special dessert all week.

*

Karen booked a consultation with Dr. MacEwan a few weeks later about the birthday meltdown and other issues. In fact, we both visited him separately to try to improve our family dynamics. In the end, he arranged an appointment with the Child & Adolescent Psychiatrist at the local hospital. At first, Jackie refused to consider it, but we remained adamant.

"I'm taking you, or your cell phone will disappear forever," Karen threatened.

She obeyed, and they updated me afterwards.

"We saw Dr. Bhatt, the psychiatrist, today," Karen said, and her voice was chipper. Jackie's head was down, concentrating on the meal on her plate.

"How did it go?"

"Well, I went into his office with her and talked about the behaviour, and he had her complete a test. After evaluating the results, he concluded that she has Attention Deficit Disorder or ADD."

I smiled weakly at Jackie. "I guess that explains why you had trouble focusing on math." But the fact that I may have misjudged her didn't register with my daughter.

"He pointed at Mother and said she has it too, ha-ha," she declared, trumpeting the news. "He said I got it from her because there's a genetic component."

"What?"

The fact that a psychiatrist would assign a medical condition to Karen without an evaluation shocked me, although his conclusion didn't. Karen was hyperactive but never had a label attached to it. Our friend Vicky called her Hurricane Karen because she was constantly in motion.

Karen nodded solemnly. "Yes, he did, and I'm angry about that. He never should have said that with her in the room."

Then she said to Jackie, "Maybe I have it, but I've controlled it with exercise. You don't exercise. That's the problem." She faced me again. "He prescribed medication to control her restlessness and increase her attention span, and we're to see him again next week."

And so, they dutifully trekked back to Dr. Bhatt. After a brief discussion, he told Jackie, "Everything is fine. You needn't see me again, but continue with the medicine, and check in with your family physician. I'll send him my report."

When they stood up to leave, Karen asked to speak with him alone for a minute. Jackie waited outside. She drew herself up to her full height and let him have it.

"I said he crossed the line and was very unprofessional," she said, recapping the conversation for me. "I told him, 'you should never have said that in front of my daughter — my teenage daughter, for Pete's sake! You just handed her ammunition to use against me.'"

I felt the feelings of respect and pride surge through me. Her courage and forthrightness constantly impressed me. She didn't care if it was a doctor, lawyer, or the Prime Minister himself; they weren't getting away with anything that wasn't right. She was one feisty woman.

"What did he say to that?" I asked, as my mind formed a picture of her lecturing the doctor.

She smiled like a cat with a mouse. "At first, he sat there, with his eyes darting around, and then he looked as if he swallowed a bug. But he did apologize. He realized he was wrong. I told him I had controlled my ADD with exercise, got an honour's degree, held many successful jobs and raised three kids — so I didn't have a problem."

"Well, good for you, honey," I stammered. "I'm glad you brought it up because I know it bothered you."

She paused with an air of satisfaction. The doctor had annoyed her, but she made him see the error of his ways and, in the end, parted on friendly terms. Karen quite enjoyed putting someone in their place. "I respected him, though, for apologizing."

They had been given a pamphlet on ADD, and the more I read about the condition, the more it explained our youngest's behaviour. Teenagers with this condition have more negative moods, such as anger, anxiety, stress and sadness. Some also have a coexisting affliction, such as Oppositional Defiance Disorder, which leads to acts of stubbornness, outbursts of temper and defiance. I put the pamphlet down and digested this information. That explained why Jackie repeatedly challenged us, often playing one parent off against the other. Defiance was certainly an attribute we experienced. Hopefully, the medication would reduce the moodiness and improve her attention. Without that and prayer, we were helplessly out of our depth.

*

After a month without visible improvement, I booked a session with Dr. MacEwan. He entered and settled in the chair at his desk. He listened as I updated him on the situation at home.

"Jackie continues to lie, disobey our rules and be very angry, often swearing at Karen. The medicine doesn't appear to be helping, and she gets everyone upset."

He leaned forward, and I noticed for the first time that he had more grey hair than I recalled on previous visits. No longer primarily at his temples, grey was streaked throughout his black mop, giving the hair a salt and pepper appearance. "The medicine needs more time to work, but it's quite possible it won't stop her rebelliousness. You may have to kick her out of the house."

I looked at the floor for a moment in shock, before returning my gaze to him. "I'm not sure Karen would agree to that."

He studied me carefully before he spoke. "Until you two are on the same page and get tough with her, nothing will change."

I nodded and shuffled out of his office, knowing he was right, but wondering how on earth I would be able to bring Karen in line. Maybe when she saw Dr. MacEwan again, the message would sink in.

The holiday had been a bright spot in the past few months and made me realize how important it was to treasure those breaks from constant conflict. In some ways, the initial period afterwards would be like the eye of a storm — that calm region at the centre where all is momentarily peaceful until the fury hits again.

THE MARATHON

"My doctor told me that jogging could add years to my life. I think he was right. I feel ten years older already." - Milton Berle

WHILE WRESTLING WITH our problems with Jackie, we maintained our exercise regime. Karen biked every day, and I jogged at least three days a week after work. Running calmed me down, helped me forget my troubles and stress for the moment and energized me. If I missed a week when travelling, the lack of exercise left me lethargic. When they were little, the kids would peddle alongside me on their bikes, receiving the odd push to keep up, and we hoped they would learn the benefits of exercise when they grew older.

Eric was the first to take up jogging as a teenager, but he didn't have the stamina. I'd jog around him in circles as we ran and say, "Do you think you'll be in as good a shape as me when you're my age? Because you're not now! Ha-ha-ha."

He'd simply grinned good-naturedly in response. And when he reached grade 12, he asked me to join a health club with him, to which I eagerly agreed. There was a club nearby that provided a free fitness assessment and an improvement plan to members, so we signed up.

The assessment was done on our first visit. A tall, athletic-looking trainer, in his late twenties, put us through thirty minutes of steps, calisthenics, treadmill and stretching exercises and then checked out pulses. After discussing Eric's results, he turned to me and perused the data.

"Sir, you have the cardiovascular fitness of a man in his twenties, and ... the flexibility of an eighty-year-old."

My son hooted while I chuckled sheepishly. I'd never been very flexible, so it wasn't a big surprise, although the comparison to an eighty-year-old was. When we returned home, Eric delighted himself in sharing my results with the family, who also found it hilarious.

Throughout the year, we attended the gym regularly, but my body never did become more limber. However, it was a successful impetus for Eric, who kept up an exercise routine at university. Recently, Meggy started jogging too, which pleased me even more. All things considered, having two out of three children in fitness regimes seemed pretty good.

*

Friday was the start of summer hours at work, so I arrived home right after lunch. I headed downstairs, brought up two bottles of beer and a bag of chips and lay on the couch to eat them, listen to music and savour the freedom of an early escape from the office.

As I finished the second bottle, Meggy jumped into the room in shorts and a T-shirt. "Come jog with me, Dad."

"What? No, I'm sorry. I can't. I just finished drinking beer. Besides, I ran with you yesterday."

"Come on, Dad," she pleaded, "you used to go with Eric, and it's better for you than eating chips. Join me. It'll be fun!"

I mulled it over. If I refused, she might think that since I had jogged with her brother years ago, I had grown older and lazier.

"Okay, okay," I said, sitting up, brushing chip crumbs off my shirt and hustling upstairs to change. She was right. This would be healthier than eating more chips. Besides, the sooner I got this over with, the sooner I could return to my lazy afternoon.

While I laced up my shoes, Meggy stretched and bounced beside me. Her enthusiasm was contagious. Maybe this would do me good after all. I locked the door and put the key in my pocket.

"Take it easy. Remember, I drank all that beer."

She was elated and zipped down the road at a steady pace. But my energy quickly waned, and I realized this was going to be an endurance test. Why did I eat all those chips and drink that beer? I felt the liquid sloshing around in my stomach and the chips began to repeat on me as I lumbered slowly down the street. Meggy enjoyed it and, for a while, ran backwards while teasing me for lagging — like I used to do to her when she was younger.

I let a belch rip, and a burning pain stabbed me under the ribcage. This was going to be worse than I thought.

In no time, she was a hundred yards ahead, so I pushed myself and lurched forward, gasping and burping while rubbing the stitch in my side. Why did I ever agree to this? Then she was back, laughing and poking me in the stomach with encouragement, before sprinting off again. How sweet her revenge must have been for me making fun of her years ago.

Thankfully, we reached a juncture where we agreed she would continue while I headed home. With a quick wave, we separated. As soon as she disappeared from sight, I stopped and walked the rest of the way, massaging my side all the way. That was bad. Never again will I jog after drinking.

*

Only a few weeks later, Meggy announced she had registered for a half-marathon run, which is twenty-one kilometres or thirteen miles if you prefer mileage, which I do. Funny, I'm very comfortable with the metric system at work but not in my personal life. Canada used imperial units when I grew up, and I still visualize human height, weight and distance better in those terms.

Karen and I sat stone-faced when Meggy told us the news; neither of us had ever run that far. But even though we had concerns, it didn't faze her. She began a daily jog through the neighbourhood and joined a running club to train for longer ranges.

Perhaps it was a catharsis for the stress and emotional strain she endured looking for work. She had graduated last year with considerable assistance from us on her assignments. Anxiety and procrastination had made high school difficult, and we celebrated this milestone with a blend of pride and relief. It hasn't been easy for her to land a job. She's not aggressive by nature. Karen, on the other hand, can hustle and always excelled at finding employment. With her drive and enthusiasm, she was often the first person interviewed and subsequently hired. One summer during university, Karen approached the Addiction Research Foundation and asked to speak to the HR manager.

Upon hearing from her that there were no openings, Karen asked brightly, "What about upcoming maternity leaves? You could hire me. I'd stay for the summer, and you'd save the agency fee for a temporary worker. It would be a win-win for both of us."

The woman blinked and gathered her thoughts. "Actually, we do have someone going on mat leave," she said and immediately offered the position to a delighted Karen. She worked there as a clerk all summer, and it was an organization in her field of study. We'd only been married a year, and even though I was a manager, I would never have thought of or had the nerve to make such a proposal myself. Yes, Karen was a go-getter, and her gumption always impressed me. If our children inherited a bit of that, it would serve them well.

Her classmates had also struggled to obtain work. So, Karen

invited a couple of school friends, Jim and Hannah, and their parents for dinner, to help them reconnect and stay motivated. She had made their acquaintances at extracurricular events and found them to be lots of fun.

"You'll like them. They're very nice," she said, prepping me as I readied the barbeque. "Jim's father, Rob, is a lawyer, and Hannah's is a firefighter. I forget what the mothers do, but they have interesting careers, too."

We were experiencing a period of early heat, but despite the hot weather, Karen had prepared the patio table for us to eat on outside. The protective cover had been removed and a plastic tablecloth pinned on it. Karen had made a couple of salads, and I was in charge of grilling chicken breasts and sausages coated with a light barbecue sauce. Soon the sounds of guests arriving could be heard, and I went into the kitchen to greet them.

"Hi, I'm Rob." A man with thinning light brown hair stretched out a hand towards me, and I shook it. Karen was right, Rob struck me immediately as an affable gent, and I knew we'd have fun together. He introduced his wife, June, who had a pleasant, maternal appearance. Behind him, a sandy-haired fellow, about six-foot-three, stood beside a short, pretty brunette and smiled from the entrance. In high spirits, Karen chattered loudly to everyone, offering drinks while I weaved my way through to meet Tom, the firefighter, and his spouse, Cathy.

The kids did their own thing while the parents sat on the patio and talked. The conversation moved to travel and holidays, which Karen had a tendency to steer it towards, and she mentioned that we had rented a cottage last summer.

She became animated as she recalled the fun we had. "Oh, and we ate dinner at this fabulous restaurant on a nearby lake. Maybe you've heard of the place. It had a great big dick over the water."

I chuckled. "I think you mean deck, dear."

Her eyebrows shot up. "What did I say?"

"You said dick — that it had a great big dick over the lake."

She squealed with laughter, and everybody joined in. Rob said it must have been a Freudian slip.

"Yes, that's what it was, ha-ha," Karen guffawed. "How embarrassing!"

It certainly loosened the group up. Talk began to flow even easier after that, and everyone seemed to enjoy the social time and Karen's beautiful gardens.

*

After dinner, we discussed the kids' prospects; none had found employment. Rob told us Jim had interviewed for a car sales position. Then he glanced around, leaned forward and spoke softly as if sharing a secret.

"I dropped him off at the dealership and parked at the coffee shop in the same plaza to wait. I'd just gotten my coffee. I hadn't even put the lid on yet when he was at my side. I jumped because I didn't expect to see him so soon. So, I said, 'Let's sit down for minute.'" Rob snickered a little, then restrained himself in order to continue. "We sat down, he put his hands on the table, leaned back and said, 'I nailed it.' I looked at my watch and said, 'Really? Because that was pretty fast.'" At this point, Rob lost control, and we all laughed with him before he regained his composure. "He's got confidence, I'll give him that. Then I said, 'Jim, don't you think they might want someone with experience to sell their cars?'" This became too much for him. Rob's head went back and he laughed loudly, gasping, "He's eighteen ... no experience ... the interview lasted less than ten minutes ... and he thinks he nailed it!" He wiped tears away, straightened up, cleared his throat and added soberly, "I do give him credit, though, for getting the interview."

Everyone smiled and became quiet until June broke the silence. "It's funny how naive young people are, and bless their innocence."

We remained outside with our coffee even after it grew dark.

Karen lit candles, and everyone revelled in the warm evening and the comradeship of other parents with teenage kids. Meggy made plans for activities with her friends later in the month before we all said goodnight.

*

At the end of the week, I left the office early to drive to the Enercare Centre at the CNE and collect Meggy's event kit from the organizers. For thirty minutes, I followed a long line of cars winding towards the city's core until I was able to exit onto Lakeshore Drive and park close to the building. A maze of booths greeted me, with exhibitors offering free handouts or selling jogging-related wares. People wandered through kiosks chattering, and it seemed like I had stepped into a different world — a fraternity of athletes. The air was filled with the cheerful buzz of excitement, shared knowledge and love for exercise. I paused by a booth for a well-known track club. These people should be savvy about the realities of long-distance events. On an impulse, I approached the middle-aged gentleman standing inside it.

He looked at me expectantly, and I started to babble. "Excuse me, but my daughter has registered for this event, and I'm worried that she hasn't trained properly. She's been sick for the past two weeks and stopped jogging completely."

His gaze shifted to the crowd, and I had the impression he hadn't heard me or didn't want to be bothered by the question. But then he spoke while still gazing at the enthusiastic passersby. "Is she doing the full or half marathon?"

Relief flowed through me because there was empathy in his voice. "Half marathon," I answered.

His eyes flickered sideways to me. "How old is she?"

"Eighteen."

"Eighteen?" He guffawed and shook his head. "Don't worry. She'll be fine. They have rubber knees at that age."

"Really, you're sure?"

He nodded and broke into a smile.

"Thank you," I said. "That's a weight off my mind."

*

I found the area where kits were being dispensed at the end of the arena, and it was the largest section with a number of stations staffed by volunteers. Sidling up to a table where a few sat with papers in front and pens at the ready, I told a blonde-haired woman Meggy's name and bib number. The lady, whom I estimated to be in her forties, checked her list, made a notation and handed over a plastic bag. I rummaged through it. Among the contents were a route card, water bottle, event running shirt, a banner with her number on it, healthy snack bars and some miscellaneous coupons. This was fascinating, but I wasn't sure what to do with the banner.

I went back to the table and enquired how the numbered banner would attach to my daughter's shirt. The woman at first seemed surprised, then appeared to deduce that I was a rookie. Smiling, she spoke patiently. "That's the bib. She has to pin it to her shirt. There should be four pins inside the bag." I searched again and nodded. "That's important because it tracks her time," she said and, noting my confounded expression, added, "There's a timing chip on the back."

My jaw went slack, and I felt my eyebrows raise. "Really? Isn't that something?" I thanked her and made my way out.

*

In the morning, the alarm went off at six a.m., and Karen and I staggered out of bed. We honestly didn't expect Meggy to get up in time for the race. She's not an early riser and often cancels things at the last minute. It'd be no surprise if she rolled over in bed and said she wasn't going. Surprisingly, she appeared in the kitchen moments later dressed in her shirt with the bib pinned on and her eyes shining with excitement.

"You look great, honey!" I cried as her zeal rubbed off on me.

We piled into the van, leaving Jackie asleep in her bed, and drove to North York. Motoring up Yonge Street, we could see the preparations for the competition had been put in place. Two lanes had been blocked off from cars, and race monitors and police stood spaced out at regular intervals along the route. I was impressed. This was more prodigious than I had expected. It was a major event.

"I'll have to drop you off and find a parking spot," I said, gesturing at the endless row of vehicles lining the curb. Karen began to protest, but I cut her off. "There's only fifteen minutes before starting time. I'll park and catch up to you."

I watched until they were safely across the street and then moved on. Locating parking wouldn't be easy; cars were everywhere. I turned off the main drag and drove down block after block of side streets packed full of cars.

Finally, I found a spot about a mile away and hurried back. I was still striding briskly along when the gun went off at Mel Lastman Square. A wall of runners surged towards me. I stepped onto the sidewalk, camera ready, and scanned the swarm for Meggy but never saw her. Once the melee disappeared, I ambled along the road, now deserted with the exception of the odd straggler. Then I spotted Karen waving with a big smile on her face.

"I missed her!" I moaned.

"So did I," she laughed. "There were so many that I couldn't pick her out."

"Oh well, we can take a picture of her at the finish line."

As we trudged to the van, I noticed Karen's limp and worried about her ability to walk all the way to the van. She had inherited the osteoarthritis that had destroyed her father's knees and now affected her.

"I had to park far away. Why don't you wait, and I'll come get you?"

She grabbed my arm for support and shrugged off the concern. "I'm fine. Never fear. Let's stay together."

*

Karen was stubborn, but she made it the whole way. I set the GPS for Ontario Place and started driving.

"Listen to that!" I gasped. "The radio said there are over 10,000 participants in this thing. Add in spectators as well, and you've got significant gridlock. Mind you, I guess we have more than that number downtown when the Leafs, Jays and Raptors all play on the same night."

But Karen wasn't listening. Something ahead on the road had her attention. "The road's closed," she said. "They're directing traffic to the right."

I altered course. "Recalculating..." Betsy, the female GPS voice announced.

This scenario replayed a few more times, and I grew concerned. "This is taking forever."

"Wait a minute. Let me get the map and figure out a better route." Karen loved maps and directing me, but I preferred the GPS. She poured over it, concentrating and muttering to herself, before yelling, "Here! Turn left at the next street." She pointed ahead.

I followed her lead. "Recalculating..." Betsy announced.

"Turn that off," she said, annoyed. "We don't need her anymore; I have the map."

"But it displays the expected arrival time so I can tell how we're doing."

The pleasant voice continued calmly, "Turn right at the second street."

"Ignore her," Karen said quickly. "She doesn't know what she's talking about."

The rest of the journey continued like this; me with my two GPSs: Betsy persistently trying to guide me, while Karen shouted alternate instructions and told her to shut up.

"But I like her voice," I insisted. A couple of times, I chose the GPS path over hers, and this irked Karen so much, I became suspicious that she might actually be jealous of Betsy.

Karen studied the map and mumbled, "Okay, I can see why she's saying that. That'll work."

Of course, it will, a voice in my head said. *She's a computer.* But I said nothing. The sunshine beat down, bouncing off store windows in blinding flashes, and we motored past outdoor fruit and vegetable stands scattered along the boulevards.

"Did you know you can change the voice?" I said while waiting at a traffic signal. "Wouldn't it be great if they had funny voices, like a German — *Achtung! Turn right, you dummkopf!* Or an insulting Don Rickles — *I said left, you idiot. Now you've really screwed up!*"

But Karen was lost in deliberation. "Yes, yes, very funny. Keep heading this way for a while, and then turn left. I'll tell you when."

Or Betsy will, said the voice again but not out loud. No need to rile her more than she already was.

*

Finally, we arrived at the Ontario Place parking lot, and I glanced at the clock. "We'd better hurry, dear."

Karen got out stiffly and gripped my hand for support. We found a terrific spot for a photo, a short distance before the finish line, where the runners rounded a corner by the lake. What a marvellous place to end the race. We gazed at the blue water and waited, camera poised, expecting her to appear any minute.

"I'm texting her to see where Meggy is," Karen said, typing on her cell.

"Good idea." I lowered the camera and relaxed.

"What? This doesn't make sense." She looked up, startled. "She said she's finished."

"She's done?"

"That's what she says."

We walked back past the finish line and found her standing amongst the dispersing masses with an aluminum foil blanket wrapped around herself. We had missed the start, and now we'd missed her finale. She had passed through ten minutes before we arrived. It took her two-and-a-half hours to jog the route and, with all the traffic, detours and stoplights, the same amount of time for us to drive it.

"Well done, honey!" I said, wrapping an arm around her. "I can't believe you ran the whole thing. How do you feel?"

She shivered but glowed happily. "Fine, just tired."

Karen high-fived her. "No wonder you're tired, but we're proud of you, honey. You were determined to run it, and you did."

It's immensely gratifying when one of your kids achieves an ambitious goal.

*

On the drive home, I reflected on how worried I'd been because Meggy didn't have a job and had stopped training before the big run. With teenagers, and life in general, it seems you have to prepare for the worst, hope for the best, and you'll usually end up somewhere in between.

THE REUNION

"Insanity runs in my family. It practically gallops." - Cary Grant

"**L**OOK AT THAT! What are they doing?"

A long flotilla with thirty to forty people of all ages drifted towards us as we walked across the bridge to a restaurant on the other side of the Rhine. Most wore bathing caps, all clung to large colourful flotation devices and appeared to be thoroughly enjoying themselves.

"Who, them?" Paul Schmidt gestured at the water. "They're cooling off," he said with the patient tone of someone explaining a simple everyday occurrence to a child.

I thought of my hot hotel room where the thirty-degree air hung heavy, and no breeze came through the window. Few buildings here have air-conditioning, and this was an old-fashioned way to adapt. I leaned over for a closer look as people passed underneath. "What are they holding on to?"

"The Wickelfisch? It's a flotation sack to put your clothes in, so you have them with you when you get out. You can buy them in town." He waved his hand towards the bank. "And there're change rooms stationed along the shore to shower and dress." His mouth curled into an amused smile, and he put his hands on the railing to observe both me and the swimmers.

"That makes sense," I said, digesting this information, "because the current's too strong to swim back upstream where you left your clothes." The sight made me grin. It was completely incongruous in a major waterway. Even now, transport barges motored by at a respectful distance from the swimmers. "I never expected swimmers to be in the Rhine. It seems like something people did a hundred years ago."

"Some people are actually quite committed to a daily swim. Bernhard Schultz, the clinical production head — you met him this week — swims every morning, showers and dresses over there," he said pointing to a station about 500 ft in front of us, "before catching a tram to the office. And he does this all summer until the water is too cold."

"Amazing! What a marvellous routine, much better than racing through traffic like I do."

We studied the bobbing heads for a few minutes longer. From the wide grins they sported, it appeared to be great fun, and I wished I were here longer so I could try it. This is one benefit of business travel that I really enjoy; the opportunity to drop in and experience the daily life of people in a foreign land.

*

When I arrived home on Saturday, as soon as I changed from business casual attire into more comfortable clothes, we took Darla for a walk. Karen was over the moon with her new pet.

"Aren't you glad we picked her?" Karen said as Darla pranced by the path. "She saved me, you know. If we hadn't got her, I would have had a nervous breakdown."

"Yes, dear, you needed her. She's your love puppy."

A constant bright spot in our daily lives, Darla had bonded the most with Karen. Whenever she went out, the dog sat by the front door and stared through the sidelight, waiting for her mommy to return. Smaller than a purebred, Darla was a black lab and border collie mix. The border collie characteristics were obvious in the way she tried to keep the family together when we walked. If someone lingered or sped ahead, Darla would strain at the leash trying to get to them and bring them back into the group.

Even though Eric wasn't home this weekend, I enjoyed catching up on the past week with the girls. But they didn't share our enthusiasm for the dog; they were still piqued at not getting their puppy.

"But see how cute she is?" Karen purred, pointing to where Darla lay watching our every bite. Fortunately, she was easily trained to stay out of the kitchen during meals. All I had to do was point and say, '*Bed!*' and she would saunter over to it and lay down.

"She met Duke the other day," Karen mentioned while we ate.

That's the small yellow lab that belongs to an older lady on the street. He was friendly and affectionate but high-strung because of a lack of exercise.

"How'd they get along?"

"Well, he tried to mount her, but she spun around, growled and chased him off."

"Oh my gosh." Jackie rolled her eyes.

Hmm, maybe Duke was too affectionate. I smiled to myself at the thought of this genteel woman, who treated her dog like a little prince, reacting in horror as he cavorted about in front of her. "What did Natalie do?"

"That was funny," Karen chortled. "She cringed and snapped, 'Stop that, Duke!' I could tell she was embarrassed so I said, 'Now,

now, Duke, Darla's not that kind of girl. You have to buy her dinner first!' That made her laugh."

"That was nice of you to put her at ease." Karen always knew the right thing to say. "While we love our pets, it's important to remember they're just animals after all," I added philosophically.

"Yes, but not you, Darla," she crooned gently to her pet. "You're part of the family." The tail started thumping at the sound of her name.

*

The next day, Karen made a trip to the local farmer's market and left Darla behind. It's too crowded, and they set the produce up outside on tables, which can tempt the beasts to help themselves.

"Boy, it was busy today," she cried, as she burst through the front door laden down with bags of fresh fruit and vegetables.

"Come on, girls, help your mother take the groceries downstairs," I instructed.

As they ran over to grab the bags, Karen's eyes widened. "Would you believe some people bring their dogs there? I saw two shoppers with pooches, and they couldn't separate them because the street was packed with people."

"It's tough when they're fighting."

She chuckled, "Oh, they weren't fighting... au contraire!"

I felt my eyes pop.

"Ewww!" Jackie wailed as she reappeared upstairs. Oblivious to most of the conversation, she managed to catch the indelicate part.

*

Towards the end of July, we were slated to visit Fort Erie for Karen's high school's twenty-fifth reunion.

More importantly, we were going without the kids. All week there was a wonderful sense of anticipation as we bustled through our activities and watched the weekend approach closer day by day.

We'd get a break, they'd have some independence, and Eric would chaperone his sisters so we wouldn't worry.

Without the girls, we packed up in record time, hardly fought at all and were now cruising peacefully on the Queen Elizabeth Way along the perimeter of Lake Ontario. The sun broke through the clouds and streamed down on the highway, and I felt myself unwinding.

"Why don't we go by the falls and take the Niagara Boulevard the rest of the way?" Karen said, relaxing in the seat beside me. "It's much prettier than the highway."

"Good idea. We're not in any rush," I said cheerfully, putting my sunglasses on.

"We don't need to stop and walk up to the falls unless you want to."

I looked at her and nodded. "No, that's fine. I'm happy to glimpse it as we drive by."

When the kids were young, we took many trips to Niagara Falls and Fort Erie. We'd walk up Clifton Hill, go through a haunted house, enjoy the winter light show during Christmas breaks and visit Karen's parents and friends. My favourite view of this wonder was at the fence directly in front of the brink of the falls, and I glanced over when it emerged on my left as I drove slowly past. With a cliff over 2000 ft wide, the sheer volume of water rushing over, thundering into the gorge below and spewing up huge mists, never failed to impress me. Karen reconnected with her inner child on those outings, soaking up the pure enjoyment of the moment.

"Isn't it beautiful, girls?" she'd shout gleefully over the roaring cascade.

We motored onto the picturesque Niagara Boulevard, with the river on one side and beautiful mansions on the other. Twenty minutes later, we reached Fort Erie, and I headed up Jarvis Street. Old shops lined the main street, which runs up the hill from the water, and evoked memories of movies set in small towns during the fifties. Even though Karen couldn't wait to leave, I'm a fan of it. It's exactly how I imagined a small town to be. It was nice that day, but autumn is especially pretty, with scarecrows, bales of straw and pumpkins on porches and leaves scattered over the lawns and streets. It stirs the imagination. When we last visited in the fall, I could almost picture Ichabod Crane plodding along the avenue on his horse.

As I reached the crest of the hill on Jarvis Street, I took a last glimpse in the mirror at the river flowing majestically on its way to the plunge over the falls. Americans flock across the border for a day trip on the Canadian side, which is one of the most scenic drives in North America. Ironic, considering the Doll House Museum in town served as a major endpoint of the Underground Railroad. President Obama visited it once, but I wonder how many tourists passed by the humble building, oblivious to its significance as a haven for escaping slaves.

*

I pulled into Maria's driveway minutes later; she had invited us to spend the weekend. Divorced, she lived with Stacey, who was the youngest of her three kids and in between our girls' ages. They've been buddies since they were toddlers.

"Hello, hello," Karen called out as we entered through the side door.

"Come in, Karen," a voice sounded as if it were from a distance. Then Maria appeared, opening the inner door with warm greetings. Steadfast friends since high school, they appeared to me like a mismatched pair at first. Although Maria was attractive with brown hair, and in her late forties, she was only five feet tall and just came up to Karen's chin. And while Karen spoke rapidly with much animation, Maria talked slowly, as if carefully weighing her words.

Karen placed a hand on her friend's head and teased her. "Look at you — you're like a hobbit, Maria!"

She giggled good-naturedly and her eyes crinkled at the corners. "Yeah, I know, but you're pretty tall too." In that moment, I saw the years peeled off Maria's face, revealing the energy and spirit of her youth.

Our friend motioned to chairs around the kitchen table. "Sit down. Would you care for a drink?" She searched our faces, and I could see whom Stacey inherited her expressive eyes from.

"Are you kidding? He's Irish — of course, he wants a drink!" Karen roared. Then wrapping an arm around my shoulders, she shook me vigorously. "Ah, the Irish, the Irish. My hoosbund!"

I couldn't help but laugh, and Maria observed us with amused fascination while I shook myself free. "The Polish aren't any better, dear," I joked.

Chuckling, we sat down while Maria brought out a bottle of wine along with a beer for me.

"So, Andrew, is it your father or your mother who's Irish?" Maria asked, and her voice rose pleasantly at the end.

I picked up the bottle and poured the beer into a glass. "My father, he was from Belfast."

"Ah, your father, I see," she said, and those dark eyes wandered around as she considered this.

Leaning back, I stretched my legs out and listened to them catch up on local gossip. I didn't recognize any of the names, but Karen was always entertaining. She moaned in empathy at some news and laughed with delight at others. But when she reminisced about the visit with Maria's daughter to Clifton Hill a couple of years ago, I jumped in to describe the experience myself of being pushed through the House of Frankenstein by three hysterical, screaming girls.

"I think he was more scared than they were," Karen declared and followed this with a burst of contagious laughter. Maria cackled so hard, she had to wipe away a few tears.

"Yes, it was hair raising," I quipped, running a hand over my bald patch.

She paused before chortling, "Oh, it was, was it? You're priceless, but it takes me a minute to realize you're joking."

All of a sudden, I felt the floor tremble. Karen's leg was shaking, a nervous habit of hers. "Stop that," I said and gave her leg a playful smack. "Are you excited?"

"I'm always excited — you wish! Ah ha-ha-ha ha!" And off she went with a crazy laugh. Maria and I exchanged surprised looks before being helplessly pulled into it.

Karen started to speak again, but I cut her off by saying something myself, and she glared at me with mock annoyance. "Now you made me lose my train of thought!"

"Sorry, dear, but it's not really a train, you know. It's more of a small caboose."

Maria giggled while Karen gave me a sarcastic laugh.

"You laugh harder at your own jokes than at mine," I observed.

"That's because mine are funnier!" Karen said with a smirk.

*

The next afternoon, we visited the high school, and Karen introduced me to former classmates, some of whom had travelled all the way from British Columbia and New York City. Then, while we toured the classrooms, hall and gym, she shared the memories that surfaced for each. The big event was tonight at the Barney, the local pub that everyone in town frequented.

"I can't believe they haven't knocked it down," Karen said, shaking her head when we were back in Maria's kitchen. "It was always a dump, but they had cheap draft. I drank gallons of it — that's why I can't stand beer today."

Maria cleared her throat, "They did remodel it."

"What with — a bulldozer?"

Maria laughed. "What about you, Andy? Are you looking forward to tonight?

"No, actually I'm not," I confided.

"Because Darlene won't be there, and he doesn't know anyone else."

"Oh."

"Don't worry. I'll have a few brews at the bar, and I'll be fine. But I am excited about seeing the Barney." I'd heard so many stories about that pub, it had acquired a legendary status in my mind.

We helped clear the dishes from the table. "Leave them on the counter," Maria instructed. "I'll do them when we get back."

As we walked through the pub doors, we encountered a mass of middle-aged partiers. The Barney was packed with an older group of ex-students, and by old, I mean our age, milling around, talking and glancing expectantly at the door whenever someone new entered. Maria and Karen found a few women they knew and introduced me. I watched them become more engrossed in conversation.

The pretty brunette spoke. "...I didn't recognize him. He used to be very handsome." She nodded her head vigorously for emphasis, and I got the impression she had adored this fellow from afar back in the day.

The other woman nodded her agreement. "People have changed so much, I hardly recognize anyone."

I stared off in boredom for a moment, and then it hit me. I could still have fun. No one looks like they did in high school, so the reunion attendees couldn't tell I was an outsider. A smiling couple came towards me, and the man, whose name tag said Fred, put his hand out.

"Hi, remember me?" I said, shaking his hand and smiling. "I'm Sam. I was in your homeroom class." He looked confused. "I was very shy then and sat at the back." He glanced at his wife, who slowly nodded her head. I continued. "Remember when I pulled the fire alarm to get out of class? Everyone got a kick out of that."

I took a satisfied sip of my beer while they stood speechless and stared at me. Then they moved on.

This was fun, I decided. As I moved towards another couple, Karen came up from behind, wrapped her arms around me and, with her head next to mine, patted my chest lovingly before disappearing. I beamed. I liked it when she was affectionate in public. She must have been enjoying herself.

I stuck my hand out to the man. "Hello, George, it's me, Sam. We were in the same class, but I sat at the end row." The man shook my hand while his wife looked at me. "Remember the time I pulled the fire alarm, and we all got out of class?"

The lady snickered, pointed playfully to my chest, and declared, "Well, your sticker says, 'I'm with Karen Wawrzynski', so I don't think so!"

I glanced at the sticker as they walked off laughing. Rats. That's why Karen patted my chest: she was putting that tag on. I swear she married me just to simplify her name. My act now ruined, I leaned against the bar and sipped my brew sadly. But another couple noticed my tag, told me they knew Karen, and we ended up having a nice conversation after all. I cheered up. My wife had been popular, and this crowd was easy to talk to.

*

After a while, I found Karen and Maria. They were conversing with a friend, who mentioned with amusement that Karen used to be a puker.

"That was a long time ago, Lindsay," she said tersely and frowned. "I'm a different person now."

She introduced me, but I remained quiet to let them catch up on each other's lives. However, I did notice that the lady was striking. Average height with short brown hair, fine features and pretty green eyes. She was a beauty and from her slightly slurred words had obviously downed a few drinks already.

"I'm sorry, I haven't kept in touch," she moaned, on the brink of tears. "I haven't been a good friend."

"You do what you can, Lindsay," Karen answered empathetically. "We're all busy. I understand." The name rang a bell. I'd heard stories about the fun she and Karen had together as teenagers. We soon learned that she was divorced, had two sons who lived on their own and had a house with a boyfriend three years younger.

"Wow, I didn't know you were a cougar, Lindsay," Karen cried, making a clawing motion with one hand. "Mmrroww!"

Lindsay laughed and her eyes twinkled. She seemed to enjoy the wisecrack.

"Do you think you'll ever come back to Fort Erie, Karen?" she asked.

My wife's gaze shifted as she considered this. "Maybe in a box."

"Oh, Karen!" Maria squealed, and they all laughed.

Then Lindsay waved at someone and headed towards another room. My eyes followed as she walked away. Karen whispered, "We did a lot together but only when she didn't have a boyfriend. Once she had one, which was often, because she had a pretty face and big boobs, you never saw her."

I nodded nonchalantly and pretended I hadn't noticed her attractiveness.

*

The buzz in the room grew louder; the booze was kicking in. A tall, sandy-haired fellow stood beside me with his elbows on the bar looking over the room. He peered at my tag and shouted above the noise, "You're Karen's husband?" I nodded, and he leaned in. "Karen was fast."

I was about to tell him to watch it; that's my wife he's talking about when he hollered, "In fact, she was faster than most of the guys."

A light bulb went off, and I yelled, "Yes, I heard she won a lot of trophies in track and field."

He nodded earnestly. "Yeah, she was very fast."

Next, I spotted a guy with a tag labelled Tony. That was a name I heard when Karen talked about old friends. I introduced myself. About my height, he was bulky like a football player, and I learned he was married. But he sighed. "I had a huge crush on Karen in those days."

I looked at him. "That's okay. I still do."

He smiled, and at that moment, Karen joined us.

When we arrived back at Maria's, both of them said the reunion was bittersweet. Everybody was older, some had passed away, some divorced, and some had done very well financially — especially the nerdy kids who became lawyers, environmentalists or government workers.

"Did you enjoy yourself, honey?" she asked me.

"Yes, I did." And I described the ruse I had used.

Maria stared at me. "You did not, did you?"

"Sure did, and it was fun, at least until Karen put my name tag on. Otherwise, I could have kept it going all night."

Maria chuckled.

"Tony seemed nice," I said to Karen. "And he told me he had a crush on you years ago."

"What did you say?" she asked and studied my face. I told her, and she beamed. "That's nice. My honey has a crush on me." She took my hand and spoke softly. "He liked me, but I only saw him as a friend. Once he drove a bunch of us to a party in his father's convertible after spending the entire day cleaning it. I got so drunk that I barfed all over the side of it on the way home. He got so mad because he had to clean it again before his father saw it. I felt bad."

*

Maria had been a great host, and even though it was fun and a nice escape for us, we were very happy when we turned onto our own street again. Moochie and the kids were glad to see us, but Darla was especially pleased. Her mommy was home at last.

As we showered our pet with affection, Meggy said to us, "That Kurt is weird!" We glanced up. No argument there. "He gave us the creeps," she emphasized.

"Yeah," Jackie jumped in, "he staggered across the front lawn, staring at the house and saying, 'They left them alone.'"

"He was probably drunk or stoned," I said and threw my bag onto the landing. "Boy, you can't even leave for a weekend without him acting strange."

Karen sat up. "I forgot to tell you, but last week when I was working in my garden, Kurt was on his front lawn." Her mouth formed a big smile, and she giggled. "He was standing there in his underwear."

"Who was in their underwear?"

"Kurt, our neighbour, on his front yard. He was watering flowers, waved and shouted to me, 'I figure they're no different than a bathing suit.' I just turned away and didn't say anything. But a car came by, and the driver stared in bewilderment. He must have thought Kurt was nuts!" Her eyes shut as she cackled.

"Not far from the truth if he thinks a pair of white jockeys can be mistaken for a bathing suit. Maybe he had a stroke?" I joked.

Karen howled louder, then let out a big sigh. "No, he's just weird." She giggled once more. "I couldn't believe it."

"Remember when he came out of the house with a red clown nose on?" Meggy piped in.

"No, I don't," I said, turning to her. "Why was he wearing it?"

"I don't know. Maybe he joined a circus?"

More laughter ensued.

*

Eric helped me take the empty luggage downstairs. And as I drew near our liquor chest, two objects caught my eye. A screwdriver and crescent wrench lay on the floor below the padlock.

I stopped for a moment before laughing. "Look, Eric — the great burglar. How can you break a padlock with these?" I asked, holding up the useless tools. I smirked. "This has Jackie's name all over it; she always leaves evidence at the scene of a crime."

Eric chortled. "I'll bet if our great-grandma and grandpa were watching from heaven, they'd be surprised to see their travel chest used to lock up booze."

"And their great-granddaughter trying to break into it."

*

When I got back to the living room, Karen was busy reading a text. "Maria said she enjoyed our company and that you were a hit with our friends. Apparently, they thought you were very funny, pleasant and sociable."

"That's nice of them," I said and smiled as I reflected on the conversations.

The experience had been enjoyable and gave me some added understanding of Jackie's behaviour. Based on what I learned about Karen's youth, the apple didn't fall far from the tree.

The weekend had been an uplifting diversion from daily strife, but tonight there was an uneasy feeling in my stomach, as if something bad were going to happen.

DRAMA QUEEN

"Best friends make the worst enemies, they know all your secrets and how to hurt you the most." - Alyson Noel

THE SAME COULD be said about family members. Eric had commented, even before the birthday incident, that there was a lot of anger in our house. As I sat at my desk, I wondered why this was. Perhaps I didn't have much patience because of the stress from my job; Karen often said so. And we were crabby with each other, bickering even when we were fighting with the girls or not.

Grabbing my coat and hat, I looked out my office window at my van four floors below and pressed the remote start. This was my first vehicle with this feature, and I loved it. Not only did it start the engine, but also the defroster and heated seats. And with the decent snowfall we had earlier, while I'd still have to clean off the windows, it'd be warm and toasty inside by the time I walked up to it. Christmas was behind us, but festive lights remained up in town, and the shop windows remained decorated. Old-fashioned black light posts line our main street, giving the quaint appearance of a small town from a by-gone era.

When I reached Maple Street, I slowed down before pulling into it. The city never gets around to clearing side streets until all the major thoroughfares are done. A car weaved towards me on the road trying to get traction, and except for the occasional sound of its tires spinning, all was eerily peaceful. A hush had fallen over the neighbourhood; the hurly-burly sounds of commuters had quieted. People moved slower after a snowfall. There was no point rushing to and from the office; the traffic would be bad anyway.

I also sensed more community spirit after a big storm. Neighbours not normally seen in the winter are outside clearing their walks and driveways. Kids play, rejoicing in the gift of a day off from school. Ruth, who lived across the road, had roamed the streets this morning with a big pot of coffee, dispensing cups to anyone that wished one. Winter is wonderful if you're wise enough to embrace it.

After pressing the garage opener, I hesitated to drive inside while I gazed at the house. Multicoloured lights hung from the eves and in the cedar bushes, blinking out from beneath a layer of snow. Bunkers of the white stuff lay in front of our bay window, which emitted a soft glow of comfort and hospitality. I breathed in winter's ice-cold air. So fresh smelling that I wanted to inhale more, but it was biting on the nostrils and back of the throat and made me cough. I couldn't live in a summer climate year-round. I'd miss the other seasons too much. The crunch of snow under my feet at -15 deg C, when you can see your breath but still feel warm from the sun on your face. I love it. The chill of the evening was hitting my bones, and everything looked warm and toasty inside, so I parked in the garage. It was Friday night, and it warmed my heart to be home.

*

The next day, the doorbell rang.

"Well, if it isn't Katie," I said, holding the door open for her to step inside.

"Hi, Kit-Kat," Jackie called from behind me, smiling.

As Katie took off her coat, I noticed her dark brown hair had been cut into a cute bob, which was very attractive. I contemplated this dynamic duo. "You two are partners in crime, aren't you?" I said.

Katie's eyes lit up, and she flashed a smile. "Yeah, fire and gasoline." She giggled, wrinkling her nose.

"Oh, Jackie told you that, did she?" I glanced at Jackie. That was how I often described them. "It's true. When you two get together — watch out!" They seemed to take turns being the fuel and the accelerator.

She laughed over her shoulder as they headed to the other room. After she went home, Jackie mentioned that Kat's mother was flying to Turks and Caicos with her boyfriend next month for a week's vacation. "She hasn't had a trip in a long time, so she's quite excited," Jackie said as she shared the news.

"That's wonderful," Karen said. "She deserves a break. Are Katie and Scott going too?"

"No, unfortunately not, but they're still happy for their mother."

Later, Karen texted Diane to wish her a pleasant holiday and suggested that she hide the car keys when away, so Katie would not be tempted. Like all new drivers, she was anxious to flex her independence, but in Ontario's graduated licence system, she would have to have an accompanying driver with at least four years' experience sitting beside her. Teenagers don't always follow the rules, so why take a chance?

Her mother texted back: *Don't worry. My brother will fix the car so it won't start. It's all taken care of.*

"See," Karen grinned, "Diane knows what to do."

*

Following the trip, we asked Jackie how Kat had managed while her mother was away.

Her face looked perplexed. "She was fine. Why?"

"Well, she must have been annoyed because she couldn't drive the van," Karen said with a smirk.

"What do you mean? She drove it."

"No, she couldn't. Her uncle tinkered with it so it wouldn't go."

"Oh, that!" Jackie snorted. "As soon as Diane left, Kat said to her brother, 'Scotty, you better get on this.' So, he fixed it and they were riding around all week in it, ha-ha-ha."

We sat there dazed while Jackie scampered off to her room. Scott was two years younger than Katie. Who would think he'd know how to fix it? Obviously, Katie was as devious as Jackie, but I have to admit that the thought of them cruising around like bandits, while their mother lay worry-free on the beach made us laugh. Score — kids one, parents two.

*

Saturday afternoon, Karen walked through the front door with her arms full of groceries, looking upset.

"What's the matter?" I asked.

She rolled her eyes. "I took Jackie and her friend Sue to the store to exchange a coat that was too big for her. Why she didn't try it on when we bought it is beyond me, but she refused. Next, she wanted to be dropped off at Carly's house and for me to take Sue home, and I said, 'No, I'm not a taxi.' But she pestered me so much I finally agreed on the condition she walk home. It's not far. I was tired, and she had been miserable and unappreciative at the mall."

The ringing of her cell interrupted us, and she glared at the number. From her frown, I guessed it was Jackie. "I'm not picking her up," she said to me before answering. Then she said 'no' several times before finally roaring, "Alright, alright!"

Twenty minutes later, they burst into the entrance, and Jackie sprinted up the stairs. Karen went straight to the kitchen and came back with a glass of wine. "I'm so mad," she fumed. "I grounded her! No friends or going out for a week."

"What happened?"

"She swore at me in the van."

"Okay, but if you ground her, stick to it. The punishment's not effective if you rescind it."

Karen stuck with it for two days but relented for a 'special' party, along with an apology and promise to be better. I didn't criticize her. She had to deal with the girls a lot more than me.

I made an appointment to talk to Dr. MacEwan again. The situation with Jackie had grown worse, and she had stopped taking her ADD medication because it made her groggy.

The doctor listened to me with a dour expression, then said flatly, "I can't see you or Karen anymore to discuss Jackie's behaviour."

I blinked in surprise. His statement baffled me. "Why is that?"

"Because nothing has changed," he moaned and glanced at the file on his desk, then back to me. "Until you and Karen are on the same page and get tough with her, nothing will change, so it's pointless to come and see me."

"You're right," I said and looked at the floor. "We've talked about it, and Karen says she'll try, but she keeps giving in. She doesn't like fighting with her."

"There you have it," he said and with a nod indicated that the conversation was finished.

My shoulders sagged as I left his office, and I leaned against the inside of the elevator feeling defeated as I pressed the button to go down. Of course, he'd still be our doctor, and we could see him for other issues, just not about Jackie. And I had such high hopes that he'd convince Karen to change her behaviour. I wasn't having success on my own. Now, what would I do?

*

Jackie continued to be rude and didn't always tell us where she was going when she went out. When Karen complained, I locked eyes with her. "Remember what Dr. MacEwan said? Punish her or the behaviour won't change."

A troubled look came over her face. "I won't ground her; girls need social engagement."

"Then, take her phone away."

"What, wrestle her to the ground and pull it out of her clenched fist?" she chortled sarcastically. "It's not so easy."

"That isn't necessary. Call the provider and ask them to suspend the service."

She raised her eyebrows. "That's a good idea. I'll do it."

Karen called me at work the following day, and I could tell from her tone that something was wrong. "They said they can't do it. There's no such thing as suspending service for a few days."

"What?" I said in shock. "Why does it matter to them since we pay for the service?"

"Well, they wouldn't," she said with a sigh of resignation.

In disbelief, I hung up. As I passed Sarah's office, I stopped in to check on a report and couldn't help venting my frustration with the cell company. She had two daughters that were a few years younger than ours, and I asked if her company had a different policy.

"I don't know," she said pensively, "but why not just tell them it's lost?"

"Tell them it's lost?" I repeated.

"Yes, say you lost it, and they need to stop the service so no one else can use it. Later, you can advise them it's been found, and they can turn it back on."

"Brilliant, Sarah, just brilliant," I chuckled. "Why didn't I think of that?"

She smiled with satisfaction, and I had the strange feeling she might have done this with her girls. I grabbed my lunch from the fridge and hurried to my desk to call Karen with this idea.

"Really?" She was skeptical. "But what happens when we want it reactivated?"

"We just say we found it," I replied smugly.

She told me later it had worked. Before dinner, Jackie arrived home upset her cell was inoperable, and we explained it had been cut off for three days as punishment. She did not receive this well and had a temper tantrum. After some verbal insults, she lost it for even longer. Despite her outbursts, at the end of the day, there was nothing she could do about it. And we were pleased; we had regained control.

And yet a day later, didn't I walk through the door after work to find Jackie sprawled in an armchair staring at her cell phone. "What are you doing?" I screeched.

"Just looking at my pictures," she said with a heavy sigh.

"Oh, okay." Relieved, I hurried upstairs to change.

Over the next two days, I grew more suspicious. She never whined about her phone and was often found staring at it. Something funny was going on, so I suggested Karen check with the company. Maybe they hadn't shut everything off.

She rang me at the office. "Her service is on again. Jackie called them up and pretended to be me. Can you believe the nerve she has?"

While I abhorred her conduct, I couldn't help but admire the initiative. She was turning out to be more cunning than anticipated.

That night we called the service company and explained the situation. The man in customer service listened patiently and then offered a solution. "I think you need to add a secret phrase to your account," he suggested and rhymed off a few ideas. I grabbed one. "Favourite author — our daughter's not a reader. Put down Hemmingway as the answer."

Now better armed, we informed Jackie that we had fixed it so she couldn't fool the cell company again.

"What did you do?" she asked suspiciously.

"Never mind, but trust us, your ruse won't succeed anymore, and it's now cut off for the rest of your original punishment period."

She said nothing, but later we overheard her talking to Katie on the land phone. "Yeah, that's right, I'm totally screwed." Obviously, she had tried again and failed.

We, however, were elated. "She must have been surprised," I joked with Karen.

"Yeah, shockerooed!" Karen said with a grin.

Score — kids one, parents three!

*

The next morning started out badly. Karen and I were in the kitchen. It was Sunday morning, and we heard fighting overhead.

"What are they quarrelling about?" Karen asked with exasperation. In the process of making coffee, she stopped and leaned against the counter looking tired.

"I'll go," I said, rising out of my chair. "What a way to start the day."

She nodded, happy to leave the intervention to me. I climbed the staircase and walked down the hall to Meggy's room, where the noise emanated from.

"Knock it off!" I roared as I stepped through her doorway. "What are you two fighting about?"

Both girls started shouting and pointing at each other.

"Quiet. Quiet!"

They both sat on the bed fuming. Jackie shot an icy glance sideways at her sister.

"Alright, now one at a time — Meaghan?"

With a sour face, Jackie turned away while her sister assumed the most patient and reasonable tone to present her case. She always made me smile when she took on this mature manner.

"I was lying here trying to sleep when Jackie marched in yelling at me and started going through my dresser —"

"She took my pants!" Jackie barked. "She always takes my things and leaves them on the floor."

"Now, Jackie," the patient voice persisted, "you wear my clothes too, and besides, I don't have your black pants."

"Liar! You always lie. Last time I found them in your closet."

"Wait a minute, Jackie," I interrupted. "You do share your clothes, right?"

"Well, I'm never sharing anything with her again!"

"Okay, and I understand you're mad about the pants, but that's no reason to shout. And if you share clothes, then isn't she entitled to borrow some?"

"You always take her side. I hate you!" she snapped and, storming out, slammed her bedroom door.

The sound was like a gunshot near my ear and got my adrenalin pumping. I walked over and shouted at her door, "Watch it, kiddo. If you bust this door, you'll be grounded for a week!"

I turned but had only taken a few steps when the door whipped open, and Jackie marched angrily towards me.

"Hold on," I shouted, blocking her path. I was going to put a stop to this disrespect right now. But to my surprise, she grabbed my arms and leaned into me. I started sliding backwards as my slippers failed to grip the carpet. It's astonishing how much strength an irate sixteen-year-old can have when they release all their pent-up anger and frustration. I dug in, leaned forward and shoved back. The force was only enough to move her sideways, but here she was before my eyes, bouncing off the wall and rolling onto the carpet in slow motion while crying, shrieking and flailing her arms to make as much noise as possible. I had to stop myself from laughing; I'd seen hockey players take better dives.

"You threw me into the wall!" she wailed, as she lay still on the carpet.

"Oh, go on. That nudge wasn't enough to do all this. Stop acting."

"Mom!" she shouted. "Dad pushed me down the hall!"

I stood there, unsure of what to do.

Her face twisted with anger and she snarled, "You jerk!"

My throat tightened in anger. "You're a little brat!" I yelled and then made a hasty retreat downstairs to calm myself down.

As I re-entered the kitchen, Karen frowned. "What's with all the hollering?"

"Jackie was pushing me, so I shoved her back, and she pretended to be thrown against the wall and onto the floor. Believe me, she faked it." I sat down and tried to slow my racing heart.

"Okay, I know you wouldn't hurt her. She could be a great actress if she wanted."

But my anger hadn't left yet, so I got up and fired another burst up the stairs, "Guess what, Jackie? No phone for the rest of the weekend!" When I came back, Karen's face was upset. "I'm sorry," I said, "but we have to discipline her. We can't let her defiance go unchecked. She's a regular drama queen, that one is."

Seconds later, there was the sound of a scream and feet running down the stairs.

Jackie glared at me from the hall. "You're an *Assxxxx*!"

"*You* can't speak to me like *that*!" I said jumping up. Rage surged through me, and I fought to control myself. "Just for that, you've lost it for a week!" I turned my back on her and sat down again, feeling the blood pounding in my head and my hands trembling.

"I'm going to kill myself!" she screamed behind me.

"No more name-calling," Karen said loudly to each of us, "and no yelling either." And then even louder, "And, Jackie, was that smart? Now you won't have your cell phone for *seven* days."

Our daughter bolted off.

"That kid has no respect," I said quietly. "I never talked to my father like that."

There was the sound of a door opening. "I'm leaving! I hate you!" Jackie yelled, slamming the door after that proclamation.

"Fine," I answered. "We don't want you here anyway if you

won't behave." Then on an impulse, I jumped up and locked the front door. I walked slowly back to the kitchen. "That'll fix her," I said with a smile to Karen. "She can stay out there and cool her heels for a while."

Meaghan had been sitting in the living room listening to the scene unfold. "She's outside pacing," she declared, as she stared out the window.

"Hah! She realizes she's outmanoeuvred." I stole a furtive glance from behind the drapes. "She's in her socks, with no jacket," I chuckled. "She really didn't think this one out."

A few minutes later, the doorbell rang.

"You wanted out, so you're out!" I yelled.

"But it's cold out there, Dad," Meaghan said softly.

"That's her problem. I'm not the one who ran out in my socks."

"She can stay outside for a while," Karen agreed.

Then there was the loud sound of her kicking against the entry.

"She'll wreck our new front door, Andrew," Karen cried out. "We have to do something!"

"We could call the police," I said evenly. A friend had informed us they'd come, not just for risk of personal injury but also for the threat of property damage.

"Alright, I'll do it," Karen said, jumping out of the chair. "Maybe they can talk some sense into her." She reached into the kitchen cupboard for her phone book.

Despite the constant noise of kicking, pounding on the door and screaming in the background, Karen was able to speak calmly into the phone, "Yes. Our daughter is out of control. She's banging and kicking the front door, and we don't want her back in." She paused to listen, and then I heard her give our address. "Thank you very much. It's a nice way to spend a Sunday, isn't it?" she added sarcastically before hanging up. She looked at me. "They're sending someone over."

*

With no phone, Jackie couldn't do anything but wait. It wasn't long before Meggy announced the arrival of the police. As we gawked out the window, a male and female officer approached Jackie on the front lawn. After a moment, the man knocked on the door, and Karen invited him into the living room to explain the reason for the call.

"Why did she act like that?" he asked.

"I don't remember what started it," I said, "but she began yelling and swearing, so I took away her cell, and she went ballistic."

Karen's gaze moved to the officer. "She's a teenager and very emotional. We've been having problems with her for some time."

Meaghan sat silently, taking it all in. But I was glad she was there because she helped present us as reasonable parents.

"Did anyone hit her?" he asked, looking straight at me.

"No. No one hit her," Karen assured him.

"Well, we don't have a reason to take her with us. Is there anywhere else she can go?" he asked, looking each of us in the eyes.

"My mother's," Karen answered immediately. "She's on the next street, but I'd rather not put that burden on her. She's old. We didn't know what else to do, so we called the police."

The officer was sympathetic but strongly suggested that Jackie go to the grandmother's. So, Karen phoned a surprised Anna, who readily agreed. And while Karen explained the situation to Anna, the officer walked outside to confer with the others.

Karen came up beside me. "That officer is very nice. He told me that he had a sister who was bipolar and put his family through hell as a teenager."

I stared in amazement. "Wow, it's nice he was that honest with you." I couldn't imagine an officer being that candid, but Karen's personality encouraged people to trust her.

In the next moment, both officers were standing in the entrance with Jackie in between, her face expressionless and her eyes impassive.

"She's ready to leave," the policewoman said, "but needs to pack some things." As if on cue, Jackie dashed upstairs and returned in a few minutes with a gym bag.

With a final nod to us, the policeman said, "Alright, we're leaving now."

Karen's hair hadn't been brushed, and her face appeared stressed, but she still managed a faint smile. "Thank you, Officer."

We watched the patrol car pulled slowly away from the curb. Our daughter's blonde head could be seen in the backseat, looking away from the house. Then we collapsed on the sofa, feeling completely drained. It had been a lot to deal with, but hopefully now, Jackie would realize we wouldn't put up with her crap and had the power to remove her. On the positive side, Karen had stood tough, which was encouraging. And maybe living at Anna's would shake some sense into our daughter. After all, if she thinks living with us is bad, wait until she tastes Grandma's cooking.

THERAPY

"Therapy helps ... but screaming obscenities is faster and cheaper!" - www.LeFunny.net

ANNA WAS A lifesaver, and having the option to send Jackie to her house made us breathe easier. Our stress level dropped, there were fewer demands placed on us, and the house became more tranquil. A bigger surprise was hearing that Jackie managed to get herself up and to school every day. Will wonders never cease? She had the occasional friend over, like Katie or Hayley, and didn't mind Grandma's lifestyle at all, which really wasn't a surprise. After all, Anna sat up late watching movies or reading romance novels and then slept in until three o'clock in the afternoon. But staying at Anna's was no picnic either; every room was full of clutter, and she wasn't much of a cook. Her fridge was packed with discounted groceries, such as day-old bread, reduced vegetables, stale donuts, pastries and cheese; and the freezer with frozen pizza, chicken wings etc. and not the expensive kind either but the cheapest ones on sale. Jackie lasted two weeks before asking permission to come back. I have to hand it to her; I don't think I could have lasted that long.

Her pretty features were contrite as she apologized and explained why she had behaved the way she did. We told her it was unacceptable, and we wouldn't put up with her verbal abuse. She nodded, and we believed she had gotten the message, so we let her return.

As we dined on a fine roast chicken dinner, she was bubbly. And her blonde ponytail bounced around as she loaded her plate and chatted about her visit at Anna's.

"Granny's food is sooo disgusting!" She laughed. "She served me these TV dinners (she mentioned a well-advertised cheap brand). Ugggh! I couldn't eat them. After two days, I started buying fast food for myself."

"Yeah, I know her meals are bad," Karen agreed. "You should have seen what we threw out when we moved her."

"Oh, and Harry left a sweater behind so she came over to get it. But when she got there, she found Grandma wearing it!"

"Grandma had Hayley's sweater on?" Karen repeated, using the friend's real name instead of the Harry Potter nickname Jackie had assigned her.

"Yeah, Harry said, 'Isn't that my sweater your grandmother has on?' and it was!" Jackie giggled. "I said that I'd get it for her later, but she told me not to bother."

Everybody laughed and I joked. "I guess it didn't look as fashionable on Grandma."

"I'm surprised it fit her," Karen added. Anna was quite overweight.

"Yeah," Jackie chortled as she fidgeted with her phone. "Look, here's a picture."

There sat Anna smiling in her living room, grey hair neatly brushed and outfitted in a pretty yellow sweater. She seemed very happy.

"I understand why Hayley didn't want it anymore," Karen chuckled.

Joking about the kids' antics helped us deal with the stress. Back in the office, I commiserated with colleagues and declared that I would write a book about the girls. I said this more and more because it always got a big laugh, even with colleagues in Montreal.

At dinner the following week, with everyone around the table in high spirits, Karen joked about the time Jackie hid beer under the bush behind our gate.

They all laughed, but when Karen started another story, Jackie bristled. "Okay, that's enough, Mom. I don't need to hear about all my bad deeds."

"She's right," I said, and Jackie smiled appreciatively. "We should stop. Besides, they'll all be in my book, anyway."

Her eyes widened. "Book? What book?"

"Oh, I plan to write a book about you and Meggy. It will be called *How I Lost My Hair Raising Teenage Girls.*"

Karen shrieked with delight. "That's a great idea. You should do it."

"You can't write about me," Jackie said indignantly. "I'll sue you."

"I'll change your name so you won't be able to," I said, dismissing the threat. "In the book, you'll be Jackeroo McKinney. No one will ever know it's you, ha-ha-ha."

She focused on her plate and said nothing more.

*

Karen glanced over her paper on the weekend. "Oh, I forgot to tell you what happened this week. It's funny."

I turned to her as she continued. "I was driving Jackie and Katie around after school — and I always listen to them talk in the back. You'd be surprised what I learn. Anyway, I heard Kat ask her, 'Is your dad really writing a book?' Jackie said, 'Yeah, he says he is.' Then Kat asked, 'Am I going to be in it?'" Karen laughed with glee. "She's worried she'll be in your book too!"

"That's so funny."

The next day, when I walked through the door, I found Katie watching a movie in the family room with Jackie and Meaghan.

I stuck my head in. "Hello, Katie, or should I say ... Chapter Three."

She giggled and Jackie quipped, "Oh, good one, Dad."

At that moment, I hadn't seriously considered a book, but it didn't stop me from having fun with it.

*

Unfortunately, the harmony didn't last long, and we were soon fighting again. In the small hours of Wednesday morning, I lay in bed with many thoughts running through my head. I was at a loss at what to do to improve our family dynamics. Life at home was not enjoyable; there were too many fights, and Jackie remained steadfastly defiant. After tossing and turning for an hour, I went downstairs and lay on the sofa in the semidarkness. Once when the children were little, my father said prophetically, 'You better get a handle on them now, Andy, or you'll have a hell of a time when they're older!'

He had been right, of course, but the question at the moment was what to do about it. Dr. MacEwan wouldn't see us anymore. Jackie had been assessed by a psychiatrist but no longer took her medication. So where did we go from here?

Later in the office, as I ate lunch at my desk, I searched for information on defiant teenagers. The term Oppositional Defiance Disorder came up a few times. I read the description: often and easily loses temper; often behaves angry and resentful; often argues with people in authority and often actively defies or refuses to comply with adult requests or rules. I whistled softly. That description fit her to a tee. I queried possible solutions. The only answer that popped up was to remove them from the house. A ranch in Arizona was mentioned, where teens could work with therapists to get back on track, but it was prohibitively expensive — something we could only dream about. By the time I finished reading, I felt defeated. The situation appeared hopeless.

At home, Karen asked me what was wrong, and I explained I couldn't sleep because I was upset. And I summarized the information I found on the internet.

Her face clouded over. "Well, not getting enough sleep won't help anything," she said. "Let's pray for guidance and try not to worry."

I slept well that night but left early for the office again before the rest of the family woke up. At least, the job was a respite from tension in the house. There, my day was driven by conference calls, projects and issues with third-party manufacturers. I plowed through the morning with a heavy heart and called Karen during lunch.

"I've been thinking about it, Andrew, and I have an idea. We can't afford that ranch, but why not take her to a therapist? The Ontario health care plan won't cover it, but it's much cheaper than the other option."

"That's not a bad idea," I said reflectively. "See what you can find. Anything that improves our relationship with Jackie would be worth the cost." By the time I hung up, I felt more optimistic. At least, now we had a plan.

As I drove home, a familiar song played on the radio. It was my father's favourite, "The Living Years," by Mike & the Mechanics.

So we open up a quarrel, between the present and the past,
We only sacrifice the future, It's the bitterness that lasts.

So don't yield to the fortunes, you sometimes see as fate
It may have a new perspective on a different day

And if you don't give up, and don't give in, you may just be O.K.
Say it loud, say it clear, you can listen as well as you hear
It's too late when we die, to admit we don't see eye to eye....

A feeling of hope came over me. It felt like a message was being sent to tell me everything would be alright. Eric came home for the weekend, and we gathered the kids in the living room to discuss counselling for Jackie. Surprisingly, all three kids insisted that the whole family should go, because they believed the problem was how Karen and I interacted with them. The girls believed our communication style and efforts to control them were the issue. Bitter feedback, but Karen and I agreed. And this decision would take us through a series of changes.

Karen found a family counselling service and scheduled an appointment after work. In the first session, each of us presented our views. Sally was in her forties, with short, dyed-blonde hair and a calm tone and manner. I noticed she ensured everybody had an opportunity to speak. Karen had a psychology degree herself and became defensive at some of the comments, but I didn't. As a manager, I was trained to listen, to be open to other perspectives and to acknowledge their views.

The therapist appeared quite experienced in dealing with families. She stressed the importance of open lines of communication and for the kids to be involved in clubs or other pursuits besides school. Eric took part in different sports at university, but the girls weren't interested in any extracurricular activities. Their only desire was to be given more respect and independence, which they expressed frequently. A lot of grumbling also centred around the internet.

When they raised this issue, I said, "If you're not using your phones at night, why do you care if the internet's off?"

The response was, "If I'm not able to fall asleep, I listen to music."

Sally echoed the view that we should regard them as adults but also stated that parents have certain rules that need to be followed. She said that rules and penalties should be stated in advance rather than 'on the fly,' which I confessed was my tendency. Then they all complained that I was impatient and quick to anger, which really bothered me.

"We have different parenting styles," I clarified to Sally. "She's more laid back, and I'm the disciplinarian."

"I'm constantly telling Andy to pick his battles," Karen interjected. Great, even my wife had turned on me.

Sally fixed her eagle eyes on me. "I agree, and that's very important. You can't fight over everything. Some things you have to let go."

It seemed there was more for me to improve on than Karen. I was wrong, and that was a bitter pill to swallow. But I nodded my understanding and acceptance. "Food for thought."

In the end, everyone agreed that the session had been helpful and enabled us to communicate without anger or fighting. We set up a series of biweekly appointments. Eric wouldn't be able to join anymore because of his studies, but we had a professional facilitator so we felt confident that we could succeed without him.

*

We made a quick dinner when we got home, and then a weariness weighed on me. The earlier discussions and feedback had been exhausting. I announced to Karen that I was taking Darla for a walk and hurried out.

As we moved onto a neighbouring street, breathing in the cool night air, I felt my vitality return. Then Darla suddenly leaped forward, nearly pulling my arm out of the socket. A rabbit had bolted across a lawn, and the great hunter had jumped in pursuit until she reached the end of her leash, that is. She strained against me, so fascinated she didn't even emit a 'woof.' To one side, another bunny sat by a bush, immobile and invisible to her.

"Don't you see him, Darla?" I watched her and pointed to the second rabbit. No, she didn't. Like Tyrannosaurus Rex, her eyesight was limited, and she resumed her pace while the second bunny raced off.

A few minutes more, and Darla stopped to pee. I stood and looked up at the moon while I waited. *My family thinks I'm impatient; it's just ridiculous.* The moon was full, a beautiful pale orange, and glowed brightly against a dark blue sky sprinkled with bright stars that hung individually and in clusters and appeared to go on to infinity.

Sitting low in the skyline, it appeared unusually large, a super-moon perhaps, and radiated light almost magically to illuminate lawns and spaces between homes. This simple wonder of nature was fascinating and seemed to make everything in the neighbourhood stand out clearer and with more meaning.

We walked another twenty feet before Darla had to stop to pee again. I jerked the leash. "Come on, Darla, for crying out loud!" *Hmmm,* I thought to myself, *maybe they were right — I am impatient!* Right then and there, I made a commitment, to myself and Darla, to try to be more easygoing and hoped my children would eventually view me as that one day.

Opening the front door, I called out, "Hello, we're back!"

"Well, somebody's mood has improved," Karen said cheerfully. "I'm glad the walk did you some good."

"Yes, it did, but you have to come and look at the full moon. It's spectacular!"

"Come, kids," Karen shouted, "your father wants us to see the moon."

*

Our subsequent appointment centred on the girls' desire to be treated as adults and not have the internet shut off. I had trouble with this, so we debated it a while before I eventually agreed to leave it on during weekends. Sally had us draw up a contract that incorporated some of my wishes.

McKinney Family Contract
1. Jackie's grounding for lying ends Monday
2. School nights, internet off at 9:30
3. Facebook, etc., off from 7 p.m.

The following session was just for Karen and me, and we were able to talk freely about our challenges.

"Jackie's amorphous by nature," I stated categorically.

Sally blinked in surprise, and I realized I had used a scientific term. My mind flickered back to a microbiology lab. I was examining a specimen of corn starch under the microscope and glanced at the description for the expected result.

"What does amorphous mean?"

"Having no defined edges or boundaries," the teaching assistant responded, hovering beside me.

That was Jackie alright, no boundaries.

I continued and was very frank with Sally about my frustration. "Karen consistently goes behind my back and shortens the punishment. This makes me the bad cop and her the good one."

"Not always. Sometimes, I don't," Karen protested.

"Only on rare exceptions."

"Yes, but Andy uses a sledgehammer approach when it comes to discipline," she said decisively.

"Okay, perhaps I do, but when you don't provide enough punishment, I feel the need to come down even harder the next time."

"It's important to follow through with punishment, or they never learn boundaries," Sally advised, "which could present greater problems as they grow older. And you need to decide what the penalties will be in advance, so they're not too harsh."

"Jackie and him are constantly fighting," Karen commented, pointing at me.

Sally looked at me. "Don't take the bait."

I mulled this over. Scientists are seekers of truth, yet we have our internal biases; I needed to consider the full picture. Was Jackie getting some satisfaction by provoking me? Could I walk away and not respond? That would be difficult, but perhaps Sally had a point.

It had been an excellent session. Our eyes had been opened, we felt more like teammates, and we had made progress. I only hoped Karen realized she had to change as well.

On the way home, she spoke up. "What the therapist said about our approaches to Jackie is true, but I found her a little smug. I wonder if she has any teenagers herself?"

I shrugged. It was hard to dispute her professional advice.

The girls attended the next meeting, and we drew up a chore schedule. One beef of ours was that they didn't help out enough around the house. The girls were less resistant than I expected, and the request was fair. If they wanted to be treated as adults, they should share tasks with the adults. I began to value Sally's agreements — everything was clearly specified, and we were accountable to her for following them. Although I'd written and approved many business contracts, the idea of creating one for a family relationship had never occurred to me.

The following appointment was solely for our blonde girl. We hoped in a private session she might open up about any personal issues that might be bothering her. When we picked her up afterwards, she was chipper and chattered about a party she wanted to attend. The therapist had drawn up an agreement for it, which she had signed, and there were places for us to sign.

Bonnie's Party Contract
Mom will not be given the home number because:
- *Jackie must keep her cell on*
- *She will answer if Mom calls*
- *Bonnie's parents are someone that my parents approve of*
- *Jackie will get picked up at 9:00-9:30 or be home by 12:00 if getting a ride with someone else.*
- *If any difficulty getting a ride, Jackie must call by 11:45 to request a ride home.*
- *Mom can call only once between 9:30 and 11:00 p.m.*

A complaint both daughters frequently vented over was that Karen calls or texts them frequently when they're out. But setting these rules for pickup should stop this. Although we didn't like the prospect of a late call to come and get her, we conceded to try it.

*

Only Karen and I were scheduled for the subsequent meeting.

"Are they doing the chores?" Sally asked.

"No," I answered.

"They are helping out more," Karen said and glanced sideways at me. "Not with everything or as often as they should, but they've been doing more so I am happy."

Sally made a note in her pad. "And how did the party go?"

We shifted in our chairs, and I cleared my throat. "We didn't let her go because she wouldn't give us the parents' landline number."

Sally appeared irritated. "But you saw the rules, and you know the parents."

"We've never met them," Karen rebutted, "and we have no idea who Bonnie is or where she lives."

"But Jackie said you knew them," Sally mumbled and blinked in disbelief. "You mean she lied?"

With a slight smile on her lips, Karen said, "In a word — yes."

A look of annoyance crossed Sally's face. She knew now that she'd been duped.

I leaned forward and said gently, "Now you see what we've been dealing with."

Score? Kids one, therapist zero.

*

Karen prepared the patio table so we could eat outside. The warm days of spring had arrived, and she and I basked in the warmth of the sunshine while sitting together with a drink beforehand. Despite being alone, we discussed the meeting with Sally in whispers.

"Did you see her face when she realized Jackie had lied to her?" I said with a grin.

Karen snickered, "Yeah, maybe in the future she won't act so superior about handling teenagers."

I took a sip from my glass. "You know, I found this beer in the basement fridge. Jackie must have hidden it there."

"Great, that might teach her a lesson."

"Of the three, she's been the most precocious, but why does she have to try to grow up so fast? Whenever people ask how old my kids are, I say Jackie is sixteen going on forty."

Karen chuckled. "That's just how teenagers are. I was like that. When you're older, you wonder why you did it." She sighed. "I'm sorry we have all this grief; it must be hard on you with a job as well." I nodded, and she continued, "It's a shame. You make good money, we're all healthy, and the kids are still at home. If we could only remove all the bullshit and aggravation, we'd have a wonderful life."

"You're right," I said and gazed at the large grey clouds in the sky. "Honestly, no one ever told me how hard it was to raise teenagers."

Jackie informed us later that the beer belonged to Katie, who had left it in our fridge. They never asked me to replace it and didn't raise the issue again. Karen read somewhere that when you're angry with your kids, you should try to picture them as little children sleeping in their beds. That helped to some extent but not as much as drinking their booze.

*

Jackie came with us to the next meeting. To her credit, Sally didn't focus on the lie but continued to discuss our overall relationship and how things were going.

"Honestly, I think we've been spinning our wheels for the last few weeks with no headway," I said.

Sally considered this (she might have thought so too), but her voice remained patient as she recapped the key changes we each agreed to make. Throughout the session Jackie stared at her phone and stroked her eyelashes, a habit she claimed was caused by mascara flaking off. Whatever the reason, the impression given was one of boredom and indifference. The therapist glanced frequently at her while speaking and, at one point, asked her a question. Jackie responded without looking up.

Sally made no comment but leaned forward with her hand out. "Can I see your phone for a minute?"

Jackie looked surprised but handed it over.

"Thanks," Sally said. "I'll just hold on to this while we work on these issues."

Jackie's eyes popped open. We finished shortly afterwards and left without the phone.

In the car, she was furious. "That bitch took my cell!"

We drove the rest of the way in silence, but my body shook with stifled laughter. And once we were alone, I howled with delight, "'Can I see your phone?' she says, ha-ha-ha. Then wham, bam, right into the drawer! I thought it was hilarious."

Karen said nothing.

Sally had been a hard nut to crack, but it goes to show you, even professionals can take only so much teenage attitude. This was even better than cutting Jackie's internet off. Teenagers may change suddenly from loving, fun children to demanding, spoiled and entitled beasts. You need to be prepared for this. Sadly, however, a parent can never truly prepare for it. Counselling helped us but met with great resistance from our youngest — the one who needed help the most. But we all gained a better understanding of the issues and how our own actions triggered them. We also realized that as parents, we must learn to accept our flaws and strive for improvements. And don't worry if you think you don't have any flaws; just ask your family. They'll be happy to point them out. Maybe Sally didn't help our relationship with our youngest significantly, but she'd bring us to the man who could.

THE TURNING POINT 26

"There's a reason why some animals eat their young."
- unknown author but often quoted by Andrew McKinney

INITIALLY, KAREN AGREED that Jackie got what she deserved from Sally for her rudeness, but our daughter started working on her to get the phone back. She wouldn't wait for the next appointment; she wanted her cell now. And she refused to meet with Sally again. I advised Karen to be strong, but of course, I escaped to the office and didn't get the daily treatment Karen did. After holding out for a week, she called Sally and picked up the phone.

When I protested, she stuck her chin out. "Sally shouldn't have taken Jackie's cell; she had no right. I don't blame Jackie for not wanting to see her anymore."

That was a shame. Sally had helped our family, but it only took two months for our daughter to break her professional cool. We switched to the only other therapist at this location, and he happened to be her husband.

"I'll bet Sally filled him in," I laughed when I learned of this, "and he probably put us in a red file." When Karen worked as a social worker, client files were colour coded to alert other workers of the volatile ones, which were red.

The irony that the new therapist was Sally's husband struck me again when the three of us trundled back to their offices for our next appointment. I shook his hand and took in his appearance. Frank was my height but huskier, with mid-length brown hair combed to one side and a moustache. Dressed in a brown suit with no tie, he invited us into his small office where he led the discussion in a relaxed and soothing manner while reclining in a soft leather armchair.

Although he knew the situation from our file (and his wife), we gave him a synopsis, and he probed us with questions. In the end, he asked each of us what we hoped to gain from the sessions and then drew up another contract.

Jackie will:
- *Set her own alarm and get herself up*
- *Pack her lunch the night before*
- *Get her breakfast in the morning*
- *Shop for her groceries for breakfast and lunch*
- *Call the school and tell them if she can't go*
- *Get a ride to the bus if she is downstairs with her coat on and ready 5 minutes before 7 a.m.*

Over the next two weeks, only the last point was adhered to, but I was still pleased. It yielded a vast improvement in Jackie's readiness for school. Watching her coming downstairs earlier, already dressed, and in good time to depart, made me wish we'd set this rule years ago. It would have saved a lot of bus chasing. Karen and I felt that our initial encounter with the new therapist had been a success, but it would take a while to really gauge his mettle. We booked a series of appointments for Jackie by herself, just Karen and I and all three of us together.

*

And throughout it all, June rolled in with its glorious sunshine and hot days. It was a big month in the McKinney household, for Eric had graduated with his degree in Mechanical Engineering. We were proud of our son and planned a party to celebrate. Karen made the arrangements, invited guests and squeezed it in just before Eric and Gloria departed for a three-week holiday.

Thirty friends and relatives filled the house, including his pals, who brought a great deal of cheer and fun to the occasion. A caterer dropped off food, which we set out in a large buffet along with salads Karen had prepared. I piled my plate high with chicken, veal, vegetables and salad and found a seat by my older cousin Eileen. Tall, with short black hair, she sat on the love seat dressed in an elegant blouse and tailored pants. Eileen always carried herself with class and dignity and was a great resource when advice was needed. We talked about the family and how proud we were of Eric's achievement.

"Where are they going for their vacation?" Eileen asked.

"They plan to backpack through Thailand," I replied, taking a mouthful of food. Karen and I had had slight misgivings, but Eric was a strapping young man and should be able to take care of both of them.

"Why Thailand?"

"Kids today want to go somewhere different from us, and it seems that Thailand is the latest trend. In my day, it was Europe, but young people have their own ideas."

Eileen juggled the plate on her lap, leaned in and spoke in hushed tones. "Have you heard about the two Canadian girls that died there last week?"

"No, what happened?"

"They don't know yet. Apparently, it's not easy to obtain information from the officials." Her voice was calm, but I saw concern in those dark brown eyes. "The officials suspect they were poisoned."

I stared at her, and the food in my mouth rapidly lost its flavour. "I'll have to look into that. We're not happy they'll be so far away. Between the distance and time difference, it would us take twenty-four hours to get there if anything happened."

"I'm sure they'll be fine, but it's good to be aware of these things so they can be careful."

*

On Sunday, I searched the internet, and the information I uncovered was disturbing.

I shared it with Karen. "Over twenty teenagers have died in Thailand over the past few months, and poisoning was suspected in each case."

We wrestled with our fears and whether we should ask Eric and Gloria to cancel their trip. But at the end of the day, we had to accept the fact that they were adults; we could only caution them and pass along the few available details.

When we dropped him off at Pearson airport, Eric put his arm around my shoulder. "Don't worry, Faja, we'll text and Skype to keep in touch."

After goodbye hugs, Eric and Gloria walked towards the security doors and, with a final wave, disappeared behind them. Energetic youths off on an adventure, and it reminded me of my own trip after university. The excitement and anticipation, as well as my innocence, surfaced from the deep wells of my memory. Despite my naivety and many blunders, I had survived, and this comforted me. My worries lessened. It turned out to be a wonderful experience for me and, God willing, would be the same for them.

We Skyped on Monday after they arrived at their hotel. It was ten p.m. in Canada, and thanks to the wonder of long-distance travel, nine a.m. Tuesday morning in Bangkok. On camera, Eric looked tired but happy, and since Gloria was occupied, we had him all to ourselves for the conversation.

The webcam technology was impressive, and there was no fee, no matter how long the calling distance.

I remembered my first video conference call twenty years ago with our American R&D team. Although primitive by today's standards, it was cutting edge at the time. The equipment was prohibitively expensive, so the call was booked with a company specialized in the technology. Sitting with my boss and the US vice president, I stared at an empty conference room displayed on a large screen and waited. Suddenly, a door opened and four men in lab coats walked stiffly to the table in jerky motions. Video transmission hadn't been perfected, so in addition to the strange body movements, their speech was out of sync. If scientists don't look nerdy enough on camera, add disjointed actions and out-of-step dialogue. It looked like a Monty Python skit. I laughed in surprise but quickly covered it up with a cough, followed by some throat clearing. I wondered if we appeared the same to them on their end.

News media at the time claimed video calling to be the new de rigueur way of conducting international business, making high-cost travel a thing of the past. It didn't, at least not in that form. We never used it again, but within a few years, video conferencing improved and became inexpensively available on desktops. Yes, today's teleconferencing technology was infinitely better.

*

On Saturday, we Skyped with Eric again. This time, our son looked worse and confessed with some embarrassment to being ill. We queried his symptoms and listened attentively while alarm bells rang in our heads.

"See a doctor, Eric. Don't fool around with this," Karen chastised him. "Remember those deaths?"

"Yeah, I know, but we think it's the flu," he said, shrugging off the concern. "But, if I get worse, I'll see a doctor."

It so happened they were heading to Phuket next to enjoy the beautiful beaches. We texted frequently over the next few days, and his condition remained unchanged. On a video call Tuesday, he delivered the news that Gloria was also sick.

"Go to a hospital. What are the chances you both have the flu?" I said, and my voice was quivering. "Very low if you ask me, and you say Gloria's symptoms are different from yours?"

"Yeah, I don't have the fever, that's true," he said and appeared to consider this. "But to be honest, I believe she has food poisoning from the restaurant the other night."

The word poison struck fear in our hearts. Although we felt encouraged that their recent stay had been at a big chain hotel, with presumably better pesticide practices, when your child is in a developing country with limited healthcare and sparsely spoken English, you imagine all sorts of threatening scenarios. Eric was certain they had a virus and food poisoning, but we didn't share his conviction.

"Dear God, please keep Eric and Gloria safe, and if they've been poisoned, help them find medical aid quickly. Please bring them both home safe," we prayed often.

*

At work, I girded myself for a sudden flight overseas. It'd be expensive on short notice, but I wasn't prepared to let them die in a foreign country without proper medical aid. Now we were talking to them every day. And then, miraculously, both of them got better. Karen and I breathed a tremendous sigh of relief. And soon we received pictures of them grinning at a golden palace and another posing with large tigers and equally large smiles. They were having a great week, and the recent tension tumbled off our shoulders.

"Oh, Faja, I told you not to worry," he said, with Gloria smiling alongside. "It was the flu or a bit of food poisoning, that's all."

Thank goodness for the visual connection because we could see with our own eyes that they were healthy and robust. I slumped in my chair after the call. With the crisis over, the tiredness from weeks of adrenalin-pumping stress sank in. Of our three children, Eric had given us the least trouble, but even an easygoing, well-behaved child brings drama into your life every now and then.

*

Then before we knew it, and before they wanted to, it was time to leave. We picked Eric up at the airport, and Gloria's parents did the same for her. Our son was in an expansive mood as he stretched out in the back of our van on the way home. "It was so cheap, Mummsy, we ate dinner each night for ten dollars in total. And funny enough, plenty of people thought Gloria was Thai even though she can't speak the language."

Since her family were five generation Canadians, it surprised him that they'd mistaken her for a local. Glancing in the rear-view mirror at Eric, I noticed he looked serene and happy; no doubt the trip had been therapeutic after the pressures of his last school year. Karen sat blissfully beside him listening, but after a while, she shot him an annoyed glance.

"You aged Father and me ten years with this trip, Eric. Please — don't ever travel to a country like Thailand again!"

He appeared ruffled by this. "What? Why did you worry? We were fine."

I couldn't restrain myself. I shouted over my shoulder as I drove, "Oh, I don't know, Sonny. Maybe because all these kids died there. And then you got sick... and then Gloria got sick. Of course, we were worried!"

"Oh, Faja, you shouldn't have. It was perfectly safe," he said breezily and gazed out the window to close the subject.

Ah, the ignorance of youth. It was months before a CBC investigative report revealed the truth behind those deaths. Twenty-four young travellers, including the two Canadians, died from exposure to a pesticide placed under their beds or in ventilation systems to kill bedbugs. One grief-stricken mother recited how her son complained of a headache on the phone and said he'd go to bed early to get rid of it. By morning, he was dead from the increased exposure of the additional sleep. Government officials were feckless, claiming the pesticide was already labelled not to be used near humans, and they hadn't the resources to police it. Even though he tried not to show it, Eric appeared rattled as he watched it with us. We could only give thanks that these two hadn't been harmed.

Both graduated, and back in Canada, Eric and Gloria started job searching. And since Eric was living at home again, he had ample opportunity to observe the difficulties we faced with Jackie, including fighting and running out of the house screaming. He attempted to mediate, but it wasn't easy. Many a day, I felt like running out of the house screaming myself. On the bright side, Meggy was still working at a retail position she found last fall, and Jackie had graduated from high school.

*

As we continued meeting with the family therapist, I found the greatest benefit from our sessions without Jackie. In these, Karen and I could talk candidly about how her behaviour upset us and the big decisions we faced. A family vacation in Hawaii had been booked for August, and Jackie wanted to attend university in September.

I fixed Frank squarely in the eye. "I have trouble with this. We love our family holidays, but why would we bring her on this trip or pay for university if she doesn't appreciate what we do for her?"

Frank considered this for a moment and then spoke. "Well, you don't have to take her on vacation, but I think it would be good for all of you." He looked at me and then Karen. "But you may come to the point where you have to kick her out. Either she behaves or leaves."

We told him about the two weeks she had spent at Anna's.

"Staying at her grandmother's isn't really the same as kicking her out. She has to learn consequences and take responsibility for them. If she doesn't learn this now, she could end up with more serious issues, like getting arrested or losing a job later in life."

"I don't want her living on the streets," Karen piped in, and her face showed concern. "My mother's isn't the best solution, but it's better than going to a shelter."

Frank gestured with his hand. "If you don't teach her that she can't cross this boundary and still live in your house, she'll continue to hold all the power." That made absolute sense to me. She did hold the power. He elaborated further, "Teenagers are self-focused with very little empathy for the parents trapped into watching a constant me, me, me show of their kids. There are many opinions on the cause; some believe it results from the massive mental and physical development they undergo. You can help minimize the behaviour by giving them opportunities to be accountable for their actions, instead of jumping to their rescue. And believe me, teenagers know how to manipulate a situation."

We listened carefully. It was a lot to take in, and he had touched on an area in which we struggled. During the ride home, we rehashed the session, and I had the impression that the need for Karen to stand tough was sinking in.

*

The first test of her new resolve came quickly. Karen picked Jackie up from Kat's house on Friday and took her to a physiotherapy appointment. Jackie was learning exercises to strengthen her muscles and reduce the effects of scoliosis. Afterwards, she texted Karen and asked to be dropped at a party. Karen had been to the place before and thought it might be a drug house. Two older men with tattoos stood by their motorcycles observing them on the previous visit. Therefore, she told Jackie she wouldn't drive her there because she had a bad feeling about the place. This resulted in a stream of abuse.

Karen texted a response: *Fine, I'm not picking you up then. Walk home or ask your dad.*

Then she called me to give me a heads up.

I listened sympathetically to her tale of the vitriolic attack. "Funny, she rarely swears at me."

"That's because when she does, your eyes bulge, smoke comes out of your ears and you rain down fire on her."

I chuckled at her description, but she was right; and I did fight too much with Jackie.

Shortly after, the phone rang just as I was preparing to leave the office. Jackie's voice sounded pleasant, so I agreed to get her. After all, I didn't relish my reputation as the tough one.

There wasn't much talking in the car, but halfway home I said, "I hear you've been abusive to your mother."

This was met by silence. When we entered the house, Jackie ran upstairs, and I joined Karen in the living room where she restated how upset she was.

"So, what did you do to punish her?"

Her face darkened. "She has no consideration for anyone else. I've been worried about my mother all week, she didn't look well, and I had to run her to the doctor. He scheduled an appointment with a heart specialist."

I repeated the question, "What are you doing to discipline her?"

"She's not going to the party."

"Yeah, that's a given, and you already told her that." I glared in frustration. "But how are you punishing her for being abusive? You can't let her treat you like this. Cut off her phone."

I handed her a folder with the information for the provider. Karen nodded and went to the basement to place the call so Jackie wouldn't overhear.

*

But she did. Seconds later, Jackie came running down the stairs. "Nooooo! Don't do it."

I blocked her path and grabbed her by the wrist as she tried to run past me. I let go when she attempted to bite my hand but cut her off again when she tried to dart around me. Then she yelled loudly so the person on the other end would hear, "No, no. Don't listen to them!"

I pushed her into the bathroom and shut the door. But the anger had given her strength, and I needed all my determination to keep it closed.

Karen was wrapping up the conversation. "Aren't teenagers fun!" she cried bitterly into the phone.

The woman on the other end had realized what we were doing but sympathetically played along with the lost phone story.

Jackie pulled on the doorknob and shrieked. I clung to it and shouted back, "You're not coming out until you stop screaming."

All at once, the noise ended. "O.K., I've stopped," she said quietly.

I opened the door, and she bolted past.

She grabbed her coat, and with blazing eyes hollered, "Now you've done it. I'm going out, and you don't know where!"

"So what!" I shouted in response.

The front door slammed, and Karen let out an exhausted moan. "Let her go. I don't care. Fine."

*

Ten minutes later, Jackie reappeared and bolted up to her room before leaving once more. I glanced out the window in time to watch her climb into a taxi. Pondering the situation, I went upstairs and found her money bank lying on the bed with change scattered around. *So that's where she got the money.* When I returned downstairs, Karen was opening a bottle of wine, so I poured myself a beer. Hours later, Jackie came back and disappeared into her room. We heard no more from her that night.

She joined us at breakfast, acting subdued but polite. There was no mention of her fiery exit, and we didn't bring it up. When she asked about her cell, Karen informed her it wouldn't be reconnected for three days and stuck to it.

This was a giant step for Karen. Before, if the girls yelled, "I'm leaving home," or "I'm going to kill myself," she'd run after them and try to make peace. I guess Karen had resigned herself to the fact they'll do whatever they want regardless, and we had to remain firm.

*

I grabbed my laptop bag and stepped into the sunshine outside, feeling as if a weight had dropped off me. The balance of power was tilting in our direction.

DECISION TIME

"Right or wrong, be decisive. The road of life is paved with flat squirrels who couldn't make a decision." - Author Unknown

JACKIE HAD LANDED a summer job in the pro shop of a local golf course, and the news lifted our spirits. Perhaps joining the working world would bring her some maturity, and it was only twenty minutes away by foot. But when I suggested she walk, Karen rebuffed the idea.

"It's a dangerous area by the high school, so she's not doing that — end of discussion."

I knew better than to argue with the momma bear, which is what I called her. The name stems from a camping excursion before we had children. Three little bear cubs wandered into our campground. All the campers gathered to take pictures and talk about how cute they were. All of a sudden, there was a loud crashing sound in the woods, and the momma bear emerged, flashing sharp teeth in anger. Everybody ran for their lives. That's the same instinct Karen draws on to protect her kids, and nobody messes with the momma bear.

Karen and I had met privately with Frank recently to talk about the latest blow up with Jackie. For the first time, Karen hadn't caved or acted as Baba, her Russian grandmother, would say, like a mouse under the broom. I told Frank how happy I was that Karen had stood firm but still didn't like the fact that she ferried Jackie around in the car.

"Karen takes her to work at seven every morning, while Jackie stares at her phone and barely talks to her. Our daughter doesn't show the slightest guilt at putting her mother out," I fumed. "And from the stories I've heard of Karen's friends, it seems that treating mothers badly is standard practice at this age."

Frank's mouth curved into a smile. "From my experience, I'd say that's quite true," he responded, much to my surprise.

We drafted another contract. And Frank saw Jackie's resistance for himself when they met two weeks later, and she grudgingly signed it.

Agreement for Living at Home
- *Be respectful (as long as I'm not being harassed*)*
- *Be grateful. Show appreciation for rides, meals, etc.*
- *Stop lying and stealing money*
- *Improve the behaviour — no more "screaming" or calling names*

* Jackie added this caveat

Two weeks later, Karen and I had our final session with Frank, and we had decisions to make. Jackie had been accepted at Wilfrid Laurier in Waterloo, and our holiday was fast approaching. While Frank realized what we were up against, he had a different slant on how to handle the issue, persisting in the view that she should join our vacation.

"If she doesn't improve, you need to kick her out, and perhaps university isn't something she should pursue," he reiterated.

Karen and I had discussed it beforehand and weren't comfortable with this step yet. Kicking her out was riskier than leaving her behind; she might end up on the street, on drugs or estranged from us.

With a glance at me first, Karen responded, "We want to threaten her with the Hawaiian trip first because leaving her behind may bring about the changes needed so she could continue with school as planned. She's quite smart, just lazy."

Frank reflected for a moment and then said, "It really comes down to your decision. I can only advise."

He wished us the best of luck, and we thanked him for all his help.

When we talked to Jackie later in the week, Karen levelled with her.

"If your conduct doesn't improve, you won't be joining us in Hawaii. Sorry, but that's the way it is."

"I don't care. I don't want to go anyway. I hate my family!" She spat the words out, and it felt like a knife was plunged into our hearts.

We stared at each other in disbelief. The flights had been booked a year ago with frequent flyer miles. It would be our grandest holiday yet and perhaps the last time Eric could join us now since he had recently landed a full-time job in his field. But Jackie wasn't going to make this easy; we felt she was challenging us.

After waiting a few more days, Karen called the airline, crying as she spoke on the phone.

"You don't have to cancel today," said the agent sympathetically. "You can wait until the day before because there's no refund or credit. Maybe she'll be better, and you'll change your mind."

"No," Karen sobbed, "we have to do this."

So convinced were we of the need to draw a line in the sand

that we didn't blink at sacrificing her ticket. There was no turning back now. Later, Karen said it was one of the hardest things she ever had to do. Our daughter, on the other hand, breezed about the house unconcerned and claimed she'd be much happier at home.

*

I sat waiting in Dr. MacEwan's examination room. He entered slowly with my file under his arm, and his brow furrowed.

"What is it today then?" he asked in that Glasgow accent as he strode to his chair. Although he had attempted to act blasé, I noticed an element of apprehensiveness in his manner. He must have thought I'd come to complain about Jackie, despite his earlier instructions.

I spoke as soon as he seated himself. "We've decided Jackie will not be coming to Hawaii and have told her this."

A look of surprise appeared on his face. "And is Karen on board with this?"

"She had trouble with it at first but has come around and cancelled the ticket. It can't be reversed."

"Yes!" He cried, punching the air with his fist and grinning.

I chuckled, and his expression turned serious. He leaned towards me. "You're doing the right thing. Believe me, it's not easy, but sometimes you have to take these actions."

As we walked out together, I noticed more bounce in his step. It must be hard on doctors when patients don't listen to their advice and a relief when they finally do.

*

The last week before our departure, Karen received an interesting text.

"It's from Katie's mom," she said, and Karen looked troubled as she read it. "Hmmph. Diane thinks Jackie should come with us, that it's a mistake to leave her behind."

With a sombre expression, she handed me her cell. It was a

long text and mentioned the importance of family bonding. I read it in shock.

"She has a lot of nerve to lecture us." I shook my head, but then something about the wording struck me as unusual. "Wait a minute. This isn't from Diane," I sputtered. "Jackie wrote it!"

"You think so?"

I nodded vigorously, and the more I read it, the clearer it became. "Yes, don't you see, that expression — *family bonding.* That's ours. Besides, Diane didn't take her kids with her to Turks, so why would she criticize us?"

Karen's eyebrows arched upwards. "You know, I think you're right." She guffawed. "Those little dickens."

"So devious," I muttered. "They must have gotten a hold of Diane's phone." I handed her cell back. "Sounds like Jackie's sorry she's not coming after all."

"Should I text a response back?"

"No. Let's wait for Jackie to bring it up."

She never did. We arranged for her to stay at Grandma's and wrote up a contract to specify what was expected of her during our absence if she hoped to attend the fall semester of university.

Then Karen arranged for a neighbour to take Jackie to and from work during our absence, and we started packing.

*

Two days later, Meggy threw us a curve. She refused to travel without her sister.

Meggy watched with soulful eyes as Karen explained the situation to her. "The ticket's been cancelled and can't be undone, even if we wanted to."

Things got more tense as the final days ticked by; our dark-haired daughter fell into a state of depression. With one day remaining, Karen called Sue and anxiously filled her in. Twenty minutes later, our guardian angel breezed through the front door and announced she was taking Meggy for coffee. Our raven-haired daughter left like a lamb with her. Not long after, they returned.

Meggy nodded silently in the entranceway, while Sue waved her arms about. "Hawaii! Aren't you a lucky girl," she beamed with a broad smile, "and isn't it nice your parents are taking you? Who wouldn't love this opportunity?"

Meggy had come on board with the idea now.

"Thank you, Sue — you're a lifesaver!" we gushed, and our hearts burst with gratitude as we embraced her and Meggy in turn.

*

On Friday morning, we left Pearson airport on route to Vancouver for a short layover before our connecting flight. This would get us into Honolulu at five p.m., in perfect time to reach the hotel, relax and go to bed.

Five hours later, we landed at Vancouver airport.

"Wowzer!" Karen exclaimed, in her best Inspector Gadget manner, as we rode the escalator down to the lower floor. An immense wooden totem pole stood before us, rising taller and taller with our descent.

When we reached the bottom, Meggy pointed to an immense sculpture and ran to it. An emerald canoe was carrying and being powered by various mythical creatures. She shouted, "It's called The Spirit of Haida Gwaii." And we joined her to study it in detail.

I looked at my watch. "It's wonderful, but I'm afraid we'd better find our gate."

The magnificent displays of art were unexpected and stunning. We hurried past so many beautiful sculptures and paintings that it felt like we were running through an art gallery.

We arrived at the gate out of breath.

"I'm afraid there's a problem," said the airline representative. She was young, with short blonde hair and a sympathetic smile. "The plane has a mechanical issue, so we're waiting for another to arrive." She presented us with coupons for the restaurants in the terminal.

We made the best of the situation and ordered food and drinks. It wasn't so bad; the free dinner definitely eased the pain.

Just as we finished, an announcement came over the PA system. "Passengers on flight AC 5158 to Honolulu, please be advised of a delay to your departure. See personnel at the gate for information."

We groaned. Our blonde friend behind the desk was showing signs of strain. "No, we don't know how long it will be, but I can offer more coupons," she said with false cheer, handing Karen another set.

I turned to survey the area and sighed. "Good luck finding anywhere to spend them. Everything's being shuttered."

Our plane had exceeded the normal end for departures and boutique operations. The agent made no response, busying herself with the next set of unhappy customers. A loud rant of displeasure emerged from a gruff man, and I felt sorry for the young agent. With no shops open, there was nothing to do but sit in the plastic chairs by the gate and wait.

I muttered to Karen, "This is exactly like business travel — boring!"

"Oh, well," my personal cheerleader chirped, "it'll all be worth it when we get there."

"I hope they don't cancel the flight," I whispered so the kids wouldn't hear.

"Do you think they will?" she asked, horrified at the prospect.

"Possibly. At a certain point, they don't allow any more planes to leave." My mind flashed back to late night shuttles from airports to hotels, followed by early morning rushes back the next day for rescheduled flights.

Finally, after a postponement of six hours, exhausted yet relieved that we were flying at all, we trundled aboard. The cabin was dimly lit and unusually quiet; no food or drink was served, save for water bottles. Passengers immediately settled down to sleep. The ETA was two o'clock in the morning local time. After landing, collecting our luggage and passing through customs, I slumped wearily inside a dark taxi.

*

When the cab stopped, I rubbed my tired eyes and stared. There must have been some mistake. Karen had booked inexpensive accommodation yet illuminated there in the blackness stood an impressive resort. I checked the name and address with the driver, but it appeared to be correct. Maybe there were cheaper cabins on the property, I thought as I paid the fare and tumbled out of my seat half asleep.

We entered the lobby hesitantly, expecting to be directed out the back or to the side.

"Yes, we have your reservation," a cheerful young man at the desk assured me. Nervously, I double-checked the rate before signing the registration card. He handed me key cards and pointed to the elevators, and my jaw dropped. This was indeed our hotel, and the rate was a steal.

As we rode up, I whispered to Karen, "How did you find this place for such a cheap price? I feel as if we robbed a bank."

A happy smile crossed her tired face. "When I booked our lodgings in Maui, I mentioned to the lady that it was very difficult to find reasonable prices in Honolulu. So, she gave me the hotel she stays at when she's here."

Karen had done it again, and her approach reminded me of the African proverb, *If you want to go fast, go alone. If you want to far, go together.* That was Karen to a tee, always aiding others or getting their assistance.

As I swung the door open, Karen's mouth opened wide in a radiant smile. "Oh, this is nice!"

"Nice?" I strutted across the room, spreading my arms out in joy at the grandeur. "It's bloody fantastic."

It was a corner unit, one floor below the penthouse, with three beds, a kitchenette and two balconies — both with ocean views. Karen opened the balcony door directly facing the ocean, and we scrambled out, breathing in the warm salty air and admiring the lights that dotted the darkness of Waikiki Beach.

"They filmed the opening scene for *Hawaii Five-O* from this hotel. Remember?" Karen gushed. "We watched it before we left."

"Yes, and I see the similarity." I let out a large, satisfied breath. "What a find!"

Each morning, we sat out there with our coffee and enjoyed the breathtaking view until the kids awoke. For over a week, we enjoyed the hotel — swimming, walking on the sand — and one day rented a convertible to explore the north shore. In the evenings, we strolled the boardwalk and picked a different restaurant overlooking the sea each night for dinner. As far as I was concerned, this was living. The only missing ingredient was our blonde daughter, and although we tried not to dwell on it, we could tell that Meggy missed her a great deal.

*

We had planned half the vacation to be on Oahu and the remainder on Maui. Therefore, we soon caught a short flight to the other island, which had a much more laid-back vibe. The condo unit we had rented on this island appeared a bit rundown, as if its former glory days had faded. But it was on the ocean and had the full kitchen we required, so we were happy.

As we sipped our morning coffee early that week, Karen jumped unexpectedly out of her chair and shouted, "Look, dolphins!"

She leaned against the concrete barrier and pointed. I followed her hand and spotted two dolphins jumping in unison every few seconds as they moved across the bay.

"Isn't that amazing!" she giggled. This was the sort of thing that really made her day.

I grinned back at her. "Amazing, and we didn't even have to leave the condo."

We went sightseeing in the area and then drove to Lahaina, which has the oldest Banyan tree in Hawaii. Possessing an aerial root system, the roots descend to the ground to create new trunks. We walked underneath the canopy and between the multiple trunks and imagined the history and stories this tree might tell, if only it could talk. After exploring the town, which wasn't very big, we headed to Fleetwood's restaurant for dinner. Although the kids weren't as familiar with the old band, Karen and I were big fans of Fleetwood Mac.

A tall young man, probably working there for the summer, showed us to a table. And before he could take our orders, Karen blurted out, "Is it true Mick Fleetwood drops in every now and then?"

"Absolutely." The waiter nodded and gestured with his hand to a corner of the room that contained a flashy red set of drums. "He comes in to play."

"When was he here last?" I asked, suspecting they put the drums on display and perpetuated the story to encourage business.

"Oh, a few weeks ago."

Karen's eyes glowed with excitement and she kept a continual watch during dinner, in case Mick made a surprise appearance. However, he was a no show that night.

After the waiter brought coffee, Karen said eagerly, "We should do the Road to Hana tomorrow. It's the main attraction on the eastern shore."

The kids perked up.

"Sure, I'm down for that," Eric said happily, and Meggy expressed her willingness too with a wide smile and a sparkle in her eyes. She had come out of the funk she'd been in without her sister and now was in full swing of the vacation spirit.

I hesitated. The idea of driving all the way across the island, down the coast and back again wasn't enticing. But they all appeared so exuberant that I agreed.

*

As we entered the scenic coastal road, it ascended the side of a mountain, and I caught breathtaking glimpses of green-blue ocean bays far below. But it became a slow journey, for I encountered a single lane bridge every few minutes and had to wait for our turn to cross. At some bridges, blind turns obstructed by tropical overgrowth waited ominously on the other side to give me an additional thrill. Finding a gap in traffic, I'd race across and then pull over to let the emerging vehicles pass. It was nerve-wracking.

Karen, however, was unperturbed and merrily read from her guidebook as we travelled along.

"It says the Bamboo Forest is a highlight, and... there are fifty-four old one-lane bridges and over 600 curves, some of which are hairpin. So be careful, dear!"

"Terrific," I wheezed, "are you sure Road to Hana doesn't mean Road to Hell in Hawaiian?"

"Ha-ha."

Karen may have been captivated by the scenery, but I felt a tension headache building.

Momentarily, I heard Eric behind me. "There's a hike I discovered on the internet that looks really good, Poppo. We should do it."

I glanced in the mirror at my grinning son, and Karen went on the lookout. Soon we were meandering down a cul-de-sac with large stately residences on one side and verdant forest on the other.

"Stop!" Eric shouted. He undid his seatbelt. "Okay, people, this is where we go in." He ushered us out of the car.

*

I surveyed the few bushes and small path before us with skepticism; there was no sign or marker.

"Are you sure this is the entrance?"

"Yep, this is it," he said, standing beside me.

"Looks like the perfect spot for a murder," I grumbled, peering nervously through the trees as we entered.

It wasn't as much a path as simply wooden planks laid over mud, but we followed it, crisscrossing a creek for about forty minutes. Just when I was about to suggest turning back, the trail opened up to reveal a waterfall. Blue water tumbled into a deep, languid pool surrounded by rocks and rainforest vegetation. It was the pacific paradise you dream about. About twenty other tourists were scattered around enjoying this hidden gem, lounging on the boulders or swimming in the pool. Some glanced over casually to check out the newcomers. At Karen's insistence, we had worn bathing suits under our clothes, so we stripped off and waded in. The water was cool and refreshing. We swam about and ducked under the falls. I joined Eric and some others climbing up one edge of the waterfall and jumping into the water.

"Well done, Sonny," I exclaimed after surfacing and swimming up to him.

He flashed a smile, which displayed his white teeth, and then dipped below the surface.

Meggy snapped pictures, and we spent an hour or two enjoying the natural pool before retracing our steps. We parked at other places on the Road to Hana and hiked inwards. And while they were all worth a visit, none was as spectacular as that first. It was definitely a highlight of our trip.

*

On Wednesday, we drove to Haleakala National Park to hike the volcano and watch the sunset from the top. The journey up was spectacular, with many photo ops of the crater below and small waterfalls. As we climbed higher, the lush greenery gave way to a more barren, almost moonlike rock surface. We parked at the Visitor Center,

10,000 ft above sea level, and admired the panoramic view of the crater and mountains in the distance. We were much closer to the clouds; it felt as if you could almost reach up and touch them. There were stairs leading to the trail we had chosen, and Karen picked up a crooked walking stick to help her. Her knees were not what they used to be.

In the late afternoon, we ate the sandwiches we had made and stored in our small cooler and found a place to watch the sunset amongst sixty other tourists spread out across the wide ridge. While we waited, I took a spectacular shot of Eric, hands over his head to give the appearance of holding the small crimson ball of a sun between them.

Murmurs rippled through the crowd as the show started. The sky glowed in hues from orange to crimson, and the sun began its descent behind white, fluffy clouds before disappearing behind the distant mountain. Even though it was gone, the clouds and sky remained lit for some time with the sun's ethereal glow. It was amazing. But we didn't linger much longer. We got up stiffly, gave one final survey of the horizon and then moved quickly to our rental car. Nighttime temperatures dip near freezing, and the cold had already crept upon us despite our long pants and warm jackets.

As we started back down, Karen turned the heater on and said, "Let's eat at that restaurant we saw on the way up. It had a flower garden and overlooked the valley."

"Sure, that would be nicer than some fast-food joint."

*

The hostess seated us in a booth against the large set of windows, but it was dark outside so we couldn't see the beautiful gardens. After a satisfying meal, we sat comfortably and chatted while waiting for the waitress to bring coffee. Meggy scanned the pictures on my camera, deleting some and showing us the odd one.

"Look at this shot of Mother," she cried abruptly, grinning from ear to ear.

Karen had been captured bent over as she was about to walk down to the trail, with one hand gripping the crooked stick she had placed on the step below. She was the spitting image of an old lady in a children's book of fables. Meggy enlarged it and passed it around again.

Eric doubled over and collapsed along the back of the booth, his body shaking. He gasped, "The... wizard... stick!"

We all howled, including Karen. It was true. With her vest and backpack, she looked like Gandalf holding a miniature staff. Our son laughed so hard the tears rolled down his face. Other customers regarded us with curiosity.

"We'd better cut it out," I said, catching my breath, "or people are going to ask what we're drinking and then order the same!"

It wasn't easy, though. We'd all fall quiet for a moment recovering, but then someone would start giggling, and we'd all roar again. It was the fitting end to a glorious day.

*

The following afternoon, as we stretched out lazily on the small sandy beach at our condo, we suddenly realized it was our last full day of vacation. The three weeks had slipped by incredibly fast. And I wondered how Jackie would greet us. Each of us had texted her frequently, especially Meggy, and the responses had been friendly but brief. At least the golf course had kept her busy. Diplomatically, we had avoided raving about the scenery and only posted a handful of photos.

When the taxi brought us home, we burst in as one excited mass pulling baggage, talking, hugging Anna and Jackie and stroking the pets. Jackie appeared subdued but smiled at each of us. We chatted about the trip, and Karen told her not to worry because we'd return one day so she could experience it.

Within an hour of walking through the door, Karen had already started the laundry. She could be a dynamo as she pushed loads through the machine. We gathered in the living room, handed out souvenirs and asked how everything had been at home. No problems occurred, and I felt relieved. Wisely, we had returned on a Saturday, so I would have sufficient time to recover from the time difference before rushing to the office.

The next day, Karen found a plastic lei of yellow, blue and red flowers on Jackie's dresser and brought it into the family room. "What's with the lei, Jackie?" she asked, looking at our blonde daughter. "I found it hanging on your mirror."

"Oh, they had a Hawaiian day at the golf club," she sighed, "and we had to wear them for the members."

Karen and I exchanged looks, kept our faces impassive, but laughed inwardly. How ironic life can be.

We never talked about Hawaii again in Jackie's presence. Like Voldemort, it became the name that should not be spoken. But we were happy with our decision not to bring her. And while we valued the professional advice to include her, we were the ones that had to live with the outcome, not the therapist. Hopefully, Jackie had gotten the message now to follow our rules. With the holiday behind us, the next hurdle would be university — to go or not to go. And the answer to that depended entirely on Jackie.

THE UNIVERSITY 28 CONUNDRUM

*"Knowledge is like underwear. It is useful to have it,
but not necessary to show it off." - Bill Murray.*

"**W**HY WOULD YOU want me here to fight with?" Jackie asked
defiantly when we threated not to send her to Wilfrid Laurier.
She was fidgeting on the couch in a pink T-shirt and pink terrycloth
shorts with the word *Pink* printed on the bottom. Meggy sat in the
adjacent wing chair, taking it all in.

I fixed my gaze on Jackie and spoke evenly, "Who says you'd
stay home? University is a privilege not a right. If you don't behave,
we can kick you out."

"I can't afford to live on my own."

"That's your problem."

Following the return from our trip, we enjoyed a brief interval
of acceptable conduct from Jackie. But within a week, she reverted

to acting rude and ungrateful: not telling Karen where she was going and treating her like a servant.

Karen and I vented our feelings about this on Saturday night when the girls were out.

I exhaled loudly. "Frankly, I find it depressing. After all our effort, and all the therapy, and having missed out on Hawaii, why won't she behave?"

Karen frowned. "Jackie's extremely emotional and a hothead. And you two are always banging heads."

"Yes, but I get mad because she doesn't treat us with respect. And I won't reward bad behaviour with university. Even though I've paid the tuition, I can still cancel with a full refund."

"Let's think about it and pray for guidance. It won't help to worry about it tonight."

But it was coming down to the wire; the move-in date for residence was less than two weeks away, yet she remained defiant. Was bad behaviour intrinsic to her nature?

*

Monday afternoon, Karen called me at the office. "I've thought about it, Andrew, and I believe we should let her go to Laurier. I talked to Sue and Maria, and both said they would send her." She gave a bitter laugh. "Besides, I can't take her living at home anymore. And maybe it'll smarten her up. After all, university is a maturing experience."

As I listened, the words my friend Mike had said came back to me. "... *staying home wasn't an option. It was either go away to school or move out.*"

"Good point," I said. "Okay, I agree."

Still, I wasn't prepared to write her a blank cheque. We wrote an agreement for her to sign, and if she didn't live up to the conditions, we'd pull her out.

Contract for University
- *Attend all classes*

- *Maintain a B to B+ average in order to qualify for the co-op program*
- *Try to get a part-time job **if** I have enough free time*
- *Be respectful*
- *Help out **if** I'm home*
- *Bus **if** I decide to come home*

The 'ifs' were added by our daughter.

Jackie had the smarts for a B+ average if she rekindled her ambition. As with her brother, I'd pay her tuition, books, room and board this year, and she'd have to pay for books in the remaining years. She also had to pay personal expenses, such as movies, trips or eating at places outside the meal plan.

After signing, she glared at us. "I hate my family. You'll never see me again until Christmas!"

Those words hurt deeply, but we said nothing. My head ached, and I felt miserable right down to my toes. Somehow, we had failed as parents, and the possibility of being estranged from her weighed on my mind. There must be a way to rebuild our relationship.

*

On the Sunday of Labour Day weekend, we packed up our van with all the things Jackie would need for first year and drove to Waterloo. When we were within a few blocks of the campus, the streets began to swarm with young people and became dotted with endless fast-food outlets — all needed to feed those teenage brains. This was a young person's town, filled with students. And September is a pretty month on campus. The hot days of summer were behind us, but the air was still pleasantly warm. I blinked at the sun, which burned brightly above green grass littered with teenagers sitting in groups or walking between buildings. We parked adjacent to Jackie's residence.

When I opened the door to her designated room, I found a pretty brunette sitting on one of the two beds and staring at me.

I smiled. "Hello, I'm Jacquelyn's father ..." My introduction was cut off as the rest of the family burst through the door with suitcases and boxes.

She smiled shyly at all of us. "Hi, I'm Sarah."

Jackie and her grinned at each other, and Eric and Meggy introduced themselves.

Karen busied herself unpacking bed sheets, making up her bed and placing things in drawers. "Look over here, Jackie, so you can see where I've put things."

Sarah had moved in earlier, so we asked her where Jackie could eat since most of the cafeterias hadn't opened yet. She mentioned a few places nearby and offered to go with Jackie later. Then she disappeared down the hall to talk to some friends and give us some privacy.

"She seems friendly," I said as I set up the new laptop and printer we had bought Jackie. I showed her how it worked and gave her a spare ink cartridge. "What's your campus log on?" I asked. "I'll connect you to their website."

"I don't know," Jackie said, stumped. "But never mind. I'll find out from Sarah."

"This must be your half of the bulletin board," Karen said, pointing to a large corkboard on the wall. The left side was bare, while the right had crisp documents neatly pinned in a pattern. "Look how tidy and organized your roommate's half is," Karen effused and turned her head towards our daughter. "Maybe she'll be a positive influence on you, Jackie!"

This brought forth a chuckle from the whole family. Then we gave hugs and said goodbye so she could meet other students on the floor.

*

With Eric we were more nervous — would he be lonely; would he make friends? But we didn't worry as much about Jackie. She was very sociable and had more pals than anyone else. Unfortunately, none had chosen Laurier, so she would start out like Eric, alone. Still, there was no doubt she'd fit in. Eric helped me load the empty boxes and suitcases into the trunk, and we headed off in high spirits. It was a relief to be finished and to know Jackie was in a good place for her studies and fun activities.

As we motored down Highway 401, Karen said, "Funny, I cried when Eric moved out, but this time was different — I would have cried if she hadn't!"

I laughed and glanced at Meggy in the rear-view mirror. She'd miss Jackie and be distressed her younger sister had moved away before her. But she seemed to be handling it well, helping with the move and appearing excited for her sister. Meggy had registered for two evening courses at Humber College and started a better job, so she had things to be proud of too.

After dinner, while we relaxed with a drink, Karen let out a contented sigh. "It'll be nice to have a break and know she's safe."

I sipped my beer and leaned back against the sofa. "I agree, and it's a load off my chest."

"We'll miss her but not tonight!" she laughed.

The unusual quietness in the house was calming. Meggy had gone to change her clothes and entered the room now, wearing a blue sweat top and grey fleece pants. Restless, she sat down in the armchair, clasped her hands around one knee, and started talking.

"I think she'll make friends quickly," she said. Meaghan was always impressed by her sister's social skills.

"Yeah, she'll be fine," I agreed, but the worry that we might not hear from her nagged at me.

Karen nodded. "I'm not concerned either, and if she doesn't come home until Christmas, so be it."

Moochie moved beside Meaghan and motioned with her head to be picked up. She seemed to sense Meggy was struggling with her sister's move away.

*

The following afternoon, Karen gave me a ring at work.

"Andrew, remember how Jackie said she hates us and won't be back until December? Well, she's already texting."

"What did she say?" I whispered into the mouthpiece.

"Here, let me read it to you," she giggled. "I don't like it here; I want to come home."

I couldn't have been more shocked if someone had slapped me. "Are you kidding?" I gasped. "We just moved her in!"

"Yeah, he-he, she also texted Meggy and Eric. Whatever happened to — 'I can't wait to get out of here!'"

I paused for a moment to consider this unexpected news. "Wow, big change. But tell her we can't bring her home right now; she'll have to wait until the weekend. Tell her to give it a chance and stick it out for a while. She's just feeling insecure right now."

"I will. She'll get to know other kids; she just needs to be patient," Karen said in a tone that oozed understanding.

I glanced out the window at the peaceful courtyard below. "Living on your own is scary in the beginning. Remember Eric? He came back every weekend for the first two months."

"I remember. Well, she's coming home this Friday, so be happy to see her."

"Of course, I will," I said indignantly, but my mind was thinking — *this is terrible!* I took a deep breath and said, "Let's pray tonight that she'll feel better and stay put."

After hanging up, I returned to the report I'd been reading before the call but had trouble concentrating. I kept chuckling to myself. Jackie had caught me completely off guard, but the fact that she missed us was a tremendous relief. I stood up, walked to the door, poked my head around and looked into Carol's office. She was working at her desk, and as I stood there trying to judge whether to interrupt her or not, she glanced up and smiled.

*

Jackie took the bus home that Friday and every one for the next eight weeks. To be honest, I had hoped for more of a break.

Karen didn't seem to mind and admonished me for expressing the desire to have a Jackie-free weekend. "This is her home; she needs to feel loved and encouraged."

Karen was certainly resilient, having sloughed off any resentment or bitterness to eagerly support her child during a difficult period. Our youngest had begun her journey down the road of appreciation, just as we hoped and prayed she would. It's traumatic when you're away from the family for the first time, and Karen understood this well. Having moved to the city at nineteen, she was often lonely despite having relatives here. So, we put the past aside and greeted our daughter enthusiastically on each visit. However, we weren't prepared to drive out and pick her up. We had to do that with Eric because there wasn't a direct bus to McMaster, but Laurier had hourly service from a nearby mall.

*

We corresponded mostly by text but also with the odd phone call in order to hear her voice and make sure she wasn't depressed. Suicide is a real concern for first-year students, and we weren't going to rely on passive texting to gauge our child's mental health. Despite having no interest in texting before Eric went to university, Karen had become quite proficient since then.

On another call, Jackie complained to me, "OMG, she writes me a letter every morning! As soon as I wake up, there's a super long email waiting. I just read the first line. That's enough, ha-ha-ha."

"You're so mean," Karen teased, having heard her on speaker.

"I'm sorry, but that's too much to read in the morning. Dad, she asks me — where are you going? Who are you going out with? And so on and so on." She had lowered her voice to imitate her mother and then giggled. "It never ends."

Karen laughed it off. "If loving you is a crime, then I'm guilty as charged!"

There was a groan on the other end.

After a few weeks, Jackie texted: *If I have to ride the bus this Friday, I'm not coming.*

Karen: *Fine, don't. There's no need to drive all the way there when transit runs hourly. If it's too much for you, then stay in residence this time.*

Jackie: *Alright I'll take the bus.*

She kept testing us, but her attitude was much improved.

*

Her brother and sister were elated whenever she arrived, although brothers have a special way of displaying affection — by torment mostly. One Saturday, for example, Jackie strolled into the kitchen while I was cooking breakfast.

Eric glanced sideways from where he sat eating a bowl of fruit. "Jackie, did you know you have man hands?"

The effect was similar to a grenade being thrown into the room.

"MAN HANDS? What are you talking about? **DAD!**"

I gritted my teeth. "Eric, you know better than to say that. Girls are very sensitive about these things. Never joke about their weight, looks or hands."

He snickered and continued eating.

I spied two empty bowls on the table beside him. "Eric, did you eat all *three* fruit bowls?"

"Yeah, why?" he asked, glancing at them. "They were for me, weren't they?"

I rolled my eyes. "Nooo. If your mother made all that fruit for you, why would she put it in three different bowls?"

He licked his spoon and laughed. "Oh, I thought they were for me. *Sorry.*"

"You're such a glutton, like Gordie the Gut."

"Who?"

"You've forgotten about him, but he had a habit of eating other people's food."

*

A month passed, and then Jackie texted me, all excited. Laurier had a private chat forum where students could post comments, and someone nominated her for most attractive student. She was thrilled, and I congratulated her. No surprise to me, though; both our girls were gorgeous. They took after their mother. As expected, Jackie had settled in, made friends, and was revelling in campus life. And for the first time in a long while, we had pleasant conversations with her again.

"So, how many hours of classes do you have a week?" I asked the next time she was home.

"Umm, I don't know. Why?"

"Just curious. When's your first class each day?"

"Uh, eleven."

I nearly spit out my tea. "Eleven o'clock? I started at nine each day."

"Ha-ha-ha, I didn't want to wake up that early, so I picked courses that start later." She jumped out of the chair. "I gotta go upstairs." Off she flew like a rocket. A few minutes later, she zipped back in and plopped back down in the armchair.

I glanced over. "Your roommate's cute and very neat."

"Yeah, ha-ha. I took a picture of her bulletin board to show my friends." Jackie said, slouching in the chair with her legs crossed. "Oh, and a boy came to my room, so I pretended Sarah's side was mine. I told Sarah that when he left, he said, 'Your roommate's very messy.'" Jackie started chortling. "She was so mad, ha-ha." Then her expression turned serious. "But I couldn't tell him it was my side because that was such a dump."

"Of course, you could clean it up," I suggested with a slight smile.

"Hell to the no. That's not going to happen. Let's be real."

*

Later in the week, Karen snickered as she showed me another text.

Jackie: *I told the other girls in our dorm that Dad's writing a book about me, but he's changing my name to Jackeroo so people won't know it's me. Now they're calling me Jackeroo and introducing me like that to their friends. It's so annoying!*

I howled. This was perfect. Here I was getting revenge without even writing the book. It's wonderful when the universe rewards you like this.

More improvements continued in our daughter. At the beginning of December, Jackie phoned, and as was our habit, Karen turned on the speaker so she wouldn't have to repeat the same conversation to me.

Jackie sounded upset. "A girl here just lost her father. Isn't that sad?"

"That's terrible!" Karen cried. "What happened?"

"He was decorating their Christmas tree, had a heart attack and *died*." Compassion flowed from the speaker. "I feel so bad for her."

"How awful," Karen said, "and right before Christmas. Now you see why we say, life is short and can change in a heartbeat."

"I know... but you and Dad are alright, aren't you?" Her voice trembled with anxiety.

"Yes, we're all fine."

"Good, 'cause I was worried when I heard about this girl's father."

After we hung up, Karen's eyes watered. "Isn't that nice? She's concerned about us."

*

Exams were scheduled, and although Jackie had plenty of days in between them, she chose to stay at university to study. The stress and loneliness can be heaviest during the end of term because there's little social activity. Everyone's busy cramming and under pressure. Some kids had already finished and left campus; even some of the cafeterias had closed. One evening, Jackie had an exam at seven p.m., and Karen worried about her walking across the campus in the dark.

She texted beforehand: *Good luck on your exam. I'm looking forward to shopping with you when you're home. Text me when you're done and back in your room. Take your time and do well.*

Jackie: *Thank you* ☺

Afterwards Jackie texted: *I aced it for sure!*

Karen: *Great! On to the next one. Study hard!*

A few days later, Karen followed up: *How did you do? Did you pass?*

Jackie: *Idk, we'll see lol.*

Karen: *Ok, as long as you pass. Good night daughter. Luv u. xo.*

Jackie: *Night, love you L3. tell daddy I love him too.*

*

The next day there were more texts.

Jackie: *I'm at the burrito place & it's so busy & they call my number to pick out what I want but I was distracted and people around me got mad and yelled* **COME ON!** *Like Chill out.*

Karen: *Ignore them.*

Jackie: *I'm surprised you & daddy still love me, I know I was a brat. I'm very thankful for both of you. I'm sorry for what I put you through.*

Karen: *Hey daughter FYI I love this new and improved Jackie. Keep it up.*

Jackie: *Thanks. Love u* ☺☺☺

Karen wiped tears away and passed it to me. "Finally, some appreciation." She blew her nose. "Being on her own has made her grow up."

I sighed as I read it. "I'm shocked, but it's marvellous, finally ... after all these years."

Karen's hand found mine, and I felt a lump in my throat. We

hadn't realized that the difficult years would end so suddenly. We had entered a new phase. One where our teenage daughter demonstrated respect and appreciation. Sending her to university was one of the best decisions we ever made.

*

But life wasn't all bliss. When I walked through the front door the next day, Karen and Meggy were fighting.

"I asked her to show me what she's done on the essay that's due tonight — and she had nothing!" Karen yelled, and her face twisted in anger.

Our black-haired daughter sulked on the couch.

"What happened, Meggy? You claimed to be working on it all week," I said as I hung up my coat.

"I can't think of anything to write."

"Yeah, we're back to the bullshit again!" Karen fumed. "She lied, and then she was calling me names."

"Mother was mean to me," she said, and her eyes pleaded with me. Then her lip curled, and she glared at Karen. "And stop nagging me!"

Meggy struggled with procrastination and often begged for help at the last minute, which stressed all of us out. After dinner, we talked more calmly and told her she had to buckle down or go to Anna's. These courses cost money, and she had to be honest about her progress. She got irritated and charged upstairs to pack.

As I watched from the bedroom window, Meggy marched down the street with a duffle bag slung over her shoulder.

Here we go again. I looked up to the sky — heaven help us.

*

After Jackie finished her last exam, I drove to Laurier to pick her up. Pulling into the parking area, I spotted my blonde girl standing by the residence building with a suitcase and a large bag beside her. Her face lit up beautifully when she saw me.

"So, you're off until the new year," I said after she had scrambled into the passenger's seat.

"Yes, and thanks for coming to get me, Daddy."

"No problem. You really can't take a bus when you have this much luggage." I pulled out onto the side street. "Oh, and to give you a heads up, Meggy isn't at the house right now. She's at Grandma's."

"Why?"

"Rude behaviour, not doing her schoolwork, calling your mother names. You know the drill."

Jackie was quiet for a moment. "I talked to her last week, and she seemed upset. All her friends are away at college or university, so I tried to encourage her. I told her she's doing well."

"That's kind of you, Jackie." Her empathy surprised me. "Don't worry. I'm sure she'll be back soon."

We drove along University Avenue in silence for a few minutes. Then she sat up quickly.

"Dad, are you really writing a book?"

"Yes, I am, honey. Not this year, but at some point."

"Well, you know how you say I inspired the stories for it?"

"Yes."

"I have an answer for that. It's a famous quote."

I stopped at a traffic light. "What is it?"

She searched her phone. "Here it is. It's supposed to be by Marilyn Monroe — *Well behaved women rarely make history.*"

The signal changed, the traffic moved on, and the van lurched forward as I pressed the gas pedal down. I chuckled.

"I guess you're going to make a lot of history then, Jackie."

THE END

LESSONS LEARNED

Chapter 1 The Day Your Kids Lie

- Accept the fact that just when you begin to excel with your kids at one stage, they will change to another. Try to be flexible and adjust.
- In your darkest hours, prayer can help. Be more spiritual. Studies have shown that people with faith are happier.
- Create rules for cell phones, parties, etc., at the beginning. Set limits early, and you'll have less pushback later.
- At times, your teens will behave like cute children again. Cherish these moments, and remember them when you're angry.

Chapter 2 Don't Bite the Hand That Feeds You

- Savour the beauty of nature, be it a snowfall, your own backyard, a lake or hiking. It's soothing and peaceful and can bring you happiness. There is a Japanese saying that means "to bathe in the forest." Relish God's creations; they restore your soul.
- One day, your child may turn on you and no longer hold you in esteem but regard you with amusement instead, such as the guy who dresses like a clown. Try not to be too upset; it is part of the process of them pulling away from you and asserting their independence.

- Adolescent girls treat their mothers badly. They bully them and are angry towards them. But one day, they will do an about-face and appreciate them.

Chapter 3 The Day It All Started
- Commiserating with other parents will bring comfort and reassurance. Everyone has problems with their kids.
- Sometimes, your teen will act irrationally, such as refusing to go to an agreed-upon school or on a family trip. Keep the lines of communication open, and try to uncover the reason behind the change, but don't push too hard. Depending on the situation, you can always say no.
- Once your child reaches high school, worries change from homework to gangs, drugs and peer acceptance.
- Don't leave a teenager at home unchaperoned. Uncontrolled parties and damage are a real risk due to social media.

Chapter 4 Go West Young Girl
- Vacations, even inexpensive ones, can break families out of the cycle of constant fighting by providing scenic distractions and excitement.
- Humour helps dissolve tension and feelings of anger and frustration.
- Accept the fact that as a parent, you are a source of embarrassment to your teen.
- Compromise on activities; some things you try to avoid may surprise and delight you.

Chapter 5 Ewww!
- Vancouver Island has sensational scenery with old-growth forests and natural hot springs. It's not to be missed.

Chapter 6 The Ride from Hell

- Near disasters are a part of family life, as I found out at Mt. Revelstoke. Accept the fact that you cannot control everything, and try to survive the calamities with grace.
- Racing down a mountain in the dark can provide more heart-pumping fear than the scariest ride at an amusement park.
- Spouses or offspring may not regard punctuality or deadlines with the same importance, and at some point, you need to realize that you are unlikely to change their behaviour. Life is much happier when you accept each other's faults, whether it's chronic lateness or being uptight.

Chapter 7 Cell Phone Mania

- Never underestimate your daughter's ability to spend endless hours taking strange, funny and even ugly selfies.
- When accidents happen, don't criticize the person. Be supportive.
- Your kids will surprise you with ingenious, devious and creative ways to circumvent your rules and get what they want.
- Sadly, a cell phone blocker isn't legal in Canada.
- Ratchet means nasty, crazy.
- Parents need to be firm. If your kids misbehave, you need to punish them and not reduce it later. As much as you may desire to be their friend, remember you're a parent first, and they need to learn boundaries.

Chapter 8 Tempers Rising

- The likelihood of having neighbours that parade around naked increases at the same rate their attractiveness decreases.

Chapter 9 Travel Hell

- Strive to be more open-minded. One can never tell what toy your children will have the most fun with. For me, the trampoline was a surprise. Who knew it could be a social forum?

- Despite the best planning, you will have bad experiences — but determination will correct them. And within hours, you can go from being horrified, as I was in the red-light district, to delighted by wine fairies.

Chapter 10 Girls Are Nuts!

- Do you eat to live or live to eat? This question can diffuse the tension inherent in dinner preparation.

Chapter 11 Milo — Fearless Dog and Noble Beast

- None of the women in my house are interested in war stories.
- Kids can quickly burst the dream a parent or teacher might have of igniting their ambition.

Chapter 12 Jackie Has a Project

- Your spouse may have quirks, such as collecting strange yard ornaments or burning a hundred candles, but accept these. We all have idiosyncrasies, and a marriage is better when you don't criticize each other.
- Beware of the three-way con: X is sleeping at Y's house; Y is sleeping at Z's and Z is sleeping at X's. This type of plot surfaces when you least expect it and is a symptom of puberty.

Chapter 13 Passages

- Some of your child's behaviour may be the result of peer attitude towards them: leaving them out of cliques or shutting them out of social circles. Even their good friends may alter their relationships with them.
- With all the stress they're under, parents may forget their teenagers are turning into attractive young adults until someone else points it out.
- Start locking up your booze before your kids become adolescents to stay one step ahead.
- Don't be afraid to talk to other parents; everyone has difficulty with teenagers. You might be surprised how honest they can be.

Chapter 14 Under Pressure

- Raising kids can be very hard on parents and a marriage. Pets add another level of stress. Make sure to set aside time for yourself as a couple and exercise regularly.

Chapter 15 The Dog Nazi

- Regardless of how good-natured and obedient your pet is, they will seize any opportunity to take your food.
- Pets have the same joy for life that small children do.

Chapter 16 Reaching Out

- Puberty causes more severe mood swings in some teenagers than in others, and they will take you along for the ride.
- Everyone has a strange and unreasonable neighbour, and one has to tolerate them.

Chapter 17 Canoeing the Credit

- The exact same canoe trip can be incredibly relaxing one time and terrifying the next.
- Married life is filled with more excitement and drama than a single person could possibly imagine.

Chapter 18 The Mooning

- Parents need to keep an eye on their teens' plans and talk to their friends' parents. In their naivety, kids will put themselves in risky situations.
- In the age of cell phones, parents have to be careful of their own behaviour in front of their kids. Avoid mooning your child no matter how irritating they may be.

Chapter 19 Auto Shop

- Most brothers will torment their younger siblings. Farting is a common tactic.
- Even though your daughter gets a good mark in auto shop, it doesn't mean she knows anything about cars. Never underestimate the ability of a pretty girl to manipulate others.

Chapter 20 Naked Girl

- Always help other young adults. Your children may end up in similar situations one day.
- Swimming with sharks is not the leisure activity some believe it to be.
- Holidays may be the only time to have your kids completely to yourselves for more than an hour.

Chapter 21 The Birthday Surprise

- Your adolescent will live in a dump at college or university, and you need to let them enjoy their freedom, even if they acquire gross habits.
- When your child has a temper outburst for small matters, such as the wrong cake for their birthday, never get even by eating their birthday cookie. It will only return to haunt you.
- Psychiatrists, and doctors in general, are not perfect and can make mistakes. Don't be afraid to call them out on it if they put you in an awkward situation with your teen.

Chapter 22 The Marathon

- If you build exercise into your lifestyle and model this to your children, they may follow your example and even surpass you when you're older.
- Never drink beer before jogging.
- Even the latest and best GPS will not prevent your spouse from giving you directions.

Chapter 23 The Reunion

- Observing daily life of people in another country can be more fascinating than museums.
- Going back to your spouse's hometown and meeting her friends can be very enjoyable if you approach it with the right attitude. And it can teach you a lot about their behaviour as a teenager.

Chapter 24 Drama Queen
- Shockeroo may not be a real word, but it certainly describes a situation well.
- The police will come when you call, even if your teen only poses a threat to property.

Chapter 25 Therapy
- Threatening to write a book about your child can really reduce your stress.
- When you're angry with your kids, picturing them as little children asleep in their beds helps. But drinking their booze is even better.
- Set rules and penalties in advance, and punish them for breaking these. It's important that teens learn boundaries, or there may be more severe repercussions when they are older.
- Even professionals can lose their cool when faced with teenage attitude.
- Family therapy will help household dynamics if one is open to constructive criticism. And if you don't think you have any flaws, just ask your family.

Chapter 26 The Turning Point
- Even an easygoing and well-behaved child brings drama into your life now and then.

Chapter 27 Decision Time
- Seek professional advice to deal with a rebellious teen, but make your own decisions. You are the one that has to live with the consequences.
- Hold your child accountable for their behaviour, and make the tough decisions. It will pay off in the long run.
- Everyone needs the support of others to help them over the difficult hurdles.

Chapter 28 The University Conundrum

- Even though your child says she hates you and won't be home until Christmas, be prepared for a call pleading to come back after only one day.

- Getting them out of the house can help them mature and appreciate you more.

- When your teen is away from home, put the past behind you, and provide love and support.

- The difficult years won't last forever. Pray, work on improving your interactions, and have faith that one day, they will return to a more loving and respectful relationship with their family.

ACKNOWLEDGEMENTS

There are a number of people that have helped with this publication and to whom I am very grateful:

-my beautiful blonde daughter Jacquelyn for providing the majority of incidents in this memoir, including the quotation at the end which she also provided in conversations. She has always been fun-loving, social and a bit mischievous.

-Karen, for standing by, loving and supporting me in all my adventures in life. And for dragging me kicking and screaming on many of them.

-the other beautiful members of my family, Meaghan, Eric and Gloria, for the events that they provided and will continue to provide as well.

-my best friend, Steven, for the many hours spent providing early editing and advice for this book. And for helping me retain my sanity during the tumultuous periods of my life.

-my pets - Moochie, Milo and Darla - for their love, colourful personalities and joy that they brought into our lives. Although I could have done without all the cat bites.

-my editor and owner of Book Magic, Sigrid Macdonald, for her sage advice and attention to detail.

-Ana Chabrand Design House for their artistic design of the front and back covers.

-AM Press, for the wisdom to publish this book.

-Chrissy Hobbs of Indie Publishing Group for the interior design.

-Andrew McKinney, an older cousin I admired and who died too young, and whose name was chosen as a pseudonym.

-and the internet, where the answer to any question can be found, and to those kind souls who generously post tips and advice for writers.

ABOUT THE AUTHOR

As an executive in the pharmaceutical industry, Andrew learned only too well the pressures of work and family. He and his wife, Karen, raised a son, two daughters, a cat and a dog. And despite some difficult years, he cherishes the good times and funny moments that occurred when least expected. By sharing his challenging yet humorous experiences, he hopes to entertain readers who have raised kids and provide a roadmap to those beginning to navigate this stage of their lives.

After living with his family in a small town in Ontario for decades, Andrew has been on the run from his daughters ever since publication.

If you enjoyed this book, please post a review online wherever you buy books. Visit www.howilostmyhairraisingteenagegirls.com, and connect on Facebook and Instagram: @authorandrewmckinney

Andrew is also a songwriter, and you can listen to his songs on YouTube @andrewmckinneysongs

Manufactured by Amazon.ca
Bolton, ON

27621719R10199